The Wall Street
Journal Book of
Chief Executive Style

The Editors of
The Wall Street Journal

CONTRIBUTORS
DAVID DIAMOND
Bryan Burrough
Cathy Crimmins
Stephen Fenichell
John Marchese
Sara Nelson
James P. Sterba
Mary Walton

The Wall Street Journal

Book of CHIEF EXECUTIVE STYLE

WILLIAM
MORROW
A   N   D
COMPANY,
I   N   C.
NEW YORK

Library of Congress Cataloging-in-Publication Data

The Wall Street Journal book of chief executive style / editors of the Wall
    Street Journal, contributors, David Diamond, Bryan Burrough,
    Cathy Crimmins, Stephen Fenichell, John Marchese, Sara Nelson,
    James P. Sterba, Mary Walton.
        p.   cm.
    ISBN 0-688-07922-9
    1. Business etiquette.   2. Executives.   I. Diamond, David, 1952–
    II. Wall Street journal.
    HF5389.W35   1989
    658.4′094—dc20   89-34468
                                                                     CIP

Printed in the United States of America

First Edition

1 2 3 4 5 6 7 8 9 10

BOOK DESIGN BY RICHARD ORIOLO

To Ed Cony,
who taught many of
us that companies are run
by real people and that writing
about business doesn't
have to be dull

Acknowledgments

The editors wish to thank Lee Lescaze, Dan Austin, and Don Moffitt, who conceived the original *Wall Street Journal Report on Executive Style*. They inspired us and set the tone. We also thank the reporters and their editors who brought the tabloid report into existence.

David Diamond directed the project through its most crucial stages and contributed the lion's share of the writing, reporting, and editing.

The contributors—Bryan Burrough, Stephen Fenichell, Sara Nelson, Cathy Crimmins, John Marchese, James P. Sterba, and Mary Walton—traveled a continent to find the CEO in his or her habitat.

Finally, thanks to Nancy Cardwell for her guidance and encouragement.

CONTENTS

WHO'S THE BOSS?

Picture poor Irving Shapiro. It's 1974, and the board of Du Pont has just tapped him to be the chairman and chief executive officer of the nation's largest chemical company. He is a smart and savvy operator and the first chief in Du Pont's 172-year history to come from outside the technical rank of the company.

But Shapiro is also the first-generation son of Jewish immigrants from Lithuania, and he is a lawyer who hasn't been to management school. So he has what he considers to be a vexing educational gap. Simply put, he has become a CEO without any training in how to behave like one.

Behavior isn't a word that crops up often in grown-up conversation. But transmogrify it into Style, and all of a sudden you're talking the topic of the decade. Style is Substance these days, and anybody who wants to get along and get ahead had better have a good one.

So, in the interest of sociology, self-advancement, and voyeurism, we have spent the past year investigating the personal lives and habits of the chief executives officers of the nation's largest corporations. These guys obviously have a style that works. We wanted to find out what it is, and where they got it.

Our quest has taken us all over the map and to places we thought we'd never see. We visited Reliance Group chairman Saul Steinberg at his Park Avenue co-op, where we rummaged around and found the skateboards stored under the center-hall stairs. We toured the best of the many drinking sites at California's exclusive Bohemian Grove, met Lubrizol chairman Lester Coleman's personal Cabbage Patch doll, and sneaked onto the grounds of a neighboring mansion with Cincinnati Reds' chairman Marge Schott. We soared into the Nevada sky with Hilton's Barron Hilton, learned the secret rites of Houston's Coronado Club and persuaded former Lockheed chairman Lawrence Kitchen to tell us his strategy for getting to the top without a college degree.

Our year of tracking down CEOs in their corner offices, executive washrooms, and living rooms—and, ultimately, getting inside their heads—has produced some startling results. Many of these privacy-possessed CEOs who constructed stone walls around themselves as the first order of chief executive business now are lonely.

They talked about their pleasures, their fears, their caution with friends and their checkbooks. They took us golfing, to dinner, and home with them. We learned how they treat their families, spend their money, decorate their offices, eat their breakfasts, and part their hair. (They may occupy the right side of the political spectrum but they part their hair on the left. According to a *Wall Street Journal* survey of 351 CEOs, 71% part their hair on the left side. And while we're on the subject, 91% get their hair cut out of the office.)

We also learned a few of their little tricks. At least one uses golf outings to size up employees and business partners. He once fired a subordinate for cheating on his scorecard.

If it isn't golf, a corporate honcho typically settles on another pastime—drinks at the club, for instance—during which he can surreptitiously size up others. Indeed, if there's one trait that binds CEOs, it's an innate ability to use their time with precision to accomplish several tasks in the time it takes the rest of us to accomplish one.

And CEOs tend to be terrific actors. Irving Shapiro went on to become one of the nation's most prominent and respected business leaders, all the while secretly taking his own measure. "Whenever I was in a situation where I didn't know how to act, I would try to imagine what [former Citicorp chairman] Walter Wriston would do in a similar situation and I would adapt that to my own style," he reports nearly a decade after his retirement.

Clear across the continent, in an office that sits perilously close to the flight path of Los Angeles International Airport, we found Peter J. Ratican, about as different from Irving Shapiro as you can get. He's young (45), tanned, a former college athlete, and a former accountant who speaks with a rock-music producer's laid-back cadence.

Ratican was called in to take over the reins of the failing Maxicare Health Systems in the hot, late summer of 1988. His difficult task put him into lots of sticky executive situations where he didn't quite know what to do. And he followed the same instincts that guided Shapiro. Ratican's words, in fact, are eerily similar to those uttered by the former Du Pont head: "I look at it and say, well what would Joe Conner [chairman of Price Waterhouse] have done in this situation? And what would Lew Wasserman [chairman of MCA] do? And usually those are very opposite. And then I say, well what would *I* do? What do *I* think is right? And I try to reconcile the three positions."

CEOs, like most everybody else, instinctively want to look to their superiors for the subtle signals that tell them how to operate. The problem is, when one finally becomes top dog, there are no superiors—just subordinates, shareholders, the fellow who hands out towels in the club locker room, the headwaiter at La Côte Basque—and other CEOS. So the elements of executive style often are gleaned from other chief executives: at board meetings, at Greenbrier confabs, at the Bohemian Grove encampment, at the 18th hole.

Despite what we've just told you, there are a few CEOs who don't seem to emulate a personal model but—for better or worse—simply act on impulse. Howard P. Allen, chairman of Southern California Edison, which supplies electricity to Peter Ratican and practically everybody else in Los Angeles, says he has always just done what comes naturally. "I love authority," he tells us, letting a grin creep across his face, a mischievous grin that convinces us he isn't lying. "And growing up in this company I took a great deal more authority than I really had, because of my nature and because nobody stopped me." Maybe it's his breakfast routine that inspires such confidence. In addition to yogurt, cottage cheese, and fruit, he downs a concoction that includes a tablespoon of lecithin, a tablespoon of safflower oil, a tablespoon of wheat germ, a tablespoon of oat bran, a tablespoon of bran mixed up with milk, honey, blackstrap molasses and hot water. ("And it works," he reports. "My cholesterol is 90.")

Not everybody picks up the rules directly from other CEOs or calls upon gut instinct. Some, like National Intergroup chairman Howard M. "Pete" Love, were virtually bred for the job. His father, George M. Love, was founder and chairman of Consolidation Coal in the 1940s and 1950s, and chairman of Chrysler in the 1960s.

And Walter Wriston, the man who was cited as the nation's number-one business leader by 11% of our respondents, doesn't recall having had a tidy vision of an all-knowing chief exec (or chief execs) lodged in his mind's eye during the years he ran Citicorp. But then, too, his father was a CEO, of sorts: the legendary president of Brown University, for nearly two decades. What Walter didn't learn about chief executive behavior from his dad, he may have picked up when he earned a master's degree at the Fletcher School of International Law and Diplomacy, which is run jointly by Harvard and Tufts.

There were many CEOs who made us stop and consider the tough life—and the special brand of caution—that comes with the corner office. One CEO confides his fear of running into people at the grocery store while he's sloppily dressed. "I can't afford to let them think I'm a slob." Later, he acknowledges that people include him in a number of business and social situations "not because they like me but because of the position I hold."

AT&T chairman Robert E. Allen addresses the same issue from a different perspective. "You have to make sure you don't take all that attention to heart," he advises. "And everyone outside the business wants you to be present everywhere. You've got to learn to say no."

In a headline typeface that was rumored to have been reserved for The Millennium, *Fortune* magazine heralded former IBM chairman Thomas Watson, Jr., as THE GREATEST CAPITALIST IN HISTORY. So we listened attentively when he told us: "Anybody who becomes a leader in his own right develops an aura around him. He can break through it, if he wants, to become Just Old Bill. But it's probably not the best way to go. There's nothing more undignified to me than for a leader to be trying to be one of the boys."

But that's the side CEOs want most to show.

Every CEO seems to have a bit of the self-promoter in him (like Lee Iacocca, Mr. Name Recognition himself), a streak of showmanship (like Sara Lee chief John H. Bryan, Jr., who let *Business Week* follow him around in a limo), even traces of that timid cartoon character, Caspar Milquetoast. But above all, they work devilishly hard at coming across as Just Old Bills.

"Sure, we go to McDonald's. I like McDonald hamburgers," offers General Motors chairman Roger Smith, telling us that while his wife is away at the summer place in Northern Michigan, "[son] Drew and I are batching it. Last night we broiled some lamb chops out on the patio, it was great. Now tonight we're going to the ball game. How 'bout that?" he says, ending the sentence with a folksy laugh.

Listening to Smith, you get the impression that his personal life is not terribly different from that of the guys down on the Chevy assembly line. For instance, on the opening day of deer season each year, he goes hunting with the same fellow he's hunted with for the past 11 years. "Heck, I have friends in this company that go back 35 years. They didn't make it to CEO but we're just as good friends now as we were 35 years ago."

But a moment later, the chairman of our nation's largest manufacturing company starts to detail the contents of his toy collection at his summer home on Michigan's Burt Lake and at the Turtle Lake Club, a 28,000-acre hunting and fishing preserve he co-owns. And it becomes obvious that he has very little in common with the commoners who install all of those fan belts. First, he waxes rapturous about his personal navy: "I love boats, we've got all kinds of boats. Slow boats, fast boats, old boats, new boats," he says. His land vehicles come next: "I've got a '36 Cadillac convertible sedan that's a beauty with the big side mounts and divided windshields. I've got a 1960 Corvette I've restored, looks like it came right off the line. I've got a '64 Corvair convertible, it's bright red with a white top. [I've got] Motorcycles. Not *big* motorcycles, I'm not a fan of big motorcycles. These are little Honda 90 trail bikes, we own some land behind our place . . ."

True, some of these guys do have a hefty streak of the ordinary in them and appear to get a kick out of eschewing the considerable trappings of their lofty positions. Kenneth Perry was chairman of American Petrofina when he chatted with us about his lunching routine of peeling shrimp at a regular old "sawdust-on-the-floor-type" joint around the corner from the company's Dallas headquarters, just like everybody else. (A few weeks later, when American Petrofina's board replaced him and made him vice-chairman, he was, in fact, just like everybody else.) *Time*'s Dick Munro, who commutes to work on Metro-North's 6:02 A.M. out of New Canaan, Connecticut, spoke fondly about the pleasure he derives from mowing his own lawn. And when pressed for the make and model of his tractor, he actually knew that, too.

Highly paid communications consultants have a term for this business of highlighting those areas of a CEO's personal life that make him seem not so different from people who do all their own heavy lifting. They call it "common grounding," and the bulk of the CEOs we interviewed were eager to participate. (Chrysler's Lee Iacocca has made an art form out if this, by forever mentioning his son-of-immigrants roots, by writing about his unbearable tenure under the nasty ol' Henry Ford II, and by telling us more than we ever need to know about the circumstances of his firing.)

By emphasizing their similarities with common folk and playing down their differences, CEOs—like other politicians—send off two powerful messages: 1) that they are simple, likable, trustworthy folks (and therefore, not to be resented or mistrusted by everyone beneath them) and 2) that they must be pretty damn smart to have gotten so far in life, since they are everyday people.

Part of the same common-grounding pattern involves publicly deflating the importance of their high-echelon jobs.

When we asked these gentlemen to discuss their heroes, we got an intriguing list that hardly included any businessmen. CEO after CEO told us that he simply didn't consider it possible that business leaders could be heroes.

In the following pages, we give you our firsthand report from the field. But before that, we have some data to sketch out a preliminary profile.

The average CEO is married (94%), has three or more kids (68.4%) served in the U.S. Armed Forces (74.9%), works more than 10 hours a day (83.4%), thinks he's overweight (63%), favors white shirts (53%) and blue/dark blue/or navy blue suits (53%), manages his own money (57.5%), owns a firearm (54.1%), believes that, in general, CEOs of major corporations are more ethical in their business practices today than they were ten years ago (71.2%) and would hesitate to promote a homosexual to management-committee level (66%).

Stability is foremost among the character traits exhibited by our CEOs. In their median 57.7 years, our CEOs rarely change wives or companies. Among those surveyed, 81.8% have been hitched to the same person for more than 20 years and 42.7% spent 16 or more years with their present company before being named CEO. (A full 80.9% have had only one wife; 30.5% have had only one employer.)

Just as the islands of the Caribbean contribute more than their share of our nation's baseball players and the South gives us many of our Miss Americas, CEOs have their own breeding ground: the Industrial North. One in four CEOs grew up in the Mid-Atlantic states of New York, New Jersey and Pennsylvania. The Empire State is the biggest producer of chief executives (14%), followed by Illinois (7.7%), Ohio (6.6%) and Pennsylvania (6.3%).

While their fathers represent a broad range of occupations, from rancher to clerical worker and from craftsman to engineer, only 16% of the CEO dads were executives. And, nearly one of every four *Fortune*-500-type CEOs (23.5%), like Lee Iacocca, is either a first- or second-generation American.

CEOs tend to favor wives who don't work outside the home for money. Only 6.7% of our respondents report having spouses with full-time jobs. More common are wives like Barbara Heckert, who is married to recently retired Du Pont chairman Richard Heckert and takes part in charities that utilize her gardening hobby. She's a master flower-show judge of the National Council of State Garden Clubs and a member of the council of the Pennsylvania Horticultural Society.

When it comes to religion, 60% of the surveyed chief execs indicate they are Protestant, 20.8% are Roman Catholic, and 6.8% are Jewish. But regular worship apparently doesn't fit into a busy CEO's schedule. Only 35% attend religious services more than 20 times a year. (A few notable exceptions: Black & Decker's Nolan D. Archibald and Marriott's J. Willard Marriot, Jr., are devout Mormons, even teachers of Sunday Bible class.)

CEOs prefer seafood to red meat, drink as much wine as they do scotch, but drink more vodka than gin (91.5% say they drink; only 3.1% say they drink at lunch). Here's another display of health consciousness: Overwhelmingly, corporate bigwigs are nonsmokers. Among the 12% of CEOs who do smoke, cigars are more popular than cigarettes. AT&T's chairman couldn't remember the name of his favorite brand, so he reached into his briefcase to find out. It's Monte Cruz American. He smokes two a day; usually one in the morning at work and one either after lunch or dinner.

Does it take brains to be a CEO? Of the 119 corporate leaders who know their IQs, more than half are in the 130–144 range. Of all the CEOs polled, 47.6% have master's degrees or doctorates (19.3% of which come from Ivy League institutions). And 19.1% have undergraduate degrees from the Ivy League.

And when we surveyed the nation's CEOs to determine their favorite ice cream flavor, the winner was chocolate, which registered 29% of the vote. We couldn't help but remember former Apple Computer chairman Steven Jobs's railing against "vanilla" corporations, his personal euphemism for IBM-type institutions. Maybe he was reflecting CEO tastebuds.

Back in the early 1980s, the upstart, outspoken Mr. Jobs was widely viewed as the prototypical Chief Executive of the Future. And—who knows?—if we check back in thirty or forty years, all chief execs may be single, working ungodly hours, avoiding any exposure to golf, and residing in immense, unfurnished homes. But the bulk of today's young CEOs aren't all that far removed from their elder counterparts, guys who got their career jump-starts in the business world of the 1950s, the heyday of William H. Whyte, Jr.'s conformity-obsessed *Organization Man.* Still, several new industries built on risk-taking not only welcome mold-breakers, but embrace them.

Our favorite specimen is Cray Research chairman John Rollwagen. Forty-eight years old, he tells us that " 'should' is not a favorite word of mine" and he appears to take pleasure in discussing his passion for Eastern philosophies. When he talks about his personal role models, he describes Cray Research founder Seymour Cray as a man who is "very well centered" and his own late grandfather, a Methodist minister, as someone who "more than anyone else reached a—Nirvana's too strong a word—but he reached a self-actualization more than anyone else I know." We couldn't resist asking if he peppers his CEO-to-CEO conversations with such noncorporate phraseology. He replied, between giggles: "No, I don't use the word 'centered' when I'm talking with other CEOs, except for one or two. I can use a different vocabulary with other CEOs," thus indicating an ability to shift gears in a flash—a trait we found prevalent among corporate heads.

Rollwagen gets his hair cut every three weeks, brushes with Crest (he accused us of being a front for Procter & Gamble when we asked him to name his toothpaste), and breakfasts on orange juice and cereal with skim milk. "What's a typical weekend for me? There is no such thing. If it's wintertime I'm going to be trying to be skiing in Alta, Utah [where he co-owns a condo]. If it's summertime, I'm going to be—although I didn't get to do it too much this summer—up at Cable, Wisconsin, at a lake place that we have. If it's spring, late in the spring, I hope it's Paris. In the fall, it's close to home, and with my wife and two-year-old son [he has two grown daughters]."

Folks have endured shabbier lives.

Talk to enough corporate heads and you hear a repetition of such fun-filled itineraries. You also hear unending mentions of other CEOs. Corporate chiefs, we've found, tend to drop each others' names freely and sometimes give the impression that they've all been buddies since kindergarten.

And why not? A new head of a large American company is expected to widen his reach, not only by maneuvering himself onto the boards of other companies, but by simply phoning up and establishing a relationship with other CEOs in a way that executive vice-presidents of finance, for example, rarely would. ("Hey, I'll be in Houston/Minneapolis/Stamford next week. . . .") So it sometimes seems like one big, happy corporate board. And membership seems to continue even after retirement has rendered a CEO ineffective (from a corporate point of view).

It was an initial impression of ours that a CEO's privileged position gives him entry to a special club, of sorts. The more chief execs tried to minimize that perception, the more convinced we remained.

As you read the following chapters, judge for yourself. And remember something else: CEOs seem to enjoy indulging, if only a bit, in the act of creating their own mystique.

Throughout the year of sleuthing that produced this book, we were repeatedly haunted by a paragraph from the early pages of Sloan Wilson's *The Man in the Gray Flannel Suit*. It was the barroom-gossip description of Ralph Hopkins, the fictional CEO of the fictional United Broadcasting Corp.:

"There are all kinds of stories about him—they say he had two children and had been home twice in the last twenty years. . . . They say he needs less sleep than Edison did. They say he's got his whole filing system memorized, practically, and can quote from any important letter or contract in it. Some say he's got a little blond girl on Park Avenue. Some say he's sleeping with some actress who flies in from Hollywood once a month. I've even heard it said that he's queer. . . . To tell the honest truth, I have no idea in the world what kind of man he is, except he must be pretty damn smart to be where he is."

See for yourself.

—DAVID DIAMOND

THE OPENING
(AND CLOSING)
OF THE AMERICAN
OFFICE

A CEO wouldn't have to be an idiot not to know about *"stimmung"*—even if it's on display in his office, right along with the crude Crayola by his four-year-old kid.

Just in case you haven't heard the word lately, it's German for "mood." It was that noted philosopher of interior decoration (that's right: Philosopher of Interior Decoration) Mario Praz who spoke of *"stimmung"* as "the way in which a room mirrors the soul of its inhabitant." In the case of a CEO and his office, his "room" reflects not just his own soul, but that of a whole organization. It provides not only a guide to the company he keeps, but also the company he runs.

It's no surprise, then, that when the American Society of Interior Designers (ASID), polled *Fortune*-500 CEOs in 1987, 95% of the 143 respondents said that the interior design of their headquarters accurately reflects the character of their companies. Moreover, reports the society: "CEOs are aware of the role design plays in influencing new client/customers and prospective employees, and are taking time out from their other responsibilities to participate in the design process."

Participate in the design process? Yes. But we're getting ahead of ourselves.

Ever since Kublai Khan, merchants, moguls and magnates have been designing their corporate domiciles to project power, prestige and position. Until fairly recently, in America at least, this was a straightforward proposition. You just threw down an old Oriental rug, hung some gilt-framed oils on the paneling above the marble mantle, and kept the ceiling high enough to impress the peasantry. The CEO's office looked a lot like his club, his living room, his favorite restaurant, his college dorm room, and the faculty lounge at his prep school.

Then modernism came along. Wives began to dream of doing the living room over to look like a lounge at Radio City. And offices started looking like they belonged in skyscrapers, instead of on the stage set of a drawing-room comedy.

The new rules were radically different from the old ones, but they still were rules. Precepts like "Less Is More" made a dim sort of sense. Those steel-and-leather Barcelona chairs (straight from the Bauhaus school and not too great to sit in) looked swell in a sleek marble lobby. Splashy abstract art fit right in with the track lighting and acoustical tile in the boardroom.

In the mid-seventies, though, the pendulum swung sharply backward, wiping out most of the comfortable rules. It could have been boredom that allowed the first invader, a sadistic variant of hypertraditionalism, to appear in the guise of the furnished-to-intimidate Power Office.

What self-important power player could resist the high-intensity lights firmly focused on a visitor's chair (all the better for giving some poor victim the third degree)? And the oversized desk fashioned from sunken ships' timbers propped on a dais, with visitors' chairs placed below like banquettes in an underground bunker?

The prototype Power Office was Columbia Pictures' legendary czar Harry Cohn's chamber of inquisition, modeled closely, we should note, after Mussolini's. Both boasted desks proportional to the size of their occupants' egos, placed at distances from the front door carefully calculated to cause breakdowns in even the toughest customers. Soon a number of variations flourished, like that of the CEO who kept a dog-eared copy of *Winning Through Intimidation* on a coffee table, to terrorize guests forced to consult it while he blithely took calls.

The Power Office rapidly declined to the status of corporate cliché, leaving a large gap in the Executive Suite—some 400 square feet per CEO. What came along as a replacement might have been dreamed up at the Esalen Institute, that haven of free thought and life-without-barriers. But its success was a sign that the Sixties had left a mark on corporate consciousness more lasting than wide ties.

We speak, of course, of the Open Office—an old idea first displayed in frenetic newsrooms. One such newsroom ushered in the end of the Nixon years, so the Open Office became, in a way, a fitting symbol for the post-Watergate era, with its emphasis on openness, equality, and the free flow of information. By packing a maximum number of people into a minimum of space, it saved money, too.

At first glance, the Open Office could have been taken for the Power Office's polar opposite. It took noted Power Author Michael Korda to detect a subtle authoritarian streak lurking in all that egalitarian open space. "Obviously, to be avoided are offices built on the open plan," he wrote in the 1975 bestseller, *Power.* "Places in which management has tried to eliminate the signs and symbols of power to encourage 'openness' are places in which the leadership is determined to retain all the power in its own hands. . . ."

The Eighties became a decade of decision on the office front, as competing styles duked it out. Open or Closed? Modern or Postmodern? Or Post-Postmodern? Some CEOs tried to steer clear of controversy by striking the right balance. But the question became: balance between what?

For every trend came a countertrend. Takeover fever was going to promote a new wave of corporate austerity. "A too lavish office," warned *The Wall Street Journal* in mid-1987, "just might signal to a bloodthirsty raider that there's a profitable opportunity to trim corporate fat."

But before very long, a new slew of office towers was being built that threatened to out-glitz the Baths of Caracalla. Not since the heyday of the robber barons had so much pomposity been lavished on monuments to mammon. Surrounded by enough Malaga marble, even the most jaded LBO baron had to be proud.

Two recent scenes from the battlefront reflect the prevailing identity confusion.

Scene One: Citicorp CEO John Reed makes a much-publicized move from predecessor Walter Wriston's 15th-floor office to a suite of "open" offices on the second floor. Strike a blow for democracy.

Scene Two: American Express chairman James Robinson's crystal sky-palace atop the new World Financial Center merits a spread in *Interiors* magazine as the outstanding example of corporate posh to come along in some time. Despite a decorator's disclaimers that Robinson rejected some specimens due to excessive cost, genuine burled-wood paneling, inlaid marble tables, authentic antiques and Oriental carpets say it all: Strike one for plutocracy.

Meanwhile, back at Citicorp Center, the brave new executive floor plan falls flat on its face. Amid all the ballyhoo, *Manhattan, inc.* magazine reports that few colleagues drop by for the expected afternoon chats, proving once and for all that mere architectural tinkering can't counter an aloof corporate style.

Since form follows function, the real question becomes: What is a CEO's office for? To impress clients? Intimidate colleagues? Provide an elegant backdrop for corporate functions? (Subtext: What is the function of a corporate function?)

Open or closed, public or private, modern or traditional, a CEO's office clearly serves three basic needs:

1) "War Room": A communications center from which a CEO can keep in contact with troops in the field.

2) Image-definer: A place where a visitor learns what the joint is about without very much having to be said.

3) Home base: It's where the boss lives and meets real human beings, live and in person, face-to-face, even one-on-one.

A description of a CEO Office (circa 1988) recently appeared in an advertising supplement called "Chambers of Commerce": "The Georgian partner's desk is still there, but it has been turned away from the window to face the front door. The Oriental rug is still there, but it has been spliced to accommodate a ganglion of communications wires. . . . The conference corner is still there, but the comfortable couch gets just as much use. . . ."

In the end, no matter how spacious or small, decorated or bare, any office is basically a box to put things in. The basic questions are placement, size and: What goes in it? According to the ASID survey, tradition still stands tall in some aspects of CEO office planning. A full 75% still have a wide view, and 73% still occupy that trademark of power: the corner. But only 61% are located on the top floors of their buildings (believed to be an all-time low) and even fewer (59%) have the largest office in the company.

About one third of the responding CEOs prefer "modern" decor. The other two thirds still cling to such predictable trappings of corporate clout as oriental rugs and wood paneling. Regardless, CEOs are "personalizing" (ASID's word) their offices now more than ever. "Moving away from institutional standards toward designs that express a certain amount of individuality," reports the Society. CEOs are "expressing their personal taste" through: original artwork (67%), custom-built furniture (36%) and authentic antiques (25%).

A minority of CEOs also are relying on other, less prevalent items to proclaim their individuality. Unlike doctors or lawyers, only 26% of the CEOs surveyed mount diplomas or awards on their office walls. A mere 13% of the corporate chiefs' offices feature photographs of famous people. Some 12% of CEOs find the need to include a wet bar in their office; 6% have a working fireplace, and 4%, like the movie *Wall Street*'s Gordon Gekko, incorporate an exercise area in their office.

Frequently a new chief has little to do with the planning and construction of his lair. He simply moves across the hall or up the stairs into the space occupied by his predecessor, and may or may not order up major renovations. So to get the clearest view of the office decisions with which a CEO must grapple, we decided to concentrate our cross-country office tour on chief execs who got in on the ground floor, so to speak, CEOs who ordered up their offices (and buildings) from scratch.

The Bicoastal Jay (Chiat/Day/Mojo) Chiat

Super Bowl 1984: "1984," a spot featuring blue-tinted zombies cheering as an icy-blue blonde smashes a huge TV screen with a sledge hammer. The Client: Apple Computer.

Super Bowl 1985: "Lemmings," blue-suited androids (IBM's Big Blue) march off down the road mindlessly chanting "Hi, Ho, It's Off To Work We Go . . ." Once again, Apple Computer.

With ads such as these, Jay Chiat rocketed Chiat/Day/ Mojo into the nation's top 25 ad shops based on billings, preserving a fiercely independent, maverick presence in a field increasingly dominated by megamergers.

Chiat/Day/Mojo is a sweatshop with a sense of humor. In 1983, Chiat took an agency strongly identified with a certain California "cool" on a daring raid deep into Mad Avenue turf. He leased five floors in a building on Lower Fifth Avenue (about five times as much as needed) that once sheltered genuine sweatshops. It was a risky move, given all that space. But Chiat/Day/Mojo grew into the New York digs.

Step off the elevator into Chiat's offices, an eclectic blend of California flash and SoHo chic. A gray paint-and-chickenwire silhouette of a messenger, in snap-brim hat and trench coat (poster tube tucked under one arm), is permanently plastered in his place on the wall above the couch.

In the darkly cavernous boardroom, Chiat and colleagues are depicted in totemic splendor on the walls, like prehistoric cave paintings. High on a wall deep in a coat closet, a pint-sized painter wields not a brush but a roller. You get the picture.

As Chiat, in the flesh, glides into plain sight, in plain white linen shirt, loose-fitting gray slacks (jacket no; tie yes), and curly white hair closely cropped but wild enough to still be a shade artistic, he remains the picture of casual elegance that *GQ* magazine once described as "Chiat's BiCoastal Style."

We're soon sitting not in Chiat's own office, but in a glass-enclosed, minimalist, postmodern living room/screening room/lounge by the boardroom. It's space reserved for the sort of intimate chats not easily had in an Open Office. Deco lavender leather sofas provide the requisite "conference corner" (a CEO special), while highbrow atmospherics flow freely from glass shelves lined with coffee-table books.

Chiat pours coffee from a chromium thermos that surely has its place in the permanent collection at the Museum of Modern Art. "Taste isn't something you've got to be born with," he avers. "It can be something you grow into, and evolve over time." A case in point: this Bronx-born, New Jersey-raised lad who admits to having grown up in a suburban home without "a decorator in sight."

Gazing across this bustling beehive expanse—which might pass for an art gallery but for its businesslike collection of shoulder-high cubicles displaying rows of MacIntoshes extending off into infinity, like a real-life cubist still life. Chiat reflects: "It's our position that physical environment has a real impact on your work. If you stay in the same place too long, you get glaucoma. You stop seeing things."

Employing an entrepreneurial formula roughly akin to Mao's conviction that a revolution should happen every ten years, Chiat stirs the soup by shifting offices. Either wholesale, or (by benefit of portable office dividers) individual transfers within the larger space. It's the same method Stalin used to control the fates of whole peoples, but at Chiat/Day/Mojo the dislocations don't cause revolts. (Sleep deprivation is another technique to achieve high-end results: Chiat employees refer to this shop as Chiat/Day & Night.)

None of that can detract from the fact that "creative types" would be breaking the doors down to work here. That is, if there were any doors.

"Give a person a fancy office with a soft leather chair, a marble desk, and a secretary to answer the phone," Chiat insists, "and before you know it they'll be sitting back and telling themselves. 'Boy, have I made it.' They'll never do good work again."

When we finally arrive at Chiat's own office, it is anticlimactic, and deliberately so. It conforms to classic CEO lines in just one respect: It fills a corner. Otherwise, with its clean white Formica counter and fiberglass partitions, it's identical to the cubicles on either side. It does contain two choice pieces from Chiat's personal art collection that no employees could afford (or dare) keep by their desks: a corrugated cardboard armchair by the California architect Frank Gehry and a papier-mâché tree in newsprint, a possible prop from *Waiting for Godot.*

"When people complained about not having enough privacy," Chiat recalls, "we put in glass conference rooms. [Which strongly resemble Maxwell Smart's Cone of Silence.] And something weird happened. Instead of people becoming paranoid about being exposed, they started realizing what was going on. Which was that nothing was going on—at least nothing negative that might affect them personally. When people stopped worrying about people plotting against them, they could relax, and start doing good work again."

David (ALCAN Aluminium Ltd.) Culver's Love of the Past

When Quebec separatists threatened to withdraw from the rest of Canada, David Culver, chairman of Alcan Aluminium, the world's leading aluminum exporter, fought the Anglo urge to leave and decided to stay. "Our roots are very deep in Montreal," he now says. Besides, in the uncertain business climate inspired by the separatist movement, real estate prices were a steal.

So Culver, whose company was nearing the end of its office-tower lease, decided to snatch up and renovate three adjoining British Empire landmarks on Sherbrooke Street, and to graft a new low-rise onto the back of them. (The major building material? Aluminum, of course.)

Until he retired in July 1989, Culver's own office was located in what once was the library of Lord Athleston, a canny Scot who founded the now-defunct Montreal Star. When Culver peered out his two towering windows, he saw the trim Georgian facade of the Mount Royal Club, built by Lord A. when he was "dinged" at the St. James.

When we visited Culver, he was reclining in suitably lordly style on a yellow silk sofa, as the morning light streamed in off grassy Mount Royal, falling gently on hand-printed wallpaper, thick Persian rugs and a splendid old marble mantle. With his well-cut tweed suit, British-style striped shirt and distinctly distinguished demeanor, Culver might be a prime example (one can't help but think) of just the sort of Anglo gent those separatist chaps were hoping to drive out of this province a few years back.

As if to reinforce this impression, Culver's secretary informed him that the Prime Minister would be free later on to discuss free trade, a subject clearly dear to both hearts. On the coffee table before him sat the newly published memoirs of a retired British cabinet member, from which Culver read us a particularly choice passage.

One enters Maison Alcan from Sherbrooke Street, passing under an old stone portal into a dazzling modern aluminum-walled atrium lined with smart shops and bars. The all-new aluminum-and-glass Davis Building housing much of the headquarters staff is perfectly comfortable, in a wall-to-wall modern way; it displays all the computer and communications equipment, audio-visual rooms and the like that a CEO could possibly want.

But step back into Culver's dream house, into a vanished century. Here, with the aid of archival photographs and the most up-to-date restoration techniques, the two old houses and the old Berkley hotel in between have been splendidly restored, a grand old Anglo Montreal brilliantly brought back to life.

Culver, not surprisingly, was pleased to point out some of the more practical aspects of what might (to an uninformed eye) resemble the devil-may-care opulence of the Vanderbilt era. Just consider, for a second, what it does for public relations. Corporate commitment to the community. Restoration of historic landmarks. Bringing a high-in-the-sky-scraper outfit back to earth, in touch with the street and city life.

Only a few doors down a hand-stenciled corridor from where we sit, the Canadian equivalent of *Masterpiece Theatre* is preparing to shoot a scene in the wood-paneled boardroom. But life on a stage set doesn't keep Culver from indulging in a few modern management methods: "I spend almost no time at that desk," he says, indicating an antique escritoir more suited to pen-and-quill correspondence than electronic mail. "In fact, the way I most like to work is just as we are now"—sitting on sofas before the fire—"or better yet, getting out and running around the different floors."

Once a halt has been called to the oohing and aahing over his lofty, high-ceilinged rooms, Culver prefers to discuss his new home in terms strongly reminiscent of Jay Chiat: How open it all is! Good grief.

"I can't tell you how wonderful it is to live in an office where you don't need to use an elevator," he says in his pre-

Industrial Revolution manner. "I've always found that taking an elevator puts a real damper on getting out and about. I'm always amazed how much I get done, just walking around, and bumping into people in the halls. . . ."

John (Hewlett-Packard) Young and His Palo Alto Pink Noise

How's this for reverse pride? John Young sits in his own semiprivate space and says: "This is a company that doesn't like offices. And this is the least office I can get away with."

His hand makes a sweep of the surroundings. We see 420 square feet of barely visible beige carpeting, a plain-Jane modern wood-slab desk shoved unobtrusively against the far wall, and a standard-issue, two-couch "conference corner." Its most notable attribute is its sheer neutrality. The furnishings could easily belong to just about any mid-level manager in Kansas City.

The most striking thing about Young's office isn't even in his office, but outside his floor-to-ceiling glass walls. It's an Oriental garden surrounded on three sides by Japanese-style security screens (referred to on the premises as "Don't Shoot the President Screens").

It's more than modesty that leads Young to describe his office as "a comfortable setting with a degree of privacy, but consistent with the accessible, open-style settings we've had over the years." It's also company tradition.

Hewlett-Packard was founded by Bill Hewlett and Dave Packard in a Palo Alto garage and should not, its culture dictates, indulge in fancy frills like private offices. HP, in fact, was designing and building genuine open offices before anyone had ever heard of the term.

Until about five years ago, senior managers at HP's operating divisions inhabited the same spartan space as their employees: shoulder-high cubicles. Then the company opened up a new headquarters building and moved the really top honchos to their own executive floor.

Young decided to separate the senior execs from their subordinates to improve management coordination. But the executive floor was designed to be just a slightly classier version of all the company's other open offices.

In Young's mind, traditional offices create an environment that is too structured and inhibits teamwork. He describes the ones he's seen "back East" as a combination of rabbit warrens, for lower-echelon managers, and huge galleries with fancy rugs and original Monets for the CEO.

"To me, all that takes the focus off what you're really about—performance," says Young, separated from his secretary by a wall that is half glass and doesn't allow for a Monet. Openness, he says, is "the kind of visual reinforcement you should be giving people with your office," and that it's counterproductive to have executives "fighting over a corner office, or a view."

It's a lovely theory. But when Young and his troops moved into the unstructured all-executive floor of the new HP headquarters, it didn't work. The griping started on Day One.

The complaints focused on the "the noise problem." One manager's voice carried to all corners of the floor. It disrupted the others, and it frightened them that their conversations might be equally public. But the underlying discontent was more complicated. It seems the offices basically were too small, too barren, and too Early HP. The accommodations were "not in keeping with the image expected at the top echelons of a major company," recalls facilities manager Jack Magry—with barely an audible huff.

To deal with the noise, the designers first installed more solid partitions. "This kind of layout requires special acoustical treatment," Young explains. "People have to be able to talk freely, without worrying about being overheard. But when we moved into these offices, they were so 'live' you could hear conversations at 75 feet. We had to baffle things down a bit . . ."

After conducting audio tests using Stanford students as guinea pigs, they finally filled in the open space between walls and ceilings with glass. This created clerestories that keep sight lines open but sound waves under control.

Another acoustical tactic HP has employed is to create electronic sounds to neutralize the human ones. The standard "white noise" is a boring *whoosh* that sounds like air conditioning. (It is often resorted to unsuccessfully by urban insomniacs.) So HP has come up with a new twist, "pink noise," which can be tonally altered to produce different effects.

But for all HP's attempts to maintain the exciting entrepreneurial spirit by creating more open offices (Jay Chiat, too, sought the Open Office as a Fountain of Youth), John Young eventually learned that he had to strike a balance between openness and privacy. He also learned that the company had finally grown up. Which maybe he should have known all along.

Mathias
(Rouse Company)
DeVito's Deskless
Office

"**P**eople tell me," confides Mathias DeVito, "that if times really get tough, we can always turn this building into a shopping mall." So far, the chairman of Rouse Company hasn't had to seriously entertain such a prospect, although the transition probably wouldn't be too difficult. When DeVito took over the helm of this Columbia, Maryland–based company from founder James Rouse in 1974, it was facing bankruptcy. It took a lot of chutzpah for the broad-shouldered, bespectacled DeVito to commission a new headquarters. DeVito wanted an Open Office, but after touring such facilities built for McDonalds and Weyerhaeuser, he came down with a severe case of cold feet. "What really fixed it for me was the way everyone had of saying how much they loved it. There was something suspect about how everyone acted like good wooden soldiers," he says.

The last straw (or straws) were the executive floors. "We finally found open offices! [But] The execs had whole football fields up there. You could drive trucks through their desks!" DeVito returned to Maryland disenchanted with the Open Office but willing to keep an open mind.

DeVito had hired California architect Frank Gehry (remember Jay Chiat's office chair?) who set about designing a classic "open" building, atrium and all. And DeVito set about filling it in. He put in walls where walls weren't supposed to be, and windows where the original plan called for open space. The result, DeVito firmly believes, is a better building, a more private building, and a less "totalitarian" building. One suited to the first developer to introduce natural elements into the artificial landscape of the shopping mall. And one that has worn well for over 15 years largely because "it can't be tightly identified with any specific architectural style."

DeVito's own office faces a serene wood-trellised patio overlooking a calming view of an outdoor man-made lake. In all seasons the place is alive with colorful flowers, shrubs, and other verdant landscaping. The company employs "what amounts to a horticulturalist" just to keep it all fresh and in bloom.

The room deliberately creates a feeling of transparency, of floating somewhere in space above the lake and the trees. Furnishings are mainly Modernist classics, sparingly grouped, except for a striking rather old cupboard parked in a corner, of which DeVito says simply, "It came from some shop in New York. The first thing I told Frank," DeVito recalls, "is, I don't need a desk." And he doesn't have one. Instead, a few papers are scattered across a broad polished-wood conference table, "Which I hardly ever use." Most of the time, DeVito runs Rouse from "right here on this couch," which he proudly points out, has been recovered only once "in the same white Haitian cotton it came in" since the day he moved in in 1974. (White Haitian cotton? How much use could it possibly be getting?) All the other furnishings have remained precisely the same.

One of the chief advantages of Modernism, DeVito remarks, is that if you like it, it never grows old, although the same could be said for any style. "Some people may find this too spare, or too sterile," he admits, casually gazing around at his clean, uncluttered surroundings. "But I like it. I find it extraordinarily calming."

Step off the elevator onto the second floor of Fred Carr's First Executive Life Center in West Los Angeles. Cool your heels (let's hope not for too long) in one of an unlikely pair of baby-blue leather couches bearing boomerang-shaped wings (like the fins on an old Cadillac), conceivably beamed down from the Starship Enterprise.

The Apples and Pinocchios of Fred (First Executive Life) Carr

Pick up your complimentary copy of the 100% rag-paper booklet "Insuring Creativity: Art At Executive Life," and find this inscription: "A sprawling metropolis with no specific center, Los Angeles defies easy description . . . it is a city constantly on the move, creating a style which thrives on the unconventional and original . . ."

One such "unconventional, original touch" is the basket of fresh apples sitting on the glass table in the lobby, beneath the "Mixed Media Piece in Mica, Acrylic, and Roplex." "When I took over this company in 1974, we were basically bankrupt," Fred Carr declares. "The first thing I did was put fresh apples out for my employees. It was a way of saying, 'Sorry, but this is all you can expect from me now.'"

The employees presumably appreciated the gesture, while the fortunes of First Executive appreciated as well. With something over $16 billion in assets, 14 years after Carr took over it's one of the top 20 life insurance companies in America. Every morning a basket of fresh apples appears on this table, no excuses accepted.

Carr located this building at the nexus of the San Diego and Santa Monica freeways. A friendly, somewhat rumpled man with a gentle smile masking the mind of a master strategist (he is, after all, a veteran of Wall Street's "Go-Go Years"), his other daring decision revolving around traffic patterns was the location of his own office.

When the 10-story building was finished, Carr chose to settle on the second floor because, he says, it virtually eliminates the potential for political jockeying among senior executives for higher floors, or proximity to some imagined "power center."

"We're not a heavily hierarchical company," he explains. "That's why this is not an executive floor. I deliberately scattered key executives throughout the various departments, because the company has evolved along functional lines, not hierarchical ones."

Several lines of defense create visual and psychological barriers blocking a visitor's casual entry into Carr's sovereign state. Behind "The Jetsons' living room" (the outer reception area) is an "inner" reception area, staffed by several hushed, polite aides, guarding the gate to Carr's inner sanctum. Carr's L-shaped large room is dark walled and dark carpeted, with windows blocked by venetian blinds (closed). It embraces you as you sink deep within soft velvet cushions. It contains all the standard components of corporate comfort. It's an executive womb.

The room would be somber if not for two treasure troves displayed on dozens of glistening glass shelves. They gleam in the low, indirect light, the now-famous (in L.A. lore, at least) Apple and Pinocchio collections. "Steuben apples, marble apples, apples from all over the world," Carr chants and then winks. Malcolm Forbes has his Fabergé eggs, Carr has his apples. The symbolic significance of the apples, Carr has explained. As for the Pinocchios, which surely lend the hushed, tomblike space a festive air, he seems genuinely stumped. But during the course of our visit, not one of their noses has grown.

"The thing I like best about this office," Charles M. "Mike" Harper cracks, "are these hidden spotlights we shine on the hot seat right there on the couch. So when I ask [a subordinate] a question like, 'Why are your earnings down in the past quarter?' you feel the heat."

Charles (ConAgra) Harper's Electronic Nerve Center

Despite this wry reference to The Power Office, Mike Harper's L-shaped corner on the 14th floor of ConAgra headquarters in downtown Omaha sure seems friendly enough. In fact, with its traditional American furnishings (comfortable sofa, deep upholstered chairs, old burnished brass lamps), it could easily be a well-appointed suite at one of the "better" hotels, maybe even right here in Nebraska.

ConAgra, founded in 1919 as Nebraska Consolidated Mills, had its first major food hit with Duncan Hines cake mix, a sure seller back in the Fifties. It then sold that product line to Procter & Gamble for enough dough to build a flour-and-feed mill in Puerto Rico. Today, ConAgra is a major presence in the global food chain, with feed-lots in Spain, catfish farms in Georgia, and the largest poultry and red-meat processing operation in the world.

This isn't a Power Office. And with his Midwestern brown suit, yellow short-sleeved sport shirt, brown tie (tacked down, of course), and scuffed brown wing-tipped shoes, this tall (6′6″), thin man doesn't appear to be Power Possessed.

What he does appear to be is an involved corporate chief. The dead-giveaway is a glowing digital console giving continuous readouts of the time in various time zones. It blinks dimly atop Harper's private terminal, itself tucked discretely off in a corner, beneath some charming prints of vintage airplanes. (Harper's a pilot.)

Unlike most CEOs, Harper spends time at that terminal. "It's a central part of my day," he says. "Reading my E mail, looking at the latest data, you know." Harper's office is really a well-furnished electronic nerve center, moonlighting as a nice place to meet. Every Monday morning at 10:30, the numbers pop out on the screen. "Now the neat thing is," Harper exclaims, "that the numbers that flash on that screen for some 50 different companies are so fresh, our corporate controller hasn't even had a chance to 'bless' them yet!" Which means, he adds pointedly, that no positive spin has been put on them by anyone.

Harper's personal power is enhanced exponentially by the quality of data that flows through that terminal, as well as by his proven ability to interpret it, and act on it accordingly. As "one of the only food companies that operates all across the food chain," Harper explains, it's his job to grasp the fundamentals of a far-flung chain of autonomous independent operating companies. But ConAgra's Harper, at the end of the food chain, is the biggest fish in the pond.

"Ever wonder where fellows like me put all those plaques and awards we get?" Harper asks. "Well, I'll show you," he says. He leads us right into his own private bathroom (some 62% of *Fortune*-500 CEOs have one, according to the ASID survey, why shouldn't he?). He points out all these crazy plaques, commemorating such unlikely events as the time he rode a B-52 on a mission above Montana and the time he celebrated his 60th birthday by setting a new air speed class record for the San Francisco–New York run in a Cessna prop plane: 159.7 average MPH, in 16 hours, 9 minutes. "Hell of a long trip," Harper assures us, in the down-to-earth, low-key manner of a corporate chief who keeps his Ego wall hidden away in the bathroom.

And Finally, **L**et's end our tour where we began, with Jay Chiat. No re-
Chiat/Day in port on his digs would be complete without stopping in, at
LA-LA Land: least briefly, at his other coast. So here we are, with Carol
Venice, California Madonna, Chiat's West Coast assistant, offering us a Los Angeles credo: "Just because we dress casually out here doesn't mean we don't work as hard," she says. Chiat/Day (no Mojo out here) in L.A. operates out of a converted Levolor warehouse across a parking lot from The Rose Cafe, the epi-center of Venice café society, just two blocks from the Pacific.

Parts of this office suite have been shown at the Whitney Museum as Frank Gehry's (him, again) last word on the Open Office. Step past the spiky splayed wooden piles guarding the reception area, stare up at the rough-lumber vaulted ceiling with exposed insulation, gaze across acres of unfinished beaverboard shoulder-high cubicles, each containing a wooden desk and a Mac, and you might be fooled into imagining that things here are strictly functional. But function (except in the sense of purely visual, visceral entertainment) cannot explain the presence of Claes Oldenburg's "House Ball"—a 14-foot (in diameter) aluminum armature covered with foam and canvas, tied up with string, and suspended high in the air from a rafter. And oh, we almost forgot—the whole soft planetary expanse covered with foam-rubber versions of common household appliances.

We waltz past a fish-shaped conference room. It rears up against the glass walls of a trio of conference room "bubbles" familiarly known as Huey, Dewey, and Louie. A red vintage Datsun pickup nearly blocks our path, representing the Nissan account. ("Our creative director's surfboard usually sticks out of the back of that thing," says Madonna. "I guess he must be out using it." It's lunchtime in California.) The Battlestar Galactica, a hulking wooden tunnel, is "just a hallway that breaks up the cubicles," Madonna says (could have fooled us) and takes us to Main Street. Here they hold a lot of meetings. Beside is a tree that could be another prop from *Godot*. A second aluminum-sided conference room (well, unlike any aluminum siding you've ever seen) called "Three Mile Island" is surrounded on all sides by cardboard sofas and chairs. Chiat offers an explanation for such environs, for the office/ stage set that is about as extreme as one can imagine:

"Does the office sell the product? Well, I think it makes an impression. What an office does is make an announcement that a place is either more creatively driven or less creatively driven, more or less safe," he says.

"These impressions are often not terribly accurate. But the office should telegraph what the place is about," he adds. "You should walk in and say, 'Hey, this place has an energy I like.'"

—Stephen Fenichell

CLUBS:
IF OAK WALLS
COULD TALK

So what's the big deal about Aunt Clara? We wondered, as Chicago Club manager Paul C. Frederick started to make good on a promise to take us to meet her on the eighth floor.

Robert D. Cadieux, president of Amoco Chemical Company, on a new-member's tour of the cavernous old club, had nary a wrinkle in his nonchalance as he brushed by the elaborate staircase of polished brass, by oak-paneled rooms, matching smoked-glass fireplaces, a squash court, a masseur who could give salt rubs, and the other fine features of this 121-year-old institution. But at the mention of Aunt Clara's name, he became suddenly animated.

"Now there's a legend that goes along with Aunt Clara," began Frederick, with unabashed pride, as we ascended in the elevator. "See, she was the organist in the village church. She and the minister disappeared from town at the same time," he said. Cadieux nodded his head as if he already knew the story.

"Nobody knows whatever became of the minister, but Aunt Clara turned up on the French Riviera and quickly became the darling of Europe's royalty," he said. We arrived at the John Black room, which looked like your standard hotel meeting room—lecturn and all—except that it had a priceless view of Grant Park.

And there, hanging on the north wall, was Aunt Clara: a circa 1920s portrait of an attractive young woman dressed in a modest red outfit, looking not unlike a church organist.

"Now, for our New Year's Dinner we take her down to the dining room. And after the president's speech, I wouldn't really call it a speech because if it lasts more than about a minute everybody starts to holler—well, after the president's speech, we say:

Aunt Clara
She's dead to us all
We turn her portrait
To the wall

And then he physically turned the portrait, which apparently was mounted with a hinge device. And there was Aunt Clara again. But this was a rear view. And in this version she didn't look at all like a church organist. In fact, she was wearing see-through panties.

It was the ninth private club we had toured in less than a week's time and through all of it the word "anachronistic" kept coming to mind. But mind reading, as well as discretion, must be a job qualification for private club managers, because the next thing Frederick said to us was: "You know, it's sort of funny, but you could see worse than this right out on Michigan Avenue for free."

It's our conviction that the walls of America's private clubs are trying to talk. What other set of structures has witnessed so rich a history of secret rituals, clandestine summit meetings, tomfoolery among the power elite?

Lost within endless halls of oak paneling and deep among the preserved visages of long-dead industrialsts, one feels a connection with those of influence and power, the forceful few who—despite an unexplained propensity to cross-dress and perform in skits—made this country mighty. You can even come face to face with Herbert Hoover's favorite fly-caster, bequeathed to his beloved Bohemian Club and encased above a special plaque.

And then the clubs themselves, like portraits of skinny-dipping power mongers, come into sharper focus. Sure, these clubs provide one more stage for asserting one's considerable status. And, yes, they shelter leaders from the ranks of the less desirable. And, yes, they're the setting-of-choice for twisting the arm of someone on the opposite side of a business deal. But the walls reveal a less-discussed purpose. These places are playgrounds.

The windowless room measures about 15 feet by 14 feet.
That's just big enough to squeeze in a round, eight-setting table with barely the space left for a pair of corner flower stands, let alone a waiter or two hovering about—this in a state that prides itself on gargantuan sizes. The walls are adorned with a red paisley wall covering and there are two doors: one leads to the kitchen, the other to a genteel bar lounge.

The Most Exclusive Little Dining Room in Texas

Yet this is the sanctum sanctorum of the Lone Star State. Secreted away on the fifth floor of one of the anonymous shiny skyscrapers for which Houston is famed, in a tiny suite of rooms that could lay claim to more ball-and-claw furniture per square inch than probably anywhere within a thousand miles, this is said by some to be the most exclusive little dining room in Texas.

It is here, in this nameless, single-tabled room, that members of the little-known Coronado Club come for lunch when they have neither a partner nor special purpose for the occasion. And if private clubs in America had a soul, this little cubicle would likely be it. A somber space that feels older and more tradition-laden and seedier than it has a right to be—the Coronado Club was formed a mere three decades ago. But centuries and continents mean nothing within the confines of private clubs.

So it isn't surprising when club manager Mehdi Ale-Ebrahim, known to all as "Abraham," his back to an exotic tapestry from his native Middle East, explains, as way of introduction to the club: "This probably reminds you of 18th-century Britain." It probably would if not for what is heard in the background, a secretary telemarketing a future business lunch to be held in one of the club's handful of larger dining rooms. "That's right," she says into a telephone. "Your fish'll run you seventeen ninety-nine."

Typically, members not attending such a lunch meeting arrive alone and head straight for the inner sanctum. No stops at the bar (the well-trained waiters know what everybody drinks and bring it directly to the table). No stops at the library. (The "library" here consists of the current *Wall Street Journal, Barron's,* and maybe a hundred dusty books. In fact, there's nothing even remotely resembling a well-stocked library in any of Houston's private clubs. Hey, this is *Texas.)*

Chief executives sit and order Crabmeat Remick or plain old steaks brought by waiters dressed in dark-green jackets bearing the Coronado symbol, a crown. From a huge lazy susan, diners retrieve A-1 sauce or their favorite salad dressing. To get this far, one has to be fairly comfortable dumping A-1 sauce on tenderloin, although "Abraham" doesn't quite understand why anyone would use the stuff.

It is mid-morning, just before the noontime rush, and "Abraham" wants to make it clear that the quiet Coronado Club, founded by a group of "top-notch" Houston business leaders, with a current membership of about 300—and a penchant for mounted waterfowl—is a cut above its more egalitarian competitors in the lunch-club business. He nods his head in the direction of the Houston Club, a nearby, 2,500-member institution that features and advertises its famous "Shrimp Shucks." That's the place where George P. Mitchell, chairman of Mitchell Energy & Development, one of the richest men in Texas, lunches with regularity. "Abraham" shakes his head as he says: "You don't see fingerbowls at the Houston Club."

What you do see over there, at the city's oldest and biggest social institution, is a rather lively gathering of workaday, starched-white-collar Houstonians. In the flagstone-floored Grill, a so-called informal dining room, some of the diners even can be spotted without coat and tie. Situated on four low-level floors of a pre-boom (and, therefore, historic) building, the Houston Club clearly is the school cafeteria for the bulk of the corner-office crowd. That's not an exclusionary statement, since this is a metropolis with an office vacancy rate so high that virtually *everybody* could have a corner office.

You could host a nifty wedding reception at the Houston Club (although the nearby and equally accessible Petroleum Club, atop the 46-story Exxon Building, affords a far more dramatic view). And, there's a tiny and underutilized health club here, complete with that Houston redundancy, a steam bath. But don't look for sleeping rooms at the Houston, or, in fact, any other local club. For some reason that old standby of the newly separated marriage partner—living at the club— never caught on in Houston.

It's lunch, more than anything else that draws executives here. In fact, a full 80% of the Houston Club's trade takes place during the midday meal. The traffic is so heavy that a few years ago, when this city was still riding the crest of inflated oil prices, the Houston Club's library—such as it was— had to be converted into a dining room to accommodate the crowds. (Even the Allen's Landing Bar, for decades the club's room for after-work drinkfests, is virtually silent in these days of abstinence.)

Probably because this is Secretary's Week, second only to the week before Christmas in clamor, it's hard to pick out the CEOs, although many of them lunch here, keeping with the Texas custom of getting started before noon. As chairman of Texas Commerce Bancshares, Ben Love, for instance, frequently made the trip across the street for the noon buffet. "He was one of the first guys to write a letter when we put in the noon buffet," says manager David Jackson. "He uses it when he has nothing scheduled for a lunch. He's in and out in twenty minutes."

The lunching CEO really doesn't mingle much with the substantial crowds. "Seldom does anybody come up to one of those CEOs and interrupt him unless he's the same on the hierarchy. But people say things to them on their way in or out, like 'How you doing, Mr. Love?'," reports Jackson.

Some clubs go to great length to restrict from membership anyone who appears a bit too eager to gain access to members for potential business deals. But that's a nonissue at the Houston Club, where few applicants are rejected for membership, and where there isn't even a waiting list. "Oh, hell," says Jackson, "They're more opportunistic here. Nobody here would look at that as being a negative."

The Coronado Club, on the other hand, prefers to keep its roster limited to about 300 of Houston's finest and, "Abraham" says with unintended hyperbole, "Usually someone has to die or resign before a new member can join." Under the semisecret membership procedures, candidates ordinarily must be invited to join.

In other words, say your friend, Winthrop, is a member, he's taken you to lunch at the club, and you think it could be a stitch to join. You don't ask Winthrop to put up your name for membership. You wait patiently for Winthrop to ask you to apply. In fact, by the time he asks you, your eligibility already has been much discussed by the board of directors. Next, you need to earn the nod of a three-person "secret committee."

Here's how that works. After you're invited to apply for membership, you are asked to meet the board of directors at a little cocktail gathering. This is an occasion for your behavior and credentials to be scrutinized by three people who will make the ultimate recommendation regarding your membership. Trouble is, you won't know who among your hosts it is you are trying to impress, since the identities of the secret committee's members are known only to the president of the Coronado Club's board of directors.

"Abraham" admits that the procedure is simplified a bit if you are about to be named chairman of a local company whose current chairman is a member. If that's the case, the outgoing chairman is likely to write a letter of recommendation to the board to get the procedure all wrapped up before you take over the company.

But just as the Coronado Club has not deigned to select every CEO for candidacy, not all CEOs choose to join. Some prefer the Ramada Club, perhaps the only other city club around with an equal exclusivity rating. And there are two local country clubs that are respectable enough for those chief executives who fancy the links, instead of the dining room, as a place to entertain clients.

First, there's the Houston Country Club, an institution with a reputation for being so blue-blood dominant that even some of the city's top chief executives can't become members. And there's the slightly less exclusive (but none the less antebel-lum) River Oaks Country Club. At River Oaks, members pay $35,000 to join—about half of which may be returned to the member as stock in the club—and $215 a month in dues. That's probably a bargain for the chief executive who enjoys playing a couple of hands of poker at the tables that line the center of a cathedral-ceilinged men's locker room. And to celebrate a hole-in-one: A bottle of Leoville Barton, 1871, goes for only $1000.

But it is the Coronado Club, and not these lesser hangouts, that best embodies the spirit of private clubs. The secrecy. The splendid isolation. The deep-in-the-heart-of-Texas-we-must-be-British-lords neo-gallantry. Cloaked in the dark in-terior here, one can achieve the separate peace so sought after by those at the top who want to mingle—at least at lunch—only with other folks at the top. Put another way, it's a spot in which a captain of industry can throw back six noontime martinis, hidden from the gazes of shareholders, reporters or rank-and-filers.

"It's easier for a man to be loyal to his club than to his planet," said E. B. White, "The by-laws are shorter and he is personally acquainted with the members." But this is not a place to put that theory to the test. "The Coronado Club?" repeated the secretary to Coastal Corporation chairman Os-car Wyatt. "Oh, yes, Mr. Wyatt used to go there for lunch all the time when we were located downtown. Now that we've moved our offices, he hardly ever goes."

Just When You Thought You Had Arrived: The Club–Within–A–Club

With 64 dining rooms from which to choose, one literally could chow down in Pittsburgh's Duquesne Club every day for two months without ever dining in the same room twice. Not that any chief executive worthy of his corner office would ever consider such a reputation-detonating move. Fact is, in this bastion of Big Steel and Big Aluminum and Big Ketchup and, indeed, Big Money, where you ingest your calories counts as much as with whom you do it. Hint: That means you do it in Little Rooms.

Unlike most of the prominent private clubs catering to cor-porate America's lunching rituals, the Duquesne *is* in its hey-day. Part of that has something to do with the fact that Pittsburgh has more corporate headquarters per capita than any other U.S. city—unless you consider Stamford, Connecticut, or Oak Brook, Illinois, to be cities. And as far as exclusive clubs, this is just about the only one anybody around here bothers with. The Rolling Rock Country Club is too darn far to travel to for lunch.

Also, when it comes to eating, no one has ever called this burgh the "Paris of Appalachia"—there simply aren't many dining alternatives in Steel City, U.S.A.

So at the Duquesne Club's stately revolving door, in the minutes before noon, one feels a surge of anticipation, like being in the right place at the right time when the right things are about to start happening. And then, they do: A steady stream of somber-suited gentlemen, representing a spectrum of ages and school ties, starts rotating on through. And since this is a progressive institution, there is a handful of women, too, though when *they* fan out for their lunch sites, it's rare to spot them heading into areas other than the Crystal (formerly "Ladies") Dining Room.

Just how up-to-date is this place? Perhaps the most telling incident has to do with an oil portrait, by artist William H. Baird, entitled "The Ram." The pleasant depiction of a ram standing guard over his flock was first hung on the library wall about four decades ago. Trouble was, like most healthy rams, the beast in the painting bore an unavoidable set of testicles. And wouldn't you know it, the women were coming in for a special social function and were bound to be Grossed Out. So the painting was sent out to a local studio where a special bleaching process managed to strip the ram of his masculinity.

Now, flash forward to 1980. Women were crashing the Duquesne Club, threatening to rotate en masse through the revolving door, not the Ladies' entrance. They even wanted to become ... members! Shockingly, the Club membership agreed to accommodate them. But, they decided the time had come to get an artist to replace the scrotum. And then management installed a discreetly placed plaque explaining the story of the library wall that sprouted testicles.

But back to the here and now. At the Duquesne Club, one can tell who's what just by mastering the lunching hierarchy.

Let's start at what is, literally, the bottom. A corporate public relations type who wants to entertain a financial reporter would likely do it in the ground-floor garden patio, where the fountain is faintly reminiscent of the (New York)

Plaza's Palm Court and where the tables are made of—what else?—steel. (Hey, this is *Pittsburgh.*) If it's a young aluminum attorney doing the lunching, sharing with a half-dozen buddies the details of last night's intimate romantic endeavor, you'd probably find him in the Men's Grill Room, where, as the name implies, testicles are still de rigueur.

One flight up, among the red leather chairs of the huge main dining room, is where you could catch a senior VP of R&D (retired or otherwise) exhibiting civic/corporate allegiance by dumping Heinz catsup on some cold roast beef.

You've got to get significantly higher to sniff out the CEOs.

Virtually every Pittsburgh corporation maintains a private dining room—or even a suite of rooms—on the upper floors of the 12-story Duquesne Club. They comprise the bulk of the dining sites here. And that's where such chiefs as Vincent Sarni of PPG Industries or Charles A. Corry of USX spend their noon hours devouring sautéed Virginia spots and/or the stewed business associate du jour.

But there's an even more impressive place to nosh, a club-within-a-club known as the President's Room. "You have to be invited to join the room," sniffs Duquesne Club manager Melvin Rex. "And once you're a member of that room, you can eat there whenever you like." (As an indication of just how business-oriented this institution is, take a look at Rex's credentials: His background isn't only in restaurant management, he's a C.P.A. as well.)

It goes without saying that almost all of Pittsburgh's CEOs are members of the President's Room and patronize it. In fact, the Duquesne Club could safely offer a cash prize to the first person to spot a significant corporate chief in the vicinity of, say, the Crystal Room.

Just when you thought membership was enough, and that it was safe to sit *anywhere*, there's the club-within-a-club business to worry about.

At many of corporate America's favorite private social institutions, it's not nearly enough to endure the lengthy (and, if done properly, humiliating) procedure of applying for membership—the years of waiting to be sponsored, the multiple letters of reference, the membership committee interview, the waiting-list years. Once you're in, you're not really in. There's always another step, always another rung on the ladder.

The Chicago Club, for example, has its Room 100. That's a collection of about 70 of the Windy City's most eminent capitalists. Just go down the list of local CEOs and they're certain to be Room 100'ers. Richards M. Morrow (of Amoco), Edward A. Brennan (Sears), James Bere (Borg-Warner), John H. Bryan, Jr. (Sara Lee), Barry R. Sullivan (First Chicago). . . . It's no coincidence this little clubette is so CEO-dominant; tradition holds that only one individual per corporation can join.

And it's not, as you can see, limited to any one industry. "Time was when these inner clubs [there are six] pretty much centered around a special interest," says Chicago Club manager Frederick. "Like Room 19 was mostly railway and railway supply people. But it's not like that much anymore. I guess at Room 100 the common interest would be the dollar."

What does this Room 100 consist of? Is it anything more than a support group for those stuck at the top of their corporate heap?

Physically speaking, the room isn't much fancier than an average podiatrist's den. It's a simple, L-shaped headquarters located directly below the room in which Aunt Clara is on permanent display. Picture worn brown leather sofas and red nubby-finish wool wing chairs. A white tablecloth draped over an old wooden table. And providing the best that Chicago has to offer, you can both view Lake Michigan and hear the El.

This meeting place sees action only on Thursdays, when members of Room 100 host their sole traditional happening: lunch. Club management mails out RSVP postcards to Room 100 types several days in advance and the members respond if they want to come for lunch. According to Frederick, only about 15 members attend any given week. So it's exclusive, not necessarily popular.

Guaranteed, you'll find a much more jovial collection of fellows over in Room 503, another club-within-a-club. There actually are two rooms there. In the outer room, a comfortable and very large lounge-type area, sit two retirees. In the adjacent dining room, which boasts secret panels in which private stashes of liquor may be stored, there is a large table elaborately adorned with two side-by-side place settings.

It is about 1:00 P.M. and this pair of gentlemen—perhaps to

relive past corporate battles, perhaps escaping boredom, perhaps merely out of routine—are meeting for their weekly lunch ritual. And they are plastered, sitting together on the couch, giggling.

"Look at our memorabilia display. You've got to see our legacy," says one, with a smirk. Hanging in a corner is an artistic rendering of "Honey Marley," red-lipped and lying on her back, and donated to Room 503 by Pullman Company magnate George Pullman when his wife got sick of looking at it. Nearby is an extensive collection of photos and clippings that pays tribute to the Everleigh Club, which in the earliest years of the century was "probably the world's most opulent bordello," according to one of the retirees.

Next he points out a few other reproduced photographs from Chicago history. "Remember that?" one of the old timers says to the other, referring to a Chicago street scene. "Remember when that was a nice place?" Then the two march into the dining room for lunch.

Chief executives and other folks who hang around in private clubs get a kick out of being out of pace with the current century. And who could blame them? Life was substantially more tolerable in, say, the early 1850s. *Back to the Garden (Without Eve)*

Back then a group of like-minded English merchants, struggling to maintain a sense of dignity and class structure amid the raucousness of gold-booming San Fancisco, could organize a club in which they could get smashed without being bothered by the riffraff. (They did. They formed the Pacific Club in 1852.) Or, in the same town, a confederation of transplanted, upper-crust Southerners could establish a similar retreat (They did, the ill-named Union Club, established in 1854. With Britishers and Southerners being on such common social footing, the Pacific and Union were consolidated in 1889.)

Even as recently as the late 1860s, it was not unusual for a group of unmarried men in New York to set up house together and incorporate as a private club. Indeed, many clubs got started innocently enough when professional men discovered it was less costly to pool a weekly $20 apiece, rent a Fifth Avenue townhouse and hire a staff to produce meals than it was to live independently and eat out.

But in the equal-opportunity-obsessed late 1980s, such

wholesome—albeit exclusive—endeavors are frowned upon. And private clubs, the proud memorials to those years of privacy and civility and Windsor chairs—have become the object of another obsession of our times: litigation.

Many chief executives won't join clubs that discriminate, and some eschew the club life altogether. But many others find themselves swept up in an ungentlemanly fervor, using up perfectly good drinking time to defend the right to discriminate against women or religious, racial, and ethnic minorities who are trying to lodge their grubby little feet in the solid oak doors.

Among the defenses for keeping out the unwanted: proving that business transactions never take place at the clubs. If the clubs don't permit the conducting of business within their walls, then the uninvited cannot claim they are denied equal access to such business dealings as publicly funded contracts. (If truth be told, some of the clubs have for years been mounting their own, internal attacks on the conducting of business in what were intended to be social institutions. In the late 1950s, when the Pacific-Union Club sent out notices to its members forbidding open briefcases or visible business papers within the club's walls, one member griped, "Next thing you know they'll be telling us not to throw up in the reading room!"—according to *Men at the Top,* a 1959 study of chief executives.)

Nowhere has the attack on clubs been so steamy as at Bohemian Grove, a 2,700-acre Northern California redwood grove at which San Francisco's Bohemian Club holds its annual two-week summer encampment for an odd coupling of the nation's power and artistic elite. The strictly all-male affair draws in U.S. presidents and librettists and captains of industry and authors and U.S. Supreme Court justices and U.S. cabinet members and jazz pianists. They stay in 125 rustic camps-within-a-camp, bearing names like "Care Less" or "Moonshiners" or "Ye Merrie Yowls" or "Derelicts," clustered like expanded treehouses along roadways and trails. Bars, often formed out of unfinished redwood planks, are a prominent and well-utilized feature of many of the camps, so it's probably a good thing that autos—like telephones—are banned. (In accordance with the in-the-wilds motif, an elephant bus shuttles men from camp to camp or event to event.)

It's so glorious a place that California's Fair Employment and Housing Department took the 117-year-old club to court so women could have the chance to *work* at the Grove. The equal-employment advocates came out ahead and the Bohemian Club's Grove committee now is in the process of figuring out how to implement a state appeals court order to hire women (without putting a damper on what Herbert Hoover called "the greatest men's party on Earth").

Part of the difficulty stems from the well-known encampment tradition in which members and guests may urinate on trees if they feel the need. Such members as William F. Buckley and former California Governor Edmund G. Brown, Sr. have testified in court against the impending invasion by female employees, claiming the presence of women (even waitresses) would destroy the uniqueness of the retreat— perhaps create some sort of performance anxiety. "You wouldn't be able to have that complete relaxation that you get in a temporary world of men," said Brown in 1980. (Face it, guys: When it comes to male-bonding extravaganzas, everything else is quite junior varsity. Even members are forbidden to photograph the goings-on.)

Mention Bohemian Grove to any reasonably sophisticated person in, say, Center City Philadelphia, and you're likely to get a response that lacks in reasonable sophistication, like, "Isn't that the place where Henry Kissinger goes to walk around naked?"

Yes, men do walk around as if this were Eden, but generally only between cabins or tents and the open-air showers—or if they're taking a skinny dip in the Russian River, which skirts the camp (in recent years, river pollutants have made swimming an unappealing activity). But nudity is not quite as prevalent as is reputed. "If anyone in *my* camp walked around naked he'd get a rotten tomato thrown at him," says a member of the "Poker Flat" camp, where members sleep in simple, golden-colored tents, four bunks to a tent, and where an Ol' West saloon-type front covers the outhouse and showerhouse.

Dressing as women, however, is tolerated. But that activity is believed to be limited to those performing in the Grove's elaborate theatrical productions, staged in open-air amphitheatres where the lighting is rigged on 300-foot-tall redwoods.

For the most part, though, the Grove is a place to hear member George Shearing perform his jazz, or hear the Grove orchestra perform "Peter and the Wolf" to member Henry Kissinger's narration, or Copland's "Lincoln Portrait" to member Walter Cronkite's narration. It's also a place in which to get magnificently drunk and see the redwoods the way they are most impressive (on one's back) or escape to one of the nearby resort towns for a discreet rendezvous, although the latter is not officially sanctioned by the management. "Yes, for years there have been rumors of dalliance. But we discourage that," says one member, adding: "But we've got 2,000 members, all grown men, and no curfew."

And with such complete freedom comes the liberty to be ambitious. It was at the 1967 Grove encampment that Ronald Reagan reportedly promised Richard Nixon he wouldn't compete for the 1968 Republican presidential nomination. At the 1979 encampment, Alexander Haig launched his short-lived bid for the presidency. And while business transactions and the signing of contracts are barred on the Grove property, who knows what takes place within the screened-in porches of "Mandalay," which is unquestionably the grove's "power" camp? (Members and guests have included the likes of former Secretary of State George P. Schultz, former IBM chairman and U.S. Ambassador to the Soviet Union Thomas J. Watson, Jr., former President Gerald Ford, Bechtel Group chairman Stephen D. Bechtel, Jr., former Du Pont chairman Irving Shapiro.)

Not that any overly zealous encampers would feel free to hike uninvited up to "Mandalay" (which is, by the way, one of the remotest and least accessible camps) or corner a high government official during a break in a lakeside poetry reading and hope to negotiate a defense contract. But the simple power-by-association can aid a chief executive in need. In his 1988 book about the Bechtel Group, *Friends in High Places,* author Laton McCartney quoted John D. Ehrlichman as saying: "Once you've spent three days with someone in an informal situation, you have a relationship—a relationship that opens doors and makes it easier to pick up the phone."

During that July encampment, as in the 50-week offseason, Bohemian Grove is a sweet-smelling and well-tended refuge for osprey and mallards, a paradise of incidental waterfalls, wild azaleas and what must be millenium-old redwoods. This is the ideal sanctuary in which to *really* be out of step with the current century. To muse about life before federal regulations and capital gains taxes and SEC filings. To fantasize about an earlier, simpler era while simultaneously hatching next year's acquisition strategy.

"**L**et's just say this is a group of friends," said an officer of The Brook, which may be New York's (and, therefore, the nation's) most enigmatic and exclusive social institution.

To the Right of Park Avenue

For men may come and men may go, But I go on for ever.

"The Brook"
Alfred, Lord Tennyson

Over at the Chicago Club, for instance, the manager will gladly issue you a copy of the bylaws and membership roster—even phone some of the members to arrange interviews. But try getting that service at The Brook! To track down the identities of members of this secretive society, you must first haul out the Social Register and painfully go down the list, name by name, seeking out and circling listees whose credentials include the symbol "B."

In all, about 500 men belong to the 86-year-old club, which maintains a strict and intentionally vague "invitations-only" membership policy. Cornelius Vanderbilt III, W. Vincent Astor, Averell J. Clark, Ellsworth Bunker, and Fred Astaire were members. Laurance Rockefeller, David Ogilvy, Henry Clay, and Drew Middleton still are.

The Brook operates out of an unprepossessing, unmarked—that means no name anywhere—four-story brick townhouse located at 111 East 54th Street. That's slightly to the right of Park Avenue, barely missing the shadow of the Citicorp building. With its street-level air conditioner wrapped in a brown plastic bag during the colder months, the place maintains a shabby appearance for passersby. But that may be intended to mask the treasures within: "Four American Students," a 1765 painting by Benjamin West that depicts a cricket scene near Cambridge College; a Benjamin West self-portrait; a portrait of Benjamin Franklin at the Court of France at the end of the 18th century; and a collection of rare English antique furniture.

Back in the 1950s a *Fortune* article on executive lunches laid out the pecking order of New York clubs: "At the Metropolitan or the Union League or the University . . . you might do a $10,000 deal, but you'd use the Knickerbocker or the

OTHER CITIES, OTHER CLUBS
Traveling? Here's a sampling of clubs in other U.S. cities.

CITY	CLUB(S)	SPECIAL ATTRACTIONS	CITY	CLUB(S)	SPECIAL ATTRACTIONS
Atlanta, Georgia	Capital City Club	Old money bankers		The Long Room	Oysters; Antebellum atmosphere; George Washington ate here
	Commerce Club	Where Old South meets New South; early remover of discriminatory practices	Denver, Colorado	Denver Club	Old money; squash courts
	World Trade Club	Import-export businessmen		Denver Country Club	Old money; mountain views
Boise, Idaho	Arid Club	Ogden split-granite boulder fireplace	Des Moines, Iowa	Bohemian Club	Insurance salesmen
	Hillcrest County Club	Proximity to downtown allows for lunchtime tennis		Des Moines Club	Midwestern friendliness; Dover sole (frozen); upper management
Boston, Massachusetts	The Country Club (Brookline)	Nation's oldest country club; where 17-year-old former caddy Francis Ouimet defeated Brits to win U.S. Open in 1913		Embassy Club	Middle management
			Kennebunkport, Maine	Cape Arundel Golf Club	Golf; George Bush
				River Club	Tennis; boats; George Bush
	Harvard Club	Main clubhouse (there are two) in Back Bay is the neighborhood's most homelike hotel	Lexington, Kentucky	Idle Hour Country Club	Golf; horse conversation; invitations-only membership
	Somerset Club	Nation's oldest city club; best place to spot a Brahmin	Nashville, Tennessee	Cumberland Club	New facility redecorated to reflect tastes of new female members; Civil War memorabilia; homemade melba toast; white bean-and-ham soup
Charleston, South Carolina	Carolina Yacht Club	On Cooper River bank, the South's most traditional club; memberships must be inherited			
	Country Club of Charleston	On Ashley River bank, view of downtown; magnolias			

City	Club	Description
New York, N.Y. (Downtown Manhattan)	The Downtown Association	One of Wall Street areas few six-story buildings; British furnishings; great rice pudding
	India House	One of Wall Street area's few four-story buildings; curry dishes
Oklahoma City, Oklahoma	Beacon Club	New England clam chowder (Fridays); rooftop views; old-money bankers, lawyers
	Petroleum Club	Rooftop views; oil businessmen
Philadelphia, Pennsylvania	Locust Club	Lavish Bar Mitzvah receptions
	Philadelphia Club	Pedigreed Philadelphians
	Union League	Snapper soup
Phoenix, Arizona	Arizona Club/ uptown	Barry Goldwater (member); Sandra Day O'Connor (member's wife); carrot bread; men's health club; one membership gets three locations
	Arizona Club/ downtown	Proximity to Courthouse; library (aka Jurists' Sleeping Room); billiards
	Arizona Club/ Scottsdale	New facility with patio dining; shuffleboard tables; electronic darts
Portland, Oregon	Arlington Club	Never a female
San Antonio, Texas	Argyle Club	Antique-stuffed former horse-ranch plantation house in Alamo Heights residential area; Murray's Seafood Gumbo is worth the 20-minute drive from downtown
San Diego, California	San Diego Yacht Club	Controversial America's Cup Victory
San Francisco, California	Franciscan Club	Females-only lunch club (male guests permitted)
	Metropolitan Club	Females-only membership but men can eat, sleep over and (on weekends) swim
St. Paul, Minnesota	St. Paul Athletic Club	Two indoor running tracks (only other is at the YMCA); lunch-time legislators and lobbyists
Washington, D.C.	Cosmos Club	Abundance of Nobel recipients: Herbert Simon (economics); Frederick Robbins (physiology and medicine); Herbert Hauptman (mathematics); William Fowler (physics); Henry Kissinger (peace)
Williamsport, Pennsylvania	Ross Club	Proximity to Allenwood; World Little League headquarters

—DAVID DIAMOND

CEOS ON THE ROAD

Where They Stay

Where They Eat

CITY	FAVORITE HOTEL	CITY	FAVORITE RESTAURANT
Boston	Ritz Carlton	Paris	Taillevent
Hong Kong	Mandarin	Washington, D.C.	Lion d'Or
Phoenix	Arizona Biltmore	Beverly Hills	L'Orangerie
Zurich	Dolder Grand	Philadelphia	Le Bec Fin
Dallas	Mansion on Turtle Creek	London	Connaught Grill
Laguna Niguel, Calif.	Ritz Carlton	San Francisco	Blue Fox
Houston	Remington	New York	Four Seasons
Singapore	Shangri La	Whippany, N.J.	La Delicé
San Francisco	Stanford Court	Honolulu	Michel's
New York	Helmsley Palace		

Union or the Racquet for $100,000, and then for $1 million, you'd have to move on to the Brook or the Links." That was when $1 million meant a great deal more than it does today.

Since women began suing to gain membership in private clubs, charging that they are denied equal access to the business dealings that take place within the exclusive walls, men's club officers everywhere have rallied a defense. Many of them have set out to prove that business matters simply are not discussed at their clubs. Some have even rewritten the bylaws to that effect. Women, they maintain, are not missing out on anything. It's not odd, then, that one of the very few on-the-record comments any official of The Brook will issue is this: "This is a nonbusiness club. In fact, there's a prohibition against conducting business here." Then he repeats: "It's just a quiet group of friends."

Fact is, The Brook wasn't always such a concealed operation. One May evening back in 1930, co-founder Thomas Benedict Clarke gave an after-dinner lecture detailing the society's 1903 formation to 28 of its members. A year later, The Brook published the speech under the title: *The Brook: Its Incentive, Incidents, Organization and Progress.*

Clarke revealed how he and a few cronies—who seemed to spend a great deal of time debating the benefits and drawbacks of the various clubs they frequented—struck upon the idea of starting a club with a character that would accommodate the best of two existing organizations: The Century and The Lambs. "One represented the dignity of club life, the other its freedom," said Clarke. And one fateful night in the late 1890s, he told cofounder Horace Robbins: "If we could organize a small club, midway between the polite Bohemia of The Century and the charm and ease of The Lambs, I believe that we could obtain the best that club life affords." At that point, the new club was a mere fantasy.

The formation of The Brook was hastened one night in 1902 when Clarke and several others were hanging out in the Century Association's main reading room. At the stroke of midnight, the lights began to dim. "Gentlemen," said Clarke, "the impatient waiters, by these signs, are telling us that it is time for us to leave this club! Evidently these footmen have *their own* engagements to fulfill. *Some of these days we shall have a small club in this town which will provide its members with continuous service!*"

And so, with roughly the same philosophy that launched Denny's Restaurants and other all-night establishments, they formed their new club, culling the name from Tennyson's poem. To underscore the 24-hours-a-day nature of the place, on opening day the founding members took the clubhouse key (the original clubhouse was on East 35th Street), fastened it to a bunch of balloons and sent it drifting skyward. *"Horace,"* Clarke observed, *"we shall never need that key again!"*

Yes, when pay scales for doormen were relatively inconsequential, members probably never did need that key. And for decades, The Brook maintained its unique service-anytime tradition. "Up until World War Two, it was possible to come in at three A.M. and get served dinner," said Patrick Cunniff, The Brook's taciturn-to-a-fault manager. "At World War Two all that changed." Why? Noted one member: "The club just isn't used the way it was back then." He paused, adding: "And with labor costs, it doesn't make practical sense to keep a chef back there all night."

If not for late-night snacks, why then, is this establishment still in business? Not likely for its scarce seven sleeping rooms, although the members (never guests!) keep the occupancy rate relatively high. And not likely for the lunch trade. On a "good" day, a scant 25 lunches are served—and at a communal table. Replies one member: "Let's just say it's a quiet club for friends."

Or maybe there's a message in The Brook's Supper Song:

Our Brook never ceases to run.
'Tis a Club for Club men
Who know How, Where, and When!
The last word when all's said and done.

—DAVID DIAMOND

CLOTHES: PACKAGING THE CEO

You see it daily in the corridors of corporate America: the would-be chief executive officer commiting the classic eager-beaver boo-boo. He comes to work early, stays late and conducts after-hours chicanery, if any, with the discretion of superspy George Smiley.

For lunch, he starts nibbling nail-bed regimens of rabbit food at his desk. His dark-blue tie stays taut. His shirt—one of those colored jobs with white collar and cuffs—stays buttoned. Sometimes his dark blue suit coat stays on all day.

With a new, paternal smile, he starts acknowledging hallway colleagues with a measured, low-decibel, "Nice to see you." Mail starts getting answered like this: "Thank you for your [pick one] kind/generous/thought-

On Becoming Dull

ful/engaging note," instead of like this: "I thought I knew the depths to which stupidity could be measured, but your letter . . ."

You'll want to keep an eye on this fellow, because he's eventually going to make your life miserable. What's happened? Somebody from upstairs has pulled him aside and whispered the chromosome-altering words: "One day, son, all this could be in your hands."

But it won't be. His highest title will be vice-president in charge of serious. (Somebody's got to do it.) He's peaked too early. He's gotten dull too soon.

To become a chief executive, you have to get dull in stages, shedding just enough humanity, whimsy, collegiality and sartorial eccentricity with each promotion to exhibit a bit more of the progress, maturation and fine-tuning required to comfort (or sedate) board members and shareholders. As a fast-rising underling, you want to excite. As CEO, you want to soothe. This reverse metamorphosis from glittering butterfly to well-turned-out worm is a delicate maneuver that requires perfect timing.

What we are really talking about here is packaging—the expensive game of visual promotion that helps determine the winners in the marketplace.

The precise choreography of this maneuver has become especially tricky in recent years because we've seen a slight uptick in flamboyance. The rise of bright hankies (pocket squares), suspenders (braces) with frolicking nudes, tie bars and that kind of stuff to higher levels in the executive suite has made it tough to gauge the pace at which one should shed them.

To help us find our way, we consulted the oracles of corporate fashion, read the how-to books, scoured the magazines and ads ("Introducing De Rigueur, for the man who has learned to wear his income properly").

We even attended a "dynamic Executive Wardrobe Engineering seminar," conducted for $2500 by Lois *(Dress for Excellence)* Fenton, who, for $900 a day, will go shopping with you. This is the same seminar Ms. Fenton gave the troops at Drexel Burnham Lambert before the firm got into trouble with the SEC, but no one is claiming any cause and effect.

For starters, we turned to columnist Dave Barry, author of the seminal work *Claw Your Way to the Top.* He says it best: "Basically, the American businessman should dress as though he recently lost his entire family in a tragic boat explosion."

This is neither cheap nor easy. Potential CEOs have to pretend they don't care about clothes. Yet they can't be just average. They have to mold the basic dull look into their own fashion statement and pay exorbitant sums to achieve it.

Suits are obviously the centerpieces of the executive wardrobe. But we deal with them elsewhere in this chapter, so here we'll tell you about the other accoutrements of painstakingly refined dullness.

Shirts: Paying through the nose is the best policy. Custommades by Turnbull & Asser (London) can skirt dandyism. Paul Stuart (New York, Tokyo) sells made-to-measure shirts for from $66 to a seemingly hefty $164 each because, among other things, their "cuffs have a personal relationship to the wrists they encircle." Any shirts that have personal relationships seem highly desirable to us.

"You will never, ever, as long as you live, wear a short-sleeved shirt for any business purpose," wrote John T. *(Dress for Success)* Molloy. This is nonsense if you live in San Diego, says designer John Weitz, who wrote *Man in Charge.*

Watches: The way science education is going in this country, it may soon be a sign of intellectual prowess to be able to tell time on an analog. So you want a watch with hands, not digital displays.

Footwear: People who wear scuffed shoes are communist. Period.

The best off-the-shelf shoes in America are at Brooks Brothers. They're British-made. So, of course, are good Church's. But our man, surely, needs custom-made. And that means John Lobb, the legendary British bootmaker. But when somebody asks, "Aren't those Lobb of St. James's?" you say, "Oh, heavens no. Lobb of Paris, of course." Older, more experienced shoemakers there, points out designer-author-purveyor Alan Flusser.

In any case, dip into your children's education fund. Lobb shoes cost around $500 each. No, not each pair. Each foot.

All shoes from John Lobb & Sons are hand-made from

waxed calf (reversed, of course). Only reversed, waxed calf can be "boned" to get scratches out. All skins are selected by specialists known as clickers, who fit the skins to a wooden last that is hand-turned from selected hardwoods—beech, maple or hornbeam. A $1000 pair of shoes is a steal compared to the $3000 price tag for a pair of Lobb dress or "Polo" boots.

Ties: There is nothing wrong with spending $50 for a necktie. When some ties start costing $100, however, you'll have to throw all your $50 ties away or risk looking cheap.

Please, no ties that tell a story, like the one we own that shows Fred Astaire and Ginger Rogers dancing. Says Ms. Fenton: Ties need names, like foulards. Our paced-incremental-dullness formula dictates that whatever gewgaw patterns you have on your foulards (diamonds, crowns, pheasants, dots, baby sharks, whatever), do this: With each major promotion, buy new ones on which the gewgaws are one size smaller. Men who wear dark blue ties with microscopic pin dots are called "Sir" a lot.

And only buy silk. (For that matter, never wear any clothes made out of petroleum, only fibers made by sheep, plants or worms).

Colors: For people who actually produce a tangible product, dark blue, burgundy and power red are in. Wall Street money shufflers can still get away with yellow. Pink is still around, but avoid it if your company makes a product with more than three moving parts.

An aside: While we are on the subject of shopping, let us toss in a couple of other pointers.

Fishermen need consider only a fine Tonkin bamboo or old Leonard flyrod, a reel by Ross, Hardy or Michel Pezon and custom-made Ranger waders. A hunter, or pseudo-hunter, who wants to be taken seriously needs the right shotguns. That's right. A brace of Purdeys or Holland & Hollands. While you may think that sacrificing your country home is a high price to pay for $100,000 worth of shotguns, just remember: There is nothing more telling than a man with a single Purdey.

—JAMES P. STERBA

Today's CEO wardrobe is still powerfully influenced by the *What They* Anglo-Saxon Sartorial Ascendency. When we peppered 351 *Wear* CEOs with questions as to their favorite haberdasheries, watch brands, shirt styles and the like, an extraordinarily high percentage came out in favor of the established Ivy League style.

For their favorite tie color, nearly 40% of CEO respondents chose red (39.6%), closely followed (nearly neck-and-neck) by blue, dark blue or navy (37.9%). Maroon, wine or dark red were favored by 8.8%, while yellow, once a power tie color, earned a mere 3.3% of available votes. Brown did even worse, favored by just 1.7% of the total. Gray drooped badly behind with 1.4%, barely worth mentioning at all but for the dismal performance of stripes, preferred by a pathetic .9% of the total, tying paisley for dead last.

White was voted most popular shirt color by a startling 53% of the total, followed by blue in second with 35%. Pink, ecru, off-white, gray, pastel, tan and yellow all did poorly, with none achieving higher than a less-than-one percentage point range.

For a revealing (and to some fashion coordinators, depressing) statistic regarding favorite suit colors, note that a clear-cut majority (53%) opted for blue, dark blue or navy blue suits, in close but cool competition with gray, charcoal or dark gray, favored by 39.6%.

Brown or dark brown earned a mere 4.3% while black or black pinstripe pulled down 2.3%, barely beating out "miscellaneous others" at .9% (that same .9%, perhaps, who also wore paisley ties.)

Given such clear-cut conformist tendencies (in this context it might be interesting to note that "suit" means: 1. "a vestment of clothes," and 2. "to fit, to be appropriate"), it's hardly surprising that the favorite CEO haberdashery, by an overwhelmingly wide margin, is Brooks Brothers. But that's another story.

The great corporate battle of 1988 was waged between RJR *Bijan,* Nabisco CEO H. Ross Johnson and Henry Kravis of the lev- *Barneys and* eraged buyout firm Kohlberg, Kravis and Roberts for control *Brooks Brothers* of RJR Nabisco, but precious few understood what was really going on: behind the scenes, a high-level sartorial struggle

PERCENTAGES OF CEOs WHO WEAR:

CUSTOM-MADE OR READY-MADE CLOTHES		MOST POPULAR CEO WATCHES	
Ready-made suits	72%	Seiko	24%
Custom-made suits	27%	Rolex	16%
Ready-made shirts	71%	Omega	7%
Custom-made shirts	25%		

between Ascot Chang customer Henry Kravis and Bijan devotee H. Ross Johnson for fashion dominance.

Henry Kravis, who has been noticed (such things tend to be noticed) snapping up 100 custom-made shirts at a pop at Ascot Chang, is known as an elegant dresser who's married to well-known designer Carolyn Roehm. (Chang also makes shirts for President Bush and has the shirts run up in the New York workrooms instead of Hong Kong, apparently a singular honor.)

H. Ross Johnson, on the other hand, was hardly a fashion plate at all until he consulted Bijan for a complete fashion makeover preparatory to making his Nabisco bid. (Well, maybe the timing is not entirely accurate, but you get the point.)

In the battle between a Hong Kong tailor—known, as are most household-name Hong Kong tailors, for flexible styling—and the Iranian-born tailor known for his flamboyant marketing strategy, the real loser somehow got overlooked.

Neither of the gentlemen shopped at Brooks Brothers.

Referred to by some loyalists simply as "The Brothers," whether it be the Madison Avenue flagship or any one of its astonishingly look-alike satellite branches in downtowns and shopping malls across the country, from Bal Harbor to Seattle, Brooks Brothers has been *the* force to be reckoned with when it comes to purveying sartorial staples to the upper-echelon corporate American male.

But in the past half decade, Brooks Brothers ownership has changed hands so frequently that even the most loyal customers are having trouble keeping the parent-company-of-the-year's identity straight. Suddenly, loyal customers are finding Samyo labels appearing on the inside collars of rain-

WHERE THEY SHOP
A Random Survey

CITY	FAVORITE CLOTHES STORE OR TAILOR
Oklahoma City	Ellis of Edinburgh
Shaker Heights, Ohio	Peer Gordon
London	Anderson & Sheppard
West Hartford, Connecticut	Allen Collins
Mequon, Wisconsin	Berman, Mark & Son
New York	Brooks Brothers
Atlanta	Muse's
Skokie, Illinois	Baskin's
Beverly Hills	Carroll & Co.
Wayzata, Minnesota	Foursome
Richmond, Virginia	Nathan's

coats on the racks. At the same time, more than one chief executive officer, swayed by the crowd of fashion-forward merchants and tailors eagerly pursuing important clients, has opted to join—not fight—the peacock revival.

Is the Brooks Brothers Century coming to a close?

For what seemed like forever, Brooks Brothers was the only place to buy a natural-shoulder, three-button suit (costing $450 to $950, if you want it custom-made in Scottish wools). Today, that suit is widely available at any decent store throughout the United States. While Brooks Brothers still is clearly in the lead in the CEO market, that gap is rapidly closing. Into the vacuum that's been created over the past decades, a number of enterprising fashion entrepreneurs have dared to venture.

We'll soon be exploring those flashier options, but first a tribute to the tried and true button-down leader:

George M. Hanley, senior vice-president for marketing and sales promotion, chalks up Brooks Brothers' success over the years to a strong "sales- and service-oriented" tradition first established by Henry Sands Brooks in New York in 1818.

In the 19th century, Brooks Brothers earned a national name as the first American company (and store) to manufacture and retail ready-made clothing to an elite male clientele. During the Civil War, Brooks was sacked by draft rioters, but still managed to outfit Generals Grant and Sheridan (this was strictly a Union shop). Its reputation, strangely enough, seems to have been strengthened, not tarnished, when Abraham Lincoln was shot at Ford's Theatre in a Brooks Brothers suit.

Given its current reputation as a bastion of changelessness in men's clothing, it might be shocking to learn that the turn-of-the-century Brooks Brothers, under John Brooks (grandson of the founder) was a veritable Fountain of Preppy Innovation.

As the century turned, John Brooks succeeded in refining and redefining a new All-American Look mixing Savile Row fastidiousness with a more casual, relaxed American style. (To think of a Brooks Brothers suit as relaxed or casual one has but to recall the stiff, high-collared outfits in favor at the time.)

In 1898, Brooks imported the first silk foulard neckwear from England, and in 1900, while attending a polo match in England, happened to notice the buttons with which polo players anchored their collar points to keep them from flapping in the wind. The result was Brooks Brothers' now famous and much-imitated button-down polo collar. (And you thought Ralph Lauren was the first to copy from polo! Ralph didn't start out as a salesman at Brooks for nothing.)

Within a decade Brooks had introduced both the shetland wool sweater and the camel-hair polo coat. If the origins of the now classic three-button natural or soft-shouldered suit are a bit more obscure, it is clear that the profound impression this comparatively shapeless style made on the American upper-class male had as much to do with what it was *not* as with what it *was*.

What the so-called sack or drape suit was *not* was: radical, bohemian, exaggerated, flashy, raffish, rakish or extreme. It was *not* meant for rubes, sharpsters, gangsters, dudes or anyone favoring the emerging Guys and Dolls Look.

What it did offer, in the deathless prose of a recent BB brochure, was "less padding, little exaggeration, and a softer-front construction."

The preppy sack suit has long been equated with "Puritan industriousness," says Clifford Grodd, president of Paul Stuart New York. Which means that when it comes to men's fashion, he points out, "dullness was always a virtue." Operating on the novel principle that dullness is simply dull, Grodd's father-in-law, Ralph Ostrove, gave Brooks its first serious competition when he brashly opened a store on the same block and named it after his son, Paul Stuart.

Brooks Brothers' volume may dwarf Paul Stuart's, but Stuart beats Brooks in two areas: It sells more suits per square foot than any other retail store in the United States (with only one U.S. branch) *and* it sells more suits in Japan. Paul Stuart has 2 full branches in Tokyo, and 23 small boutiques inside Mitsumini department stores throughout Japan.

Paul Stuart's main claim to fame was (and is) to supply a touch of Savile Row flair to the classic American soft-shouldered Brooks Brothers suit. Paul Stuart's basic model features a more suppressed waist, a center vent, and two buttons, not three. Which may seem like small potatoes to you, but on such minute differentiae, fashion fortunes are made. A typical Paul Stuart suit costs $700; the top of the line, an off-the-rack cashmere-and-wool blend, runs $2200.

In a series of print ads that boldly imitated *The New Yorker* (in both typeface and prose style) and paid homage to Strunk and White's famous *Elements of Style,* Paul Stuart took an opportunity to poke fun at its staider elder cousin up the block by advising, "Be sparing of the tried and true. . . .

"A wardrobe built entirely of classics is as tiresome as a vocabulary of clichés," the ads coyly concluded. (Take that, Brooks Brothers!) But perhaps the ultimate tribute to Paul Stuart's single-minded drive toward success (despite its refusal to franchise itself) comes from Debrett's *Cities of the World,* which commends PS as "the best place for an intelligent presentation of American style. . . . This is no fashion smorgasbord: it is one distinctive and totally consistent approach—its genesis Brooks Brothers, but transmuted through a more refined Savile Row sensibility."

Brooks Brothers also provided the genesis for another fashion success story, cut from much the same all-natural cloth as Paul Stuart. The Bronx-born son of a mural painter, Ralph Lauren—née Lifschitz (his parents changed the name when he was 16)—has grown exceedingly rich and famous as the great all-American designer. One of the few names in fashion that does not and never did end with a vowel.

Lauren served as a Brooks Brothers salesman for a brief

stint after leaving the army. Actually, the store was something of a finishing school for the Yeshiva University grad, who has referred to himself as "the preppiest kid you ever saw." Brooks Brothers was the foundation for Lauren's self-declared "old-money look." His Polo style takes up directly from where John E. Brooks left off: cunningly adapting the staples of British haberdashery, particularly of the sporting variety, to a more down-home Yankee life-style.

Ralph himself was a loyal Brooks Brothers customer until he was shocked to find the store pushing such heretical yarns as—ugh!—dacron and polyester. (Lauren's "better" suits generally start at $700.)

In a different departure from Brooks Brothers, Barneys New York picked up the torch of the 1960s Peacock Revolution back in 1968 by offering what did amount to a fashion smorgasbord in its pace-setting International House.

Long after Carnaby Street mod, medallions and Nehru jackets had come and gone, Barneys' success has proved that the globalization of fashion is here to stay.

If the strength of the great "Preppy Triad" of Brooks Brothers, Paul Stuart and neighbor J. Press lies in purveying a strict, austere, tightly controlled and entirely risk-free version of "Good Taste," Barneys sets out to offer something different: everything under the sun, all under one roof.

Just about every item of clothing Brooks Brothers sells is either its own make or turned out exclusively for it by manufacturers of "long standing." Paul Stuart's wares are manufactured under its own label, Stuart's Choice, tailored by Southwick, or turned out by its Canadian tailors.

But Barneys offers no dogmatic definition of generic good taste. The style here is free-wheeling eclectic. While its Madison Room sells conservative suits by Norman Hilton and Ralph Lauren (for $475 to $700), the Oak Room features Hickey-Freeman and Louis Roth (for $525 to $885), the English Room offers "the cream of British haberdashery" (by such tried-and-true Savile Row names as H. Huntsman & Sons, Gieves & Hawkes and Chester Barrie), generally in the $850 to $1000 range. And the International Collection spotlights all those Big-Name Designers like Stefano, Lanzetti, Bally, Armani, Valentino, Piatelli, Marzatto, Ungaro, Versace, Paciotti, Pellinacci, and Radaelli (to name just a few). These designers' suits command sharply steeper prices: $1075 to $1500.

On the one hand, the success of designers in defining the forefront of men's fashions seems to suggest a complete globalization of corporate style. But out in the Corporate Heartland, it's the rare CEO who's willing to brandish an Italian-designed suit.

The most popular suits ordered by non-avant-garde CEOs from stores like O'Neills in Akron, D. H. Peer in Dayton or H. Stockton in Atlanta (all stores our CEOs named as favorites) are bound to be virtually identical in fabric quality, weight, color and overall appearance to the top-of-the-line suits sold at Littler's (Seattle), Maroni's (Kenosha, Wisconsin) or Todds (San Antonio).

In fact, the "top-of-the line" suit sold throughout the country today is being turned out by just a tiny handful of manufacturers, typically featuring English or Italian fabrics and American finishing and tailoring. The best known of these is the Chicago-based Hartmarx Corp., founded in 1872 by the Marx Brothers—Harry and Max. The company sells suits from both ends of the spectrum, including the top-of-the-line Hart, Schaffner & Marx and Hickey-Freeman ($525–$1000).

Other important American manufacturers include century-old clothier Norman Hilton; Boston-based A. H. Freedberg; ultratraditional Kilgour, French & Stanbury. (Suits by each of these manufacturers run between $500 and $1000).

Mid-weight suits, says Brooks Brothers' George Hanley, have become runaway best-sellers across the country, ever since air conditioning rendered regional climatic boundaries virtually obsolete. (Okay, if you're going to New Orleans in the sultry midsummer, you still can pack a cotton seersucker or two.) At the same time, stylistic variations have also gone out of style, since television, shopping malls, constant air travel and superior marketing efforts by major national manufacturers have spread the archetypal East Coast Establishment Style blandly and evenly from coast to coast.

But this near-universal consensus has put executives in a tasteful but boring box. While it's all very well to have your wife and/or clothing consultant simply order up 20 standard new suits every season in one's "usual" style but in a wide range of weights, hues, and fabrics (an experience GM's

Roger Smith freely admits to), what if a newly minted CEO feels like being a bit more adventurous when it comes to selecting his fall or winter wardrobe?

In this globe-trotting age, a foreign-fashioned custom-made suit can be the ticket to adventure, combining the pleasures of foreign travel (whether on business or pleasure) with the thrill of bringing home a useful, practical souvenir. A good many of our 351 CEOs report they've shopped for suits in such relatively exotic locales as Paris (Balenciaga, Bardot), Nürnberg, Germany (Stamm), Hong Kong (Ying Tai, Ricky Bo, Medoq, George Chen, Fat Tai, A-Man Hing Cheong, Ascot Chang, Jimmy's and Daniel Leong) and London (Strickland & Sons, Huntsman and Turnbull & Asser, to name just a few.)

But if you don't have the time or the urge to go "over there," a number of well-established tailors will happily come over here via an institution known as the trunk show. When a tailor goes on a trunk show, he sends out cards to his regular customers (in cities all over the country) announcing the date and time of his arrival. If you are a regular, he will have all your basic measurements on file, will turn up to take fittings and orders from a rented hotel suite, and send your suits (and/or shirts) on when they are done.

One of the best-known Hong Kong tailors, Ascot Chang (Mr. Kravis's Main Man), started out doing trunk shows back in 1967, quickly earning a name for himself as one of the world's premier custom tailors. Chang's suits range from $650 for an ordinary wool worsted to up to $1500 for something special, like a wool-and-mink blend.

Tom Yu, manager of the new Ascot Chang store in New York—there are two others, both in Hong Kong—points out that one advantage of the Hong Kong style of tailoring is that Hong Kong doesn't have a distinct style. While a Savile Row tailor will only cut you a Savile Row suit (either that, or face opprobrium from his peers at home), a Hong Kong tailor will cheerfully turn out a modified Italian-cut jacket with a touch of Brooks Brothers about the cuffs and lapels, all the while gently suggesting minor details or touches but never adopting the "I know what's best for you" attitude of a Savile Row bespoke tailor.

Then there's Bijan, carrying on the one-word-name tradition of Prince, Cher, Madonna and Vanity. Born Bijan Pakzad to a well-established Persian family, he's been hailed by George Will as "the Bernard Berenson of the fine art of excess" and as a "fashion genius" by Malcolm Forbes. But designer Alan Flusser is convinced Bijan's true genius lies in his marketing—not aesthetic—zeal.

Bijan launched his hype-filled American career by building himself a sumptuous "By Appointment Only" boutique in the only location where such a place might not only survive, but thrive: Rodeo Drive in Beverly Hills. By offering such fashion exotica as mink-lined denim jackets ($1500) and three-thousand-dollar white flannel suits, Bijan brazenly attempted to corner the market in a sort of hyperelegant clothing that might well be described as Robin Leach Style. The standard Bijan suit runs about $2000.

Stray *by appointment only* into Bijan's Beverly Hills boutique and the first thing you'll stumble across is a golden gun straight out of James Bond (Bijan's signature engraved in black) displayed in a Lucite case, wrapped in mink. Along the rear (the same goes for the Fifth Avenue shop), a wall of clocks, each bearing the name of someone Bijan claims as a customer beneath his national flag, are all set to the customer's correct local time.

Via a less-than-discreet display of photos of possible customers (King Juan Carlos of Spain, Teddy Kennedy, Giovanni Agnelli, Julio Iglesias, Jack Lemmon, H. Ross Johnson and the late shah of Iran, in addition to countless lesser-known Middle Eastern prime ministers, Saudi sheiks and half of the leaders of the Third World), one might get the impression that Bijan's primary customers are members of the international corporate and political jet set.

But catering to the American upper-echelon corporate executive, Bijan roundly insists, is his *real* mission in life. To be a "doctor of clothes" to the notoriously underdressed and badly served American male, who desperately needs (though may not know enough to seek out) Bijan's brand of attention.

"You know, being a 'clothes surgeon' to these corporate 'biggies' " (as he likes to call them, though perhaps he means bigwigs) "can often be difficult," Bijan admits, with a bit of a Cheshire grin. "These tend to be difficult men. They have twenty secretaries and twenty assistants and thirty executives, and all day they are barking orders. But when they come to see me, sometimes I have to tell them, 'Mister, you need my help.' Occasionally, they get upset, and I have to ask, 'Mister Biggie, am I being rude?' "

Rude or not, H. Ross Johnson (whom Mr. Bijan describes as "a very big man," particularly when compared to his foe Henry Kravis, a notoriously small man) wasn't insulted at all when Bijan declared that his fashion statement had to be completely revised. "First I always find out what the man is about, who he is, what he needs. And then I don't say to him, 'Be flashy.' I make sure he is tasteful, but chic. Do you not agree my clothes are tasteful?"

Yes, surprisingly so, given that *controversial* and *chic* are Bijan's two favorite adjectives. With the possible exception of the mink-lined denim jacket, Bijan's corporate wardrobes are surprisingly restrained. In pattern, not price.

Now, if the spirit of adventure just happens to strike twice, but you don't want (or need) an appointment with Bijan for a full-fledged fashion consultation, Louis of Boston (branches in Boston and New York) represents a continuation of the trend in American corporate clothing toward a mixture of Continental couture and archetypal American style.

A number of our CEOs named Louis of Boston as their favorite clothier, which comes as something of a surprise to Murray Perlstein, whose father, Louis, founded Louis of Boston some 65 years ago.

Now, Murray doesn't think any more highly of the archetypal American corporate style than does Bijan. He just tries to do something a little different about it. "I'm on the New York–Boston shuttle two, three times a week," Perlstein says, "and I see these CEOs and corporate types on the plane. Maybe one out of fifty puts himself together with a little bit of taste and sophistication. I would never presume to say to a CEO you *should* dress this way. But I am here to say you *could* dress in a different way; that there are alternatives and opportunities where you can be well dressed but still show yourself to be capable of some imaginative thought." After all, if you expect a guy to be creative in all his other worldly pursuits, why should he stop at his clothing? For such creativity in a nailhead-woven gunmetal wool suit by Luciano Barbera, you'd pay $1700. Louis's suits begin at $795.

To be "a little creative," in Murray Perlstein's view, is to abandon the "bill of goods" sold to the American businessman by generations of uptight Yankee tightwads. (This is strictly an interpretation, not a direct quote). One has to be willing to take a few risks. Nothing exaggerated or extreme, he insists. Just an occasional spirited excursion into new fashion territory.

For example: wearing a suit day in and day out is bad for the soul; Perlstein can be zealous on this subject. "A well-tailored sport jacket with elegant trousers, and maybe even a pair of well-made brown suede shoes, presents at least as elegant an appearance as the most conservative navy-blue pin- or chalk-stripe three-button job. It makes a fellow stand out a little, which come to think of it, isn't always so bad.

"People who wear consistently uninteresting clothing are paranoid," is Perlstein's way of putting it. "It's a way of saying subliminally, 'I don't rock the boat. I don't make waves. Maybe if I don't look too good, I won't get noticed.' "

Which is all very well for the little guy at the bottom. But is this any way for an American CEO to behave? "There's always this climate of fear about clothes in American business," Perlstein says. "A CEO is supposed to be this strong-willed, independent, powerful guy, so why should he dress in a uniform? A sanitation man wears a uniform!"

It's an emotion, a sense of frustration and distress, echoed by Chris Ryan, who runs corporate clothing programs for Barneys New York. "Some companies try to get me to set up a cut-and-dried dress code for their employees," Ryan recalls, in indignation. "It's a natural control tendency I try to fight tooth and nail. I try to explain to these guys, 'Some inconsistency is a small price to pay for self-expression.'

"In a Brooks Brothers suit, you don't have to worry about being criticized. But it doesn't do anything for your image but neutralize it." For Ryan, perhaps the saddest sight of all is South Street Seaport on a Friday night, when all the young blades of Wall Street are out in force, parading around in their navy-blue pinstripe suits, as if on a bankers' holiday.

It's a perfectly rational response to a competitive job market for young guys just starting out, or setting out for their first job interviews. But that's hardly a reason for the man doing the interviewing to feel just as circumscribed as his timid, camouflaged candidate.

Ryan used to manage Brooks Brothers' Washington, D.C., store before being recruited by Barneys. "They had a party around here when my pants touched my shoes," Ryan recalls. "They used to joke that even my diapers must have had cuffs."

But Ryan sounds like St. Paul just back from Damascus when discussing his own personal clothing conversion. He tells a little fashion parable to illustrate the fact that in some areas, at least, times have changed.

"Four years ago, *Business Week* did a cover story on IBM. And it just showed one image: a white button-down shirt. It was an image as strongly identified with IBM as the company logo itself. Two years ago, *The New York Times* Sunday magazine did a story on 'The New IBM.' They showed painters painting stripes on that same white shirt."

Yes, but we couldn't help asking: Was the collar on that striped shirt still button-down? We couldn't help thinking of a page in a J. Press corporate catalogue that proclaimed: "Button-downs forever!" "Well, yes," Ryan admits, "the collar was button-down . . ."

Anachronisms on Parade

"It is nonsense to undervalue dress: I'm no more the same man in my dark blue paletot, trimmed with astrakhan, than I was a month ago in my green fustian shooting jacket. . . . There is an indescribable connection between your coat and your character."

–James Dodd
(English dandy and diarist),
1853

Take a good hard look at the modern CEO marching into a board meeting. Flanked by deferential cohorts and courtiers, he and they (from a fashion standpoint) form a walking, talking tableau of anachronisms, as vestigial as the tailbones we're all supposed to have "back there" somewhere.

When it comes to costume, from tip to toe our respectable corporate Joe is a compendium of archaic details derived from such hidebound aristocratic pursuits as fighting (on horseback), hunting (on horseback), playing polo, going off on safari, taking long walks (gun in hand) on the moors and other respectable sporting activities such as golf, cricket and tennis.

The very vents slicing up the back of his well-appointed business suit were originally designed so that his coat could slide more easily over a saddle while jumping. The heels on his shoes were fashioned to catch stirrups, and to proclaim that the well-shod man walking by the curb could afford to ride into town, if so inclined.

Ties: The necktie draping his neck has its own royal lineage, dating back to Louis XIV, who admired the neckerchiefs worn by his Croatian mercenaries and adopted the device as his own. He phonetically transposed *Croat* into the

French *cravat,* successfully establishing the adornment for masculine throat-lines up to the present day.

By the mid-18th century, the cravat had crossed the English Channel and turned into the four-in-hand, named for the men who sat high on top of a coach-and-four (horses), ties knotted tightly against the wind.

The British dandy Beau Brummell gained considerable fame (and fortune) by devising 32 ways to tie a necktie, and for offering this stern injunction to all his fashionable followers who aspired to being "well dressed":

"If John Bull [John Doe] turns to look at you in the street, you are not well dressed. You are either too tight, too stiff, or too fashionable." Words of advice still followed by many a CEO who never heard of Brummell or Bull.

Sleeve buttons: Today, a sure sign of a bespoke, or custom-tailored, sport or suit coat is that the buttons on the sleeves really button. But how many know these apparently meaningless buttons once had an actual function? They were placed there at the order of Napoleon Bonaparte, who had the imperial tailors sew buttons on his men's sleeves to keep them from wiping their noses on them while on parade.

Cuffs: T. S. Eliot, the banker-poet, once wrote: "I grow old . . . I grow old . . . I shall wear the bottoms of my trousers rolled," as if to wear cuffs conferred a badge of timid respectability. But turn-ups were introduced by active sportsmen and hunters in England, who rolled their trouser legs up a few turns to keep them from dragging in the dirt.

Lapels: Even the rolled lapels on the modern suit coat are vestiges of our corporate leaders' ancient warrior past. When soldiers overheated in the field, they rolled back the flaps of their high-collared tunics and anchored them with buttons, the sole remaining echo of which is that buttonhole piercing your left lapel.

Suits: The suit itself, a garment of strictly British invention, didn't conquer the Continent until the 1850s, when Henry Creed, Savile Row tailor to the Count d'Orsay, was made official tailor to the court of Louis Napoleon.

Its predominantly dark color is also of recent origin, dating back to the Industrial Revolution, when cities became too sooty for bright-colored clothes. What we now call a suit was once only a lounge suit, unfit for business or in-town attire, best "suited" for long walks in the country.

STICKING WITH
THE GOLDEN FLEECE

Crossing Madison one winter morning, we encountered Fred Knapp, creator of the FKA Executive Seminars and a speech and personal-image consultant so well known for both impeccable taste *and* diplomacy that a client company once transported an ill-dressed, corner-office-bound manager clear across the continent so that Knapp could tactfully issue the following ultimatum: Trade in your signature red socks for more appropriate dark ones that we'll shop for together, or find your career road-blocked.

Knapp agreed to take us on a mini-shopping trip that would illuminate some of the finer points of CEO Style as it applies to dress. Before he was finished, he had made many significant points, carefully and emphatically stressing each one by ticking it off with his right forefinger on the fingers of his left hand, board-meeting style.

"With regard to the CEO," Knapp began, "the relevant dress code depends on the industry, on the individual, and on the geographical location of the company." But, he added, wherever a CEO may work, go or happen to turn up, some form of dress code is bound to apply.

A chief exec ignores this fact at his peril. A CEO who views his elevation as an opportunity to break out of the mold is, our guide insists, bound to get shot down, but quick.

The most important thing for a CEO to know (and you thought it had something to do with greenmail) is that he is an actor as well as a leader, a performer as well as a decision-maker.

"It is vitally important," Knapp reiterates, "that the CEO grasp the importance of projecting the strength of the office he holds." Which is why we soon find ourselves at the corner of 44th Street and Madison Avenue, at the very gates of the Temple: Brooks Brothers.

So our first lesson takes place in an open classroom vented by cold winter air sweeping between the cars. Displayed in a great plate-glass window facing Madison Avenue is a suitably distinguished pair of three-button, natural-shoulder, single-breasted business suits. One is a navy-blue pinstripe, the other a lighter shade of gray.

Both are executed in the increasingly popular mid-weight wool suitable for all climatic conditions south of Nome, north of Machu Picchu. The dark blue pinstripe one on our left "says CEO" to Knapp, loud and clear. The suit speaks with "power, authority and credibility." Why? Because of its dark color. That's why.

Still, we aren't home yet. Picking a "safe, correct" suit is rarely the problem for most men not born in a barn. Problems crop up in the details.

Take, for example, that white cotton "pocket square" (otherwise known as a handkerchief) coyly peeking out of the breast pocket of an otherwise staid and bankerish costume. It's a "pretty typical three-point treatment on the pocket square," Knapp says. Such accessories are highly respectable. Still, he notes a minor problem. Those three points are sticking themselves out just a little far for Knapp's taste, which is, as he would be the first to admit, exceedingly strict. "That's at least an inch and a half out of the pocket," he judges. "Which is just about the outer limit when it comes to projection for the pocket square."

Lest one begin to believe Knapp is a man overly obsessed by pocket squares, he quickly assures us that the whole point of this exercise is that when in doubt, look to the CEO for proper dress cues. (CEOs, it goes unsaid, should look to someone like Knapp.)

"If the CEO wears a pocket square," he remarks, "it might mean he wants his subordinates to wear one." Then again, it might not. What is the insecure manager to do? Get a Reading, of course.

To Get a Reading, you must be able to Receive the Signal. Which means you have to understand the Code. A code defined, for the most part, by offhanded remarks, casual quips and mumbled asides around the water cooler. The corporate world, in this consultant's view, is a highly indirect place. If you expect to have things put more bluntly, you'd be better off playing football. "In the corporate world a great deal of extremely serious information is transmitted by means of jokes," he says.

Moving on past pocket squares, we come to the critical issue of "shirtings." On the Brooks Brothers front, we spy a number of prime examples before us, all sporting "plain point collars," which Knapp says "comprise the standard of current collar treatment." The button-down, he adds, is perfectly acceptable, "even if some find it a little too sporty."

Passing through the great wood-and-brass doors of the Temple of the Golden Fleece, he takes a moment to spell out some rules of thumb to follow when confronting,

as we all must from time to time, the ever-present Color Question.

"In the shirt department, go with a solid color, the safest color, preferably white or blue. White projects a sense of credibility, security and openness of thought." And blue? Much the same, only less so—with a touch of wild bohemian passion.

As for patterns, well, Knapp has something of a problem there. Or rather, too many of his clients do. "In certain specified situations, a patterned shirt and a patterned tie will do just fine."

Such as? "Well," he cheerfully concedes, "I'd say when a CEO is not circulating among his peers or facing the public." In other words, not too often.

Shirts are naked without ties, so we step smartly up to a vast counter liberally shirred with ties in a dazzling array of styles.

Knapp leans away from the more dazzling reds and brightest yellows. He favors the subdued "middle ranges—your wines, your reds, your burgundies, your maroons." In other words, if it doesn't look like you could drink it, pass.

We exit the store and once again focus on the window display. The two suits before us are both dressed (if not to the nines) with yellow silk foulard ties, considered by our instructor to have passed their prime as a Power Look. There's nothing wrong with Power Looks, he patiently explains. But they can not be readily identified as such, or the entire program is blown. In fashion, as in other realms, it is better taste to keep one's agenda hidden.

Before we move on, Knapp fixates for a brief period on one final detail: the brown English wing-tip shoes on display beneath the trousers of a dark blue suit, as if to suggest that the two might make a winning combination.

Not in Knapp's opinion. "If a CEO were going to fly first class," he intones, "that would not be a first-class combination." Black shoes with dark suits, period. And brown suits—not at all.

Crossing Madison again, we stumble across another impulse the well-dressed CEO should feel honor-bound to ignore: Cost Cutting, when it comes to his wardrobe, that is, as opposed to operating costs across the board.

In full view of its betters up and down the street, a store called Bancroft announces "Two Suits $250" without a hint of shame, by means of a not very well muted billboard.

"Well," Knapp sighs, not exactly from relief, "this is a low-cost operation. You can't beat it as far as price goes, but where is the trade-off?" In this case, it comes in the quality of the fabric, and the quality of the construction.

When a cheap suit is put together, it can't have as many stitches in the seams as its more expensive cousin. Which means that the suit won't tend to give as much with the body's motion. Which in turn means that a cheap suit will begin to sag, bag and drag—in other words, look like hell—ages before a good suit will.

As we began to head for opposite paths, and as a parting shot, the man who prides himself on stressing "positive and credible communication and image projection" imparts a few final words of wisdom: "Business has to have a structure. Society has to have a structure. An organization has to have a structure. So if you want to be a successful CEO, making a statement is not the point. Fitting in is."

–STEPHEN FENICHELL

It took a Prince of Wales to make the lounge suit respectable by defiantly wearing his houndstooth tweed version (with a soft turned-down collar, begad!) into town after a Scottish holiday.

The radical playwright George Bernard Shaw had no such luck when he tried to turn the rules of fashion topsy-turvy. He showed up at his own opening night in a brown knit one-piece "Socialist Suit" (an item of his own devising) and was sent home to put on proper evening dress (not a simple tuxedo or dinner jacket, but full formal regalia.)

(Shaw suffered the ultimate indignity when his own Socialist party refused to adopt Shavian sartorial principles, voting instead to wear Basic British Black suits because even "dyed-in-the-wool" radicals wouldn't gain votes if not suitably attired.)

This time-honored tradition of equating sobriety, honesty and respectability with darkness, dullness and conformity in clothes is directly traceable to the Protestant Reformation, when elaborate ornamentation of any kind came to be associated with Catholic "popery." The Puritan strain, which took root in this country, only made matters worse (from a fashion standpoint). But the staying power of the Puritan-Protestant sartorial tradition is still inexplicable, seeing as how Protestants or Puritans never held themselves up as fashion plates.

Which is, of course, precisely the point.

–STEPHEN FENICHELL

ACCEPTABLE
BEHAVIOR

James Robert Moffett, the loquacious chairman and CEO of oilfield giant Freeport-McMoRan, is known in New Orleans social circles for his impersonation of Elvis Presley. In fact, Jim Bob, as he's called, once performed "You Ain't Nothin' But a Hound Dog" on a public wharf—complete with tight black slacks, shiny white shirt and fake sideburns.

But, not surprisingly, such behavior is frowned upon by many stockholders, bankers, boards of directors and others who dictate the unwritten code of acceptable CEO conduct. And for every Jim Bob Moffett, a CEO who feels comfortable letting down his hair, there are hundreds of corporate chiefs who find they must, in fact, clean up their acts.

On Learning to Dress Up, Keep Quiet and Say No to the Church Music Committee

Edwin Lupberger, also a New Orleans CEO, is a perfect example. Shortly after assuming the top position at Middle South Utilities, one of the nation's largest electric utilities, he stopped dressing sloppily on weekend trips to the grocery store. "I might run into somebody," he says, "and I can't afford to let them think I'm a slob." (Or, he might add, that Middle South is sloppily run.)

As scores of new chief executives discover every year, stepping into a chief executive's shoes is much more than a change in jobs, much more than assuming new responsibilities, much more than acquiring a new vacation home, much more than joining a better country club. "It's like you put on a suit of clothes and you can't get out of it," says Lupberger. Then he amends: "The better analogy is you've put on a different skin."

Suddenly, an executive who dwelled in relative obscurity for years is presented anew to thousands of employees, community leaders, financial advisers and assorted hangers-on. From the moment he becomes the top man, co-workers and others with questionable motives flock to his side like moths to a flame. Every action he takes is scrutinized; every sentence he utters is analyzed for the hidden message; every gesture, too, is subject to interpretation. And in a whirlwind of changes, both business and social, the executive often finds himself playing by a completely new set of rules, the code of the chief executive.

The new chief executive begins by watching—and controlling—virtually every aspect of his public behavior. He discovers he must ignore his personal interests for the corporate good. He generally will isolate himself from former buddies who are now subordinates or others who demand time and favors. He's courted to join a host of new organizations, and he's got to figure out which ones will be the least waste of his dwindling time, which ones will prove most beneficial to him and his company. And to endure all the loneliness that's bound to result from his new position, he'll seek the support of fellow CEOs, others who've survived the period of adjustment from mere executive to chief executive.

Take Mitchell Fromstein, for example. He didn't feel like a different person when he took over the reins at Manpower Inc., in the mid-1970s, but deep inside, he knew now he *was* different.

The Milwaukee advertising executive was a board member of the big, worldwide temporary-services concern when other directors turned to him to replace the company's departing chief executive. Fromstein was an expert on speech-writing and public relations and had even run a small company in his field. So, being chief executive of a major international personnel company couldn't be that different, could it?

"Boy, was I wrong," Fromstein recalls. "Overnight, my life changed. It was probably the most radical change I underwent in my life. It required a total change in style.

"I tried to adopt the attitude that I *was* the company, and not me, not Mitch Fromstein. My style, both in and out of the office, had to be reflective of what I wanted the company to be," he says.

He sat down and outlined his goals. He wanted Manpower, the conservative, well-run industry leader in temporary services, "to look solid, successful. I wanted it—and me—to appear to be on a high-trajectory growth path," he says. Needless to say, what looks "solid, successful" within the advertising industry would be too frivolous for Manpower. So Fromstein's first order of business was to overhaul his wardrobe. He threw out the flashy clothing of the advertising world; Manpower was to be blue and gray business suits, conservative ties and shiny black shoes.

But that part was simple. Next, Fromstein had to modify his behavior to meet both the quirks of a new industry and the demands of his new position. The advertising world Fromstein knew was populated with glib, shoot-from-the-hip types who wouldn't fit in at Manpower. It was a style he had subconsciously adopted, but which held hazards for his new job. Even more than other chief executives—who often are amazed at how their throw-away lines are transformed to gospel by their subordinates—Fromstein knew he had to watch himself. From the boardroom to the country club locker room, every word he said would be picked up, amplified and relayed until its echoes bounced around every corner of Manpower's 32-country empire.

Rule Number One became: "Watch what you say," he recalls. "Everyone lower down seizes on every word out of a CEO's mouth. It has a message for them." Yet Fromstein resisted the impulse to clam up altogether. "If you become silenced, you cease to be a leader," he says. "If you're a leader, you've got to say things. People want to know what you're thinking because it changes their lives."

Fromstein knew he needed a role model. So, for inspiration, he thought of Vince Lombardi, the legendary coach of the Green Bay Packers. Fromstein reasoned that Lombardi projected leadership, sometimes calmly, sometimes vigorously, and he drew the best out of people. So, with an image of the coach planted firmly in his mind, the new Manpower quarterback donned his helmet.

Exercising **I**ndeed, the making of a brand-new CEO often means con-
Self-Control sciously honing down sharp edges—at least in public. Some don't want to be seen or photographed hoisting a beer, for instance, for fear of alienating employees or community officials who look down on alcohol. Other chiefs simply don't like being seen having fun—from dancing to jogging—in the sometimes-mistaken notion that such displays belittle the office of the chief executive.

A critical part of keeping control is watching what you say. All too easily can an offhand remark be twisted into a dictum that spreads throughout the corporate hierarchy, sometimes with disastrous results. "Anything you say plummets down through the organization like a dead weight," said David Sheehan, chairman of Chicago-based Axia, Inc., a maker of various commercial and industrial products. "You need to be very conscious about what you're saying."

Not surprisingly, a lot of CEOs refrain from thinking aloud, preferring instead to prepare remarks for coworkers as carefully as for an analyst's presentation. "You have to be so careful: Every word, every nuance, every gesture is interpreted by almost everyone," says Henry Silverman, chief executive of Atlanta-based Days Inns. "Even if it's a joke, or a throwaway line."

And most CEOs put a renewed premium on emotional control. For example, losing one's temper, even cursing, is sometimes seen as a sign of a leader who isn't in control of his surroundings. Says Abraham Zaleznik, a psychologist and Konsuke Matsushita Professor of Leadership at Harvard University: "The rule of the game is never show anger. Don't show emotion, or you're dead in the water. If you get to be known as somebody who can't keep his cool, you're a loose cannon."

To many CEOs, that notion of control is the first tenet of leadership. Lose that, some reason, and you lose respect, and before you know it, you're losing the company. "I couldn't afford to lose control of my emotions with subordinates," says William Douce, the former chief executive of Phillips Petroleum. "It's a luxury the CEO doesn't have. If you're angry, upset and excited, you're just not effective."

M ost CEOs also soon learn that they can be about as con-   *Shunning*
troversial as a stone wall.   *Controversy*

For example, during his climb through the corporate ranks at companies like IBM and Motorola, Jim Risher had always enjoyed outside activities, including church and politics. But as he settled into his job as the new chief executive of Exide Electronics, a medium-sized concern in Raleigh, North Carolina, Risher soon discovered he would have to curb these interests, and not because he didn't have the time. His personal interests were too easily confused with the company's, he found.

So when political parties sought his support, Risher reluctantly demurred. "We don't want to back a particular senator or congressman," he said. "We have to support both parties." The same went for church activities and some charities. "You realize for the first time that you represent a constituency," Risher says. "And you don't want to get that constituency tangled up by exercising your personal beliefs."

For Risher, stepping into the chief executive's shoes "means you lose some sense of individuality," he says. It's a complaint voiced by many, but not all, corporate leaders: They've got more power than ever, but, as never before, they must be careful how to use it. Most CEOs find they end up guarding their public image as carefully as does a presidential candidate.

"There are certain things that maybe I could have gone to before, but now I can't," complains Middle South's Lupberger. "A political rally. Any partisan political thing. I can't go out and take a position on abortion if I wanted to. I might have wanted to go picket on a situation if I were 20 years younger, but I can't now. You give up a little of your citizen's rights as a person."

The need for such caution is born from the fact that a chief executive's corporate power easily translates into civic or political power. For example, Tod Hamachek, the 42-year-old chief executive of Penwest Ltd., a medium-size Seattle-area manufacturer, doesn't think much of a certain top official in the state of Washington. One of the executive's close friends, however, is related to the government official.

"This puts me in a hell of a box," says Hamachek. "I'd like to support this guy's opponent. I'd like to be a hell of a lot more vocal than I am. [But] I'm chicken. Frankly, right now I'm just sitting back. I don't want to risk losing a close friend." Not to mention, he adds, the impact such a high-profile decision might have on his company.

The Loneliness at the Top Ascending to the rank of chief executive opens up a new world outside the boardroom for many. CEOs are in demand at parties, ribbon-cuttings, industry functions, celebrity golf tournaments, you name it. Great places and tremendous opportunities to make friends, right?

Then why do so many CEOs complain about their inability to make new friends? Listening to some, one would think they inherited leprosy along with the chairman's gavel. "You are severely limited in the number of personal relationships you can have," says William Douce. "It's all right when you're down the line and you and I go out and have a few drinks and get schnockered. When you're CEO, you can't do that anymore. You have to act like a CEO."

Add to those considerations the normal demands and long hours required by the office and you get an idea of the chief executive's problem. Many say they're happy just to keep hold of old friends, a responsibility they generally hand off to their spouses. "You tend to have a few close friendships, many acquaintances, people you tend to feel comfortable about, but not that many close relationships," says Exide's Risher.

Often left behind are second-tier executives nosed out for the top job. "New CEOs suddenly don't have the same level of interest in the old cronies," notes Patricia Cook, a partner at the New York executive recruitment firm of Ward Howell International. "Many feel they have to be moving on up."

And too, many chief executives develop that wariness born of suspicion of sycophants and favor-seekers. The moment they become the top man, coworkers and others flock to their sides. Old grudges are instantly forgotten. Some CEOs compare it to being a movie star or political candidate.

For Middle South's Lupberger, "The most obvious change [in becoming chief executive] is in how others react to you. People that I never even knew or had met in past years, who maybe would have a hard time knowing who I was from meeting to meeting, all of a sudden remember who I am. They may instigate the conversation where before they may not have spoken. There are situations, either socially or businesswise, where I know I'm being included not because they like me but because of the position I hold."

These kinds of concerns are intensified tenfold for the small-town CEO. "You hear people say, 'It's lonely at the top.' Nowhere is that better demonstrated than with a top corporate executive in a small town," moans Phillips's Douce, who found himself the most powerful man in Bartlesville, Oklahoma. "When you look for outside relationships, you don't have the opportunity to develop them like you would in a bigger town. You just don't have the people." And the people you have, he adds, are too closely affiliated with Phillips to allow him free speech.

When Irving Shapiro became chairman of Du Pont in 1974, among his first moves was to give up his weekly poker game with friends from work. Indeed, the act of shying away from after-hours relationships with subordinates is virtually a ritual among new CEOs.

Steering Clear of Subordinates

"If you socialize with one [executive] and not another, you're sending messages to the ones you don't see that maybe they shouldn't be getting. They feel you don't like them, or won't promote them. It's a risk you don't want to take. And then wives get involved, and you have no control over that," explains Manpower's Fromstein.

Former CEO Douce says, "You can't play golf with a man on Saturday and lay him off on Monday morning." Concurs Silverman of Days Inn: "If you get too close to a person, when you have to terminate that person, your judgment may be altered."

Even CEOs who push openness and candor in the office often don't promote relationships outside the office. At work "you have to be informal, as open as possible, and have easy accessibility," says Douce. But it's a thin line to tread. He adds: "I don't want you close enough to me to know my shoe size, my collar size and the time I shower. That doesn't help anybody."

The standard exception to the no-fraternizing-with-the-help rule may be occasional dinners with the Number Two, though even those meetings are eschewed by many CEOs.

So, most top executives limit social ties to the dreaded company picnics, Christmas parties and the like, outings where the average CEO feels about as comfortable as he does in a roomful of hostile stockholders. In the minds of many, such social affairs serve no useful purpose, and the chief executive finds himself on display, like another package under the tree. "It's the single worst time of the year," admits one CEO, "with the possible exception of the annual meeting."

Clinging to Other CEOs

What's a CEO to do?

Form a CEO support group.

David Sheehan was corporate secretary to four separate New York Stock Exchange companies before being named Axia chief executive a few years ago. He had never palled around with other chief executives, and didn't see any need to.

Then, at an institutional investor conference in Florida, he struck up a conversation with several other chiefs sitting at his table. To his surprise, they were astonishingly frank in discussing their business problems. Sheehan took the cue, and before long he was pouring his heart out to virtual strangers. Ever since, Sheehan has sought the counsel of other CEOs in working through his own dilemmas.

"These guys relate their own problems and give advice very easily," he says. "I've never found anyone being cagey or cynical. They'll give you a lot of time."

CEOs love to debunk the myth that the top office carries with it entry into a special club. But to listen to many chief executives tell it, it's true. To a surprising extent, American CEOs need each other's support.

Some do it, of course, merely to rub elbows. But many find that, unable to discuss the details of problems with subordinates or nonbusinessman friends, other CEOs are the only ones they can turn to who will understand their problems.

"I can only really feel comfortable with other chief executives," says Manpower's Fromstein. "The higher up in the organization you go, the more difficult it is to totally relax with staff people. But if you talk to another CEO, you find your problems are quite common. You find it's not you," he adds. "Without that contact, you hit a problem and think, 'What's the matter with me?' "

Echoes Penwest's Hamachek: "When you first become CEO, everything is fine and moves right along until you hit your first crisis. Then you realize, I don't have anybody that I can sit down and talk with about this. You think, Oh, God, this whole pile is going to come down on me. It's hard for other people to conceive of what it's like to sell off a division, fire a couple of key people, or close down a plant. Who are you going to talk to about those things? You end up talking to other CEOs who have had other similar experiences."

"I never realized this until I got into this position, but as a CEO, there aren't many people you can talk to," says Middle South's Lupberger. "This idea that it's lonely at the top, it's true. You are restricted with the people that you can be open with. [But] with CEOs, there is a trust level right away. They are extremely open and frank. So much so that I'm shocked. They think, 'Here's a guy I can open up to, get some feedback about some problems, and know it doesn't go any further.' There's an instant empathy. It's almost an unwritten rule. These are people who can't talk with that many other people, so now they can talk with each other."

The opportunities to make friends among fellow chief executives are legion. The Business Roundtable remains a clubby bastion well know for allowing chief executives a chance to commiserate with their peers. A slew of lesser groups also exist, including regional and industry groups. Many CEOs initially join these organizations because it's expected, but later find themselves hooked on the friends they make there.

Socializing with chief executives is one thing. But what if they're competitors? Frowned upon in some industries, it's standard operating procedure in others. Investment bankers, for example, are notoriously clubby, while oil-industry executives may belong to the "All-American Wildcatters Club," the centerpiece of that industry's extensive old-boy network.

In the natural-gas business, a strong Washington lobbying effort helps bring together CEOs in a common cause that also produces some lasting friendships. "We're all in competition and, kind of, all of us are not in competition," says Thomas F. "Mac" MacLarty, chief executive of Arkla Inc., a big Little Rock, Arkansas-based gas supplier. "It's not the headup competition like you see in Ford versus GM. We may be going after the same market that another pipeline is going after, but we're still friends."

Such relationships have traditionally been unacceptable among the big three automakers. "For as long as I was working for Ford, [I] had to obey the unwritten rule that if a Ford and a GM guy were seen playing tennis or golf together, it was a sure sign they were price-fixing or otherwise plotting the overthrow of our free enterprise system," Chrysler chief Lee Iacocca recalls in his book, *Iacocca.*

One of the few good things about his firing from Ford, Iacocca adds, was that it allowed him for the first time to entertain his neighbor Pete Estes the then-president of General Motors.

Detroit's antifraternization tradition apparently isn't as strict as it once was, however. GM Chairman Roger Smith says he's proud to have dinner with longtime pals at Ford and Chrysler and does so on a regular basis. "I see people from Ford and Chrysler all the time," Smith says, including Ford chief Donald Peterson, whose 40th wedding anniversary the GM head was invited to attend last fall.

Given the government's tight antitrust regulations, is it wise for the auto industry's two titans and their wives to go out alone?

"Would we go out with [the Petersons] alone? Sure," Smith says. "We bumped into them the other night. That antitrust thing is . . . We're all grown up people around here. We don't go out and sit down and discuss competitive issues."

How about Mr. Iacocca, his telegenic Chrysler competitor? Smith recalls that he and Iacocca used to sit and watch their daughters play field hockey at the private school they attended. But today, Smith says, shaking his head slightly, "Let me tell you, he's on a different circuit."

CEOs find themselves being courted to bring their power, prestige, and management talents to a host of organizations. And it's not necessarily a bad position to be in, since, with their new-found status, fledgling CEOs love to join things. Corporate boards. Museum boards. Opera boards. College trustee boards. CEO clubs. The Bohemian Club. The United Way. The problem is, these groups often become a quagmire for the unsuspecting CEO, a drain of time and energy and a constant distraction from more pressing corporate chores. And the CEOs don't always get to rub shoulders with the movers and shakers they hoped to befriend.

So new chief execs learn another lesson: They must watch what they join.

"The first thing you notice about the new CEO is they get absolutely maniacal about being on boards," says Patricia Cook, of the recruiting firm Ward Howell International. "There's a tremendous preoccupation with getting on the boards of big, prestigious corporations and not-for-profit organizations."

Ask them why they do it, and most chief executives will start to sound a bit self-righteous. "I'm trying to give back a little to the community that helped me on my way up," is one refrain. "I've never had time to help the less-fortunate people in life, and now I can," is another.

Some chief executives actually harbor such desires. But in other cases the need to join organizations is a creature of far less altruistic motives: the need for prestige, both for the chief executive and his company; the need to mix with other powerful chief executives; and, not least, the insecure new CEO's subconscious need to reassure himself of his new stature.

As Harvard's Zaleznik sees it, the desire to join the United Way or other boards or become trustee of the local hospital or bank is all part of the new chief executive's all-consuming need to belong. "They're desperate to belong to things—it's all part of being established in the network," he says. "It's part of being in the know."

So Many Groups, So Little Time

It's very easy to fall into the trap that, "Gee these people really like me. [But] they tend to want you there for a reason. It's incumbent for all of us to really analyze, not necessarily be suspicious, "Do I want to be involved in this? Is it good for me and the company? Do I want to be used?"

—**Middle South CEO Edwin Lupberger**

HOW TO TALK LIKE A CEO

The men who run America's corporations are known for speaking their minds—or are they?

A closer examination of the phrasing of CEO language reveals that the *real* message almost always is glossed over with diplomatic double-talk. Here's a sampling of what a CEO may really mean when he talks like a nice guy. Note: the translations don't apply for Wall Streeters and CEOs of small, rough-and-tumble companies; both groups generally have little use for diplomacy.

The following was compiled with the help of Paul Hirsch, professor of Management at Northwestern University's Kellogg Graduate School of Management and author of *Pack Your Own Parachute: How to Survive Mergers, Takeovers and Other Corporate Disasters;* Ross Webber, professor of Management at University of Pennsylvania's Wharton School; Wharton School Dean Russell Palmer; and Michael Maccoby, management consultant and author of *The Gamesman, The Leader,* and *Why Work?*

For the new chief executive, Zaleznik says the question is, "How do you know you count? You count by associating with other people who count. That's why so many chief executives desperately want to get into places such as Bohemian Grove. They want to feel they count. They need to belong."

And not to just any group. Belonging to the right organization—keeping in mind such matters as prestige and likely contacts—can be crucial to a new chief executive's development. It's sad but true: The most effective chief executives don't waste their time on the local planning and zoning board.

Turning down those lesser invitations is an art form for some CEOs, especially those with high community profiles. "People who don't have a corporate involvement don't appreciate what it is you do," says Middle South's Lupberger. "They will say, 'Will you serve on the music committee at the church?' You say, 'Yeah, I'm interested, how often does it meet?' [They may say] it meets monthly. That isn't an efficient use of my time. But the little church lady who asked me doesn't understand that. I have to be very careful not to make them feel unimportant."

Not turning these invitations down, however, can quickly bog a CEO down. Ronald O. Perelman, the investor who

When a CEO Says . . .	*He Really Means . . .*
"We'll think about it and let you know."	"We decided against it three weeks ago, you idiot."
"Let me know if I can help."	"Don't bother me."
	"I don't want to expend any of my time or political capital on this."
"Are you comfortable with him?"	"He's going to know how to act, isn't he?"
"I don't disagree with that."	"It sounds all right, but I'm not committing myself to anything."
"My door's always open."	"You can try to see me, but it will cost you some respect and brownie points."
"It's your ball, I want you to score the touchdown."	"If you fall down I'm not going to support you."
	"Even if you score the touchdown, I want to know which yard markers you're passing when you pass them."
	"Report back for clearance at each step."
	"Keep me informed so I can exercise veto power—I think you're going to screw up."
"We don't like surprises."	"This is an autocratic organization. Unless I know about your screwups in advance, you're in trouble when they happen."
"How does he move?"	"I'm not going to be surprised when he acts like a jerk, am I?"

—DAVID DIAMOND

became chairman of Revlon Group Inc., is one of those chief executives who believes he is spread too thin. "My problem is I respond to these situations because I feel for the person who asked me or for the cause," he says. "A lot of time I don't have the time to get into it" after agreeing to.

Penwest's Hamachek, too, is up to his neck in the outside groups he started joining soon after he took his company's helm four years ago. As president of a division in Portland, Oregon, he had joined the Young Presidents Club and was somewhat active in community affairs. Moving to Seattle to become CEO, he figured he would beg off outside involvements to afford more time to get his arms around his new job.

"That lasted about six months," says Hamachek. "Now my problem is I'm too damn involved. I guess I wasn't discriminating enough."

Joining boards was a way for the novice CEO to make himself as well as his company—a spinoff of a larger firm—better known and established in Seattle. He was already heavily involved in Outward Bound programs. Next came involvement with the Washington Research Council, a political think tank, and the Seattle Community Foundation. He became trustee of tiny Lewis and Clark College, where he headed time-consuming reviews of the president's office as well as of the institution. He also got involved in a nature group. Finally, he joined the boards of a big Washington bank and a large Northwestern energy company.

"I thought it would help me and my image," Hamachek says. "Now it's all getting to be too much. I'm wasting my time."

Most frustrating, he finds, are the not-for-profit organizations where "I'm really not contributing. Most non-profits are not very well managed. They don't know how to use their board of trustees well. They expect them to come and shoot the breeze on issues that management should really take care of. You end up with a very long meeting—two, three, four hours once a month—that should take 20 minutes. As a result, I find it very, very boring."

Worse, Hamachek found the movers and shakers he wanted to rub elbows with didn't move and shake nearly as much as he had hoped. "A lot of times," he admits, "you go on these boards to be associated with someone. You think, 'Oh, look who I'm going to be associated with.' And then you go and see, oh Lord, what a disaster they really are."

Corporate boards can be just as bad. Hamachek describes one of his board memberships as "absolutely fascinating," and says it has brought him added stature. But the other, he laments, is packed with outside directors who "rubber stamp" management decisions. "If I had do it all over, I wouldn't have joined that board," he says. "It's really a bore. I've never seen so much Mickey Mouse stuff in all my life. The board itself is just too damn dull."

Fortunately, Hamachek's company limits him to three corporate directorships, so he's picky about the last one. "I've been asked to go on four boards, and I've turned them all down," he says. "The last one had better be a damn plum."

–Bryan Burrough

NEIGHBORHOODS: WHERE THE CEOS LIVE

When civic disaster strikes in Greenwich, Connecticut, the ultimate executive suburb springs to action.

Take the wave of European au pairs and Japanese businessmen's wives that washed into the neo-Colonial households here a few years back. At one point the numbers of foreigners got so unwieldly that the smooth performance of the local ballet classes was threatened by the noncommunicative and confused newcomers.

So the local YWCA started offering special classes aimed at teaching the au pairs and other foreign newcomers the English language.

Then came the mass of brioche-fed Canada geese who abandoned their migration pat-

Life in Greenwich, Connecticut: 100,000 Canada Geese Can't Be Wrong

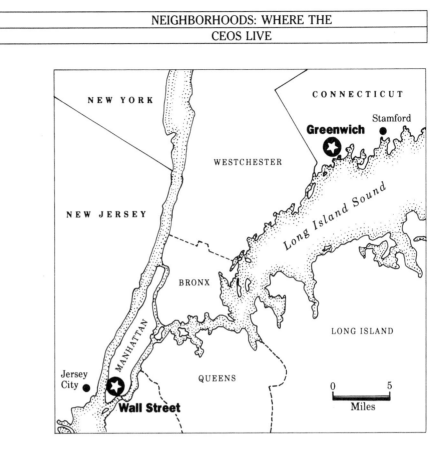

terns to take up residence in Greenwich's ample parks, golf courses, beaches and expansive lawns.

The fowl made no self-effort to halt the considerable flow of droppings (which, when freshly dropped, take on the color of old money). So a ceremonial yacht-club cannon shot several rounds of blanks to scare them away. But it failed.

Since (on paper, at least) Canada geese are afraid of swans, some of the thriving country clubs that dot this Long Island Sound community installed tastefully crafted swan decoys. The success has been minimal. Some added gizmos that shoot jets of water (Perrier?) over golf-course greens, in the hopes that an absence of the droppings (not to mention the unmelodious goose honking) will enhance golfers' concentration.

But like the two settlers who bought Greenwich from the Indians for 25 coats in 1640, au pairs and Canada geese know a good deal when they see one. So do the hordes of business leaders who've landed here in the decades since World War II.

For New Yorkers fleeing the Empire State's tax on personal income, Greenwich, 51 minutes from Grand Central Station, is the nearest haven in income tax–free Connecticut. Granted, even a modest dwelling here goes for a great deal more than does a similar home in Rye or Scarsdale. Yet taxes here are about one third what you'd pay over the border in New York's Westchester County. And the Board of Estimate and Taxation, the town's fiscal control body, is planning to reduce, not raise, the mill rate, according to First Selectman John B. Margenot, Jr., the town's equivalent of a mayor.

If low taxes and proximity to Manhattan are not enough, Greenwich's sheltered harbors and yacht clubs make it a weekend-sailor's paradise, something that can't be said for such neighboring, high-status Connecticut communities as New Canaan or Wilton. "We looked at a few other communities before moving to Greenwich, but we sort of gravitated to the town," recalls Thomas Watson, Jr., the legendary former IBM chairman who moved here after getting his U.S. Air Force discharge in 1945. A sailor, Watson says the waterfront location was a major inducement; even before moving to Greenwich he belonged to its Indian Harbor Yacht Club. ("Back then dues for servicemen were only $50 a year," he reminisces.) Over the course of the next four and a half decades, the Watsons lived in four different Greenwich houses—and raised six children. His wife, Olive, was a Cub Scout den mother.

Extending over 50.6 square miles and home to 60,000 residents, Greenwich is the nation's most CEO-dominated town. In addition to Watson, the past or present heads of American Brands, American Express, Exxon, UPS, Combustion Engineering, and an assortment of other companies live or lived here in harmony with celebrities ranging from Victor Borge to Diana Ross to David Stockman to the Empress of Iran (the late Shah's wife) to Ivan Lendl.

The names and locations of important citizens speedily roll off the lips of virtually any Greenwichite, although life here doesn't necessarily insure meeting the power or glitz elite, or even spotting them. (Okay, okay, you can see Mrs. Stockman any morning you want, as she marches down Elm Street toward her office. And to observe Diana Ross in her black convertible Rolls Royce, you need only hang outside, say,

Woolworth's on Greenwich Avenue, in the warmer months; she's always driving by.)

When word comes to town that yet another CEO or high-profile type has laid down roots, locals can confirm where the newcomer lives simply by consulting the somewhat-larger-than-pocket-size phone directory. It's rarely out of reach in Greenwich households.

There's a special spirit one acquires after living in Greenwich for a while, the same spirit of civic pride that's exuded in tiny, prosperous, European monarchies. For instance, even those who don't send kids to the public Greenwich High School (where the principal is called a headmaster and many teachers earn salaries in excess of $50,000) can recite the statistic that 72% of its seniors go on to attend four-year colleges. (About one quarter of the local students are educated at the town's private schools.) It's common knowledge that the median price of single-family houses in Greenwich is $450,000. And even a below-average second-grader (should there be any, which is unlikely) could point out the line demarcating one-acre-lot zoning from four-acre-lot zoning. (As if to downplay any overt elitism, most folks express pride in the town's public housing complex and senior citizen residence.)

The pecking order of status is something one picks up shortly after birth, something that's reinforced over lunches at Bertrand's or between nibbles of afternoon *éclair pontneuf* or *Saint Honoré* at Versaille.

The municipality of Greenwich contains several distinct unincorporated villages, such as Old Greenwich, Riverside, Cos Cob, Byram and Glenville. Although many fine people live in those villages, they are, for the most part, situated on the wrong side of the tracks. The far more statusy place is the area known as "Greenwich" (aka "Greenwich Itself"), defined by the ZIP code 06830.

Within Greenwich Itself, the most prosperous locales are the Round Hill Road area in the Mid-country (between Route One and the Merritt Parkway) or the Back country (north of the Merritt Parkway). The other favored area consists of the Shoreline neighborhoods of Belle Haven and Field Point Circle.

With the possible exception of a few burglaries and car breakins and the occasional dead body dumped off I-95, crime isn't a major issue here—although that may be changing. For example, even though Belle Haven and Field Point Circle have their own private police check-points to deter nonresidents and the noninvited, burglars recently have taken to sneaking up to the Sound-front mansions by boat.

Indeed, Greenwich is slowly evolving from a safe, civilized and well-groomed executive ghetto into a place of traffic snarls and high school drug use. And then there's an unwelcomed result of feverish real estate values: Many who spend their childhood in Greenwich won't be able to afford to live here as adults.

True, CEOs may be somewhat immune to some of these problems. "I'd say the biggest change over the decades has been the people. There are many more people," affirms Watson. "But we've always either lived on dead-end roads or on the Sound—we didn't want to get into an area that would be surrounded by suburban development, so we're not as affected as most. My wife shops a lot so she sees the effects of all the people, but I can't say I notice it at all."

CEO residents are probably unaware of another change: The rich are getting richer. In the past, the average Greenwich family was lucky to belong to one of the town's 24 private clubs. Now multiple memberships are almost a necessity. "People belong to one club for golf and tennis, a racquet club for squash, maybe a yacht club," says Bett McCarthy, executive vice-president of the Greenwich Board of Realty. "And then there's skeet shooting at the Greenwich Country Club, Round Hill and Riverside."

Like elsewhere in the U.S., health club workouts have become a part of the daily routine. "Women are dropping off their kids at school and going to the health club, whereas in the past they would have played bridge," says McCarthy. Of course, the sweat mingles with conversations that sometimes make heads turn. "I was tying my sneakers the other morning and I overheard a woman tell her friend that she didn't make it into the club last week because she had been in Antarctica. Her friend was talking about going skiing in Switzerland. And another woman mentioned that she was taking her eight-year-old child to Disney World—for the third time."

Kids raised amid such affluence don't always turn out for the better. A recent survey revealed that 5% of the town's eighth-graders said they were getting drunk at least once a

THE SORRY PLIGHT
OF GREENWICH STRIVERS

Call them Greenwich Strivers (everybody else does).

They squeeze their families into salt-box houses here for the chance to have their kids befriend the Trump youngsters among the children's books at the library. Or, maybe for the opportunity to run into Ivana herself as she, on the way to lunch with (Primerica CEO former wife) Marlyn Tsai, stops to change her own flat tire—an event that made it into the newspaper. Or, maybe to join one of the charitable organizations that will put them in close proximity to the boss.

It's well known that most wealthy communities have folks wanting to cozy up to powerful neighbors. This being perhaps America's prime CEO suburb—and a sizable town offering more real estate—may have more of that sort of thing than anywhere else. Affirms Greenwich newspaper publisher William J. Rowe: "A lot of strivers move in to run into CEOs in Woolworth's."

According to David Ogilvy, Jr., a local realtor whose Christmas card list reads like a Who's Who, a Greenwich Striver typically will spend about $400,000 for a three- or four-bedroom house in the less statusy neighborhoods of Cos Cob or Old Greenwich. "If they're good at it," he says, "they'll trade up quickly to a larger house as they move up the ladder. We've seen people move up through four or five houses during the course of ten years."

But such hyperactive mobility, he qualifies, is the extreme. The sad truth is that your average Greenwich Striver doesn't get very far in his pursuit of success, status and acquisitions simply because he settles into this rarefied community.

"Yes, we have people driving up here who want to join our club," confirms Dennis Meermans, manager of the Round Hill Club, perhaps the most desirable country club in Greenwich and certainly the one boasting the highest concentration of CEOs. "But I tell them they can't join unless they are invited to join by a member. They're in a Catch-22 situation because they don't know anybody to invite them and I'm not going to give them a list of members." He adds: "And if they knew about clubs they'd know that they weren't what's called a 'desirable commodity.' "

Oh, yes, it is possible for a Striver, over the course of several years and considerable social jockeying, to become the sort of chap Round Hill considers worthy. ("They'd probably have gray hair by the time they did," scoffs Chamber of Commerce Managing Director Sidney Willis.) Such a social-climbing strategy involves joining one of Greenwich's less-exalted country clubs first and then continually trading up. "There are some clubs in which a few well-placed phone calls will get you voted in at the next board meeting," says Meermans, who can't afford to live in Greenwich. "The Burning Tree Club is relatively easy to get into," confides publisher Rowe. "So if you move in from Cleveland you can join the Burning Tree for two and a half years before moving on to something else."

And if career advancement, a smart marriage, participation at the right charity, or whatever, eventually puts the Striver within striking range of the Round Hill Club social circle, he should get a friend to invite him. (But, by all means, heed Meermans's warning that a careless Striver may just blow it all by listing on his membership application his connection with lower-status clubs.)

Most CEO-level newcomers already know the big-wigs *before* they come to Greenwich. If they don't, their company probably has a relationship with a banker or insurance person in the neighborhood who can get them acquainted with the right folks. "Typically, somebody who comes in at that level has many people who are interested in entertaining him, introducing him around," explains realtor Ogilvy, who sometimes takes it upon himself to invite newcomer clients to private cocktail gatherings or lunches, as a get-acquainted measure.

But the lowly Striver, eager to put the social-climbing process into motion, may be reduced to volunteering at a local charity. And Greenwich has literally hundreds from which to choose. There are the old standbys, such as the Red Cross, Boy Scouts, and Meals on Wheels. Also some unique ones, such as GAPS (Greenwich Association for Public Schools) or a group called Greenwich Green & Clean.

Of course, selecting the proper charitable organization takes some careful homework. Greenwich Green & Clean is headed by Peter Malkin, son-in-law of the late New York real estate mogul Lawrence Wien. Not a bad connection for some. Until recently, Greenwich's Republican Roundtable was headed by Pendleton James, who was the White House personnel director in the early days of the Reagan administration. The United Way is presided over by Ralph Pfeifer, the retired president of IBM's international operations. And PepsiCo Chairman D. Wayne Calloway and his wife are active in the Historical Society of Greenwich.

For some, the way up the social ladder is to send a kid to a private school. But that strategy, too, requires a careful selection process. The Greenwich Country Day School, where President Bush learned to fingerpaint, has a fine reputation for its educational program. But Striver parents would be distraught to learn that it doesn't provide all that many opportunities to mix with fellow parents. It lacks a PTA and it offers only one annual parents get-together (although many parents gather for Field Day). "Of course you could become a trustee," consoles Sidney Willis of the Chamber of Commerce, "but to do that you'd have to give a lot of money."

And you'd have to devote a lot of time if you wanted to heed the advice of Greenwich's equivalent of a mayor, First Selectman John B. Margenot, Jr. He suggests that eager-beaver (our words) Greenwichites join the town government. With an unusually large legislative body composed of more than 230 members, there's ample opportunity to participate. Trouble is, it's not an efficient way to gain exposure to corporate chiefs. "Most of the CEOs, except for one or two of them, go their own way," says Willis. "I guess they're busy."

—DAVID DIAMOND

week; 18% of the ninth-graders said it was easy to buy amphetamines and 25% of the twelfth-graders said it was easy to buy crack, according to Del Eberhart, coordinator of research and evaluation for the Greenwich Board of Education. The adults, too, can be a bad influence: Ivan Boesky used to live in Greenwich.

Moreover, most residents and public officials agree that development has gotten out of hand since the invasion of office buildings that began around 1970. To control the growth, the Planning and Zoning Commission established a host of restrictions. For instance, today if a developer wanted to build an office building in Greenwich, it would be restricted to three stories and there are strict requirements for the amount of parking space that must be built, and how much of the parking space must be hidden.

To circumvent the tough zoning, developers are putting up office buildings across the border in Stamford. To fight the increasing traffic such buildings create, Greenwich leaders talked about dead-ending the road leading to the Stamford site of a new office tower housing Conair Corp., or making the road one-way in the wrong direction during rush hours—but such proposals never became law. "We didn't want to get into a border-war situation," explains First Selectman Margenot.

Today, twice as many people commute *into* Greenwich than commute out each day, and the rush-hour traffic on Putnam Ave. (aka Route One and Boston Post Road) generally is backed up for blocks. Traffic on that thoroughfare was expected to get even worse had a proposed truck weigh station been opened on I-95. Colgate-Palmolive chairman Reuben Mark led successful opposition to the weigh station. But there's no sign of the traffic letting up: Increasingly, folks who take jobs in Greenwich's 1,229 office and business buildings are deciding to move into the community. That's created a boom in construction of tasteful, new condominiums (but even these "low-cost" accommodations typically may cost $350,000 for a two-bedroom unit).

–David Diamond

A Power Suburb's Silly Restrictions   When the village of Indian Hill, Ohio, tried to outlaw dog-barking between the hours of 5 P.M. and 8 A.M., it didn't sit well with Marge Schott, whose 19-room estate contains gold-framed portraits of her St. Bernards, Schottzie and Siegie. There's even a photo of former President Reagan, autographed, with a personal, presidential note to one of the dogs.

As majority owner and chairman of the board of the Cincinnati Reds, Schott is a tough-talking widow who isn't easily fazed. (She once presented the Pope with a Reds jacket bearing the name John Paul II.) But the ban on barking, which village leaders proposed would carry a $250 fine and 30-day jail sentence for owners of offending dogs, was enough to get her German blood boiling. This, despite the facts that more than 70 acres surround her home and that her closest neighbors, the family of the late margarine magnate Julius Fleischmann, are rarely in town.

Schott and other opponents rallied themselves into a frenzy at a number of raucus village meetings. (One opponent demanded to know what the village council could do about migrating geese that land on his pond.) Finally, the council was pressured to table the measure. But the bitter struggle, known locally as the "dog fights," points out a distinct characteristic of independent CEO enclaves such as Indian Hill.

Silly, silly restrictions.

Indian Hill imposes limits on the size of the sign you can erect on your property to identify your name and house number. Such signs can be no larger than two square feet. Other village ordinances prohibit solicitors, salespeople and the discharging of firearms. And New Yorkers who feel constrained by Manhattan's alternate-side-parking regulations would find themselves even *more* hassled in Indian Hill. Since all of the village's roads are of the two-lane variety, there's virtually *no* on-street parking.

But Indian Hillers do get a few breaks. Unlike other select communities, this village does not require cat leashes (as in Hinsdale, Illinois). And when asked if homeowners are permitted to erect fences to separate their properties, City Manager James D. Jester replied, "Oh, sure, you can build fences if you want to."

This select community covers nearly one third as much territory as neighboring Cincinnati, but in all its 20 square miles, there are no businesses—unless you consider the horse riding academy and other schools to be businesses. There's not even a post office. It's strictly a community of single-family residences.

It's ironic, then, that in discussing the values embedded in Indian Hill, Mrs. Schott, a sixth-generation Cincinnatian, says: "Heck, I'd rather talk to the butcher and the baker than half of my friends." The sad fact is that neither butchers nor bakers are permitted to operate in this community.

–DAVID DIAMOND

CEO GHETTOS

Chicago

Barrington Hills **Who lives there:** Navistar's James Cotting and Motorola's George Fisher.

Home price range: $500,000 to $2 million.

Special attractions: Lake-studded far Northwest suburb 36 miles from Loop; horses; five-acre minimum homesites and 4,000-acres of farmland make this a pleasant mix of millionaires and farmers.

Historical context: Village encompasses 28.6 square miles and extends into four counties; as new high-class developments sprout up, this continues to be a community in transition; since five major roads cut through the village, it's become a convenient site for gory crimes: in 1960s one estate was the locale for a random triple murder by Chicago's De Mau Mau gang, also scene of crime for a double infant stabbing by a mother driving through.

Reason to live there: For people who prefer horses over people.

Reason not to live there: Dreadfully quiet.

Who lives there: Sears' Edward Brennan.   *Burr Ridge*

Home price range: $600,000 to $2 million (since it's all new construction, buyers get more square footage for the dollar than in Hinsdale).

Special attractions: Brand-new executive enclaves with guarded entrances.

Historical context: Community (pop: 6,876, size: 7 square miles) formerly named ''Harvester'' for Case IH (formerly International Harvester), largest landowner and operator of a huge research and development facility here; land is being sold off for development of mansard-roofed nouveaumanses.

Reason to live there: Quick access to Oak Brook corporate hub; new golf clubs; no old-money social strata.

Reason not to live there: No community identity; no village center; no old-money social strata.

Who lives there: Borg-Warner's James Bere and Interlake's Fred Langen- *Hinsdale* berg.

Home price range: $600,000 to $2 million.

Special attractions: Charming small-town appeal; on Burlington line 25 miles southwest of Loop; attractive business district.

Historical context: Built in the 1860s by businessman William Robbins; suburban sprawl encircling Hinsdale has never ceased to expand.

Reason to live there: Short hop from Oak Brook corporate hub; healthy atmosphere; availability of relatively inexpensive homesites, but first you must knock down the existing homes.

Reason not to live there: Too far from Lake Michigan.

Who lives there: FMC's Robert Malott.   *Kenilworth*

Home price range: $750,000 to $3 million (on lake).

Special attractions: Tiny town (pop: 2,208, size: .6 square mile); Lake Michigan shoreline; Richardsonian and Queen Anne-style train station; broad-shouldered homes on shady lots; Illinois' highest per-family mean income ($97,220 in 1980).

Historical context: Developed in 1891 by Joseph (no relation) Sears; site of 1966 murder of Valerie Percy (daughter of former U.S. Senator Charles Percy).

Reason to live there: Since streets are laid out at Northeasterly and South-westerly angles, the sun reaches every room sometime during the day; a mere 30-minute trip by C&NW train to the Loop's many attractions.

Reason not to live there: Stuffy atmosphere.

Lake Forest **Who lives there:** Quaker Oats' William Smithburg, Brunswick's Jack Frank Reichert, and Walgreen's Charles Walgreen.

Home Price range: $600,000 (on West Side) to $6 million (on lake).

Special attractions: Market Square shopping center, built in 1916, resembles an English village; tasteful gas lamps; Mister T lives opposite the Owensia Club; newly refurbished beach, marina and lakefront park.

Historical context: Where the Swifts, Armours and (Marshall) Fieldses settled with their millions; when the Owensia Club denied membership to advertising executive Albert D. Lasker, a Jew, he built his own golf course; when Lasker died in the 1950s, his widow carved up his property for middle-class housing; the ensuing tide of middle class has never subsided.

Reason to live there: Great grocery shopping in Lakeside Foods (carpeted, and designed with nautical motif); two all-male golf clubs—the Old Elm Club and the Bob O' Link Club—are across the border in Highland Park; creative residential renovations of private-school chapels and servants' homes; access to Wisconsin.

Reason not to live there: Too long a trip to Loop (driving time is 45 minutes, C&NW train commute is 1 hour) to visit cultural institutions.

WHERE DO CEOS REALLY WANT TO LIVE?

1. San Francisco
2. London
*New York
3. Boston
*San Diego

WHAT CITIES DO CEOS LIKE TO AVOID?

1. New York
2. Chicago
3. Los Angeles
4. Miami
5. Detroit

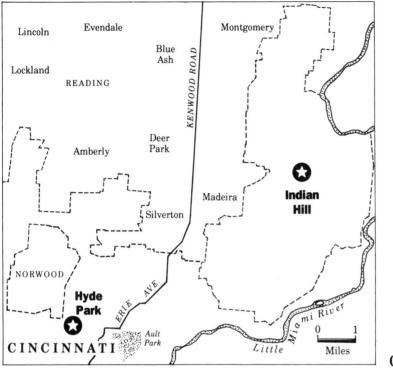

Cincinnati

Who lives there: Procter & Gamble's John Smale.

Hyde Park

Home price range: $250,000 to $2 million.

Special attractions: 1920s splendor; large old homes on hilly lots.

Historical context: Within Cincinnati city limits; originally consisted of six estates; annexed by the city in 1908; Nicholas Longworth, who married Alice Roosevelt, had a vineyard in adjacent Mount Lookout (Alice lived there for part of the couple's rocky marriage).

Reason to live there: Quick access to old book stores and other cultural institutions of "pulse-quickening downtown Cincinnati" (Tom Wolfe); access to parks; business district on Erie Avenue (Hyde Park Square) is Cincinnati's Rodeo Drive.

Reason not to live there: Proximity to nonexclusive areas of Cincinnati.

Who lives there: American Financial Corporation/United Brands/Penn Central's Carl Lindner, Cincinnati Reds' Marge Schott, Cincinnati Milacron's James Geier, and Cintas' Richard Farmer.

Indian Hill

Home price range: $350,000 to $3 million.

Special attractions: 150 miles of riding trails within municipality; fox hunts every Tuesday and Saturday.

Historical context: Founded in 1924 by fox hunting enthusiasts who built huge mansions on big lots. Almost all have since been subdivided; to keep Cincinnati from annexing it, the community set up its own water supply; noting the municipality's unusually large number of unemployed residents (and not knowing that the unemployed were idle rich), the Federal Government once offered the community Federal funds.

Reason to live there: Open spaces, Marge Schott.

Reason not to live there: Highly restrictive atmosphere of municipality (businesses of any sort are prohibited within the town's 20 square miles). Highly restrictive atmosphere of socially prominent Camargo Country Club (Carl Lindner wasn't accepted for membership until *after* he moved next door).

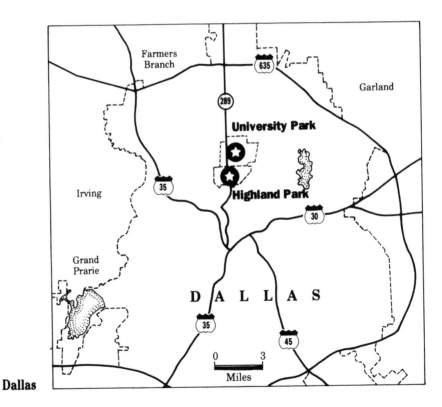

Dallas

Highland Park **Who lives there:** Southland's Jere W. Thompson, NCNB-Texas's Buddy Kemp, and Trammell Crow's Trammell Crow.

Home price range: $800,000 to $3 million (although a rare $12 million home was recently listed). The bust economy encourages serious price negotiating.

Special attractions: Insular, old-money (for Texas) community (pop: 8,817, size: 2.6 square miles); foliage imported from other U.S. regions makes the town appear almost New England-esque; Dallas Country Club.

Historical context: Incorporated in 1913 (a dozen years after the country club was formed); mission revival style shopping center is among the nation's first.

Reason to live there: Everybody else does; convenient to downtown Dallas; excellent police; all-you-can-play tennis for $15 a year.

Reason not to live there: Postage-stamp properties; socially self-conscious residents.

Who lives there: Haliburton's Thomas Cruikshank.

University Park

Home price range: $500,000 to $3 million (but the bust economy encourages price negotiating).

Special attractions: Insular town (pop: 22,300, size: 3.6 square miles) that's less exclusive than adjacent Highland Park; Southern Methodist University academic community; well-manicured Volk Estates section.

Historical context: Incorporated in 1924 on farmland and orchards adjacent to SMU.

Reason to live there: Less exclusive than Highland Park (except the Volk Estates section).

Reason not to live there: Less exclusive than Highland Park.

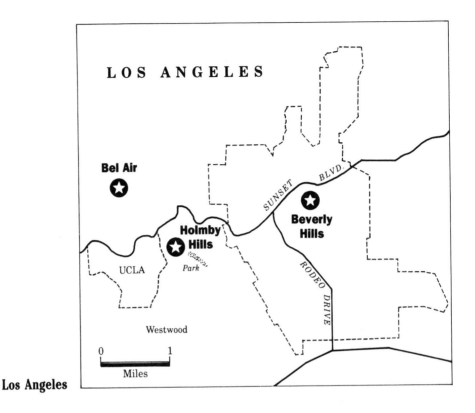

Los Angeles

Bel Air **Who lives there:** Northrop's Thomas Jones and Disney's Michael Eisner (and former President Ronald Reagan).

Home price range: $2.5 million to $16 million.

Special attractions: Privacy, landscaped hills, wooded canyons, winding drives with names like Bellagio or Perugia, incomparably lush Bel Air Hotel.

Historical context: Within Los Angeles city limits; developed by Alphonzo E. Bell in the early 1920s.

Reason to live there: Live-and-let-live privacy, attractive surroundings.

Reason not to live there: Isolation; tourists in search of celebrity homes; little community atmosphere; trash day means unsightly trash containers at iron-gated driveways.

Beverly Hills **Who lives there:** MCA's Lew Wasserman, Great Western Financial's James Montgomery.

Home price range: $2 million (for anything you'd want to live in) to $20 million.

Special attractions: Swimming pools, movie stars, rich third-world newcomers who pay up to $100,000 over market value for homes once owned by celebrities.

Historical context: Gabrielino Indians who once inhabited Beverly Hills flatlands and hills used local mud as sunscreen and to increase hair sheen (but they were all but wiped out by syphilis); city named for Beverly Farms, Massachusetts, vacation site of President William Howard Taft; Beverly Hills Hotel (1912) was popular attraction; city incorporated in 1914; Gucci opened on Rodeo Drive in 1969.

Reason to live there: Nation's most legendarily upscale community. Ample opportunity for community involvement. Great library, unsurpassed shopping. Proximity among mansions fosters friendly atmosphere.

Reason not to live there: Proximity among mansions gets old quickly, fosters little privacy (even in $4 million homes); transience born of the here-today-gone-tomorrow nature of the entertainment industry and prominent divorce attorneys.

Holmby Hills

Who lives there: Occidental Petroleum's Armand Hammer, Hilton Hotels' Barron Hilton.

Home price range: $2 million to $12 million.

Special attractions: Less crowded than Beverly Hills, less isolating than Bel Air; pretty little park; afternoon joggers from nearby UCLA; Playboy mansion.

Historical context: Within Los Angeles city limits; the more exclusive subdivision of the old Rancho San Jose de Buenos Aires, developed in 1929 by Arthur Letts and named for his English birthplace. (Westwood was the less exclusive section.)

Reason to live there: Not overrun by tourists.

Reason not to live there: Lack of community (not even a Civic Association).

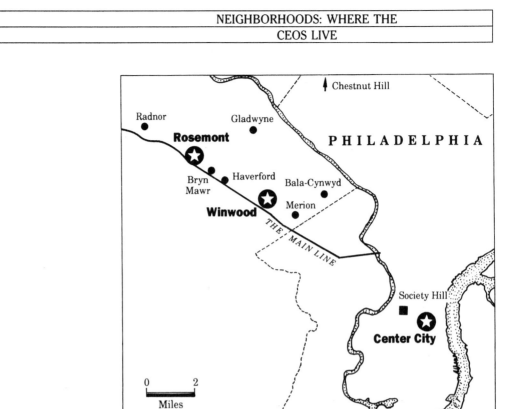

Philadelphia

Center City **Who lives there:** Campbell Soup's R. Gordon McGovern (Society Hill), Pennwalt's Edwin Tuttle (Society Hill), and SmithKline Beckman's Henry Wendt.

Home price range: $500,000 to $1.8 million.

Special attractions: City living.

Historical context: Birthplace of lending library (1731); birthplace of fire departments (1736); birthplace of insurance companies (1752); birthplace of American Revolution (1776); birthplace of U.S. Constitution (1787); birthplace of American Urban Redevelopment (early 1960s).

Reason to live there: Walk to work; endless tiny parks and charming walkways in Society Hill historic district; world's largest collection of restored 18th-century architecture.

Reason not to live there: City wage tax of 4.9% of income for anyone who lives or works in Philadelphia; tourists; largely inept city government.

The Main Line **Who lives there:** Sun Company's Robert McClements, Jr., (Malvern), Rohm & Haas's J. Lawrence Wilson (Rosemont), Cigna's Wilson H. Taylor (Malvern), and, at least in May, former Triangle Publications CEO Walter H. Annenberg (Wynnewood).

Home price range: $400,000 to $3 million.

Special attractions: Secluded wooded properties; marvelous Welsh names (Bryn Mawr, Bala-Cynwyd); expansive garden supply stores; restaurants in old mansions.

Historical context: Area encompasses four townships: Lower Merion, Haverford, Radnor, Tredyffrin. Tiny towns developed around stations of the Pennsylvania Railroad's Main Line, most of them have a college or private academy; site of *The Philadelphia Story* (Katharine Hepburn went to Bryn Mawr).

Reason to live there: Ivy-covered manor houses; easy train or auto access (via Schuylkill Expressway) to Center City; Patti LaBelle; Chaim Potok.

Reason not to live there: Lack of creative stimulation.

—DAVID DIAMOND

A CEO
AND HIS
HOME(S)

Saul Steinberg, the megamillionaire head of Reliance Group Holdings, has a home befitting a captain of industry: a baronial, three-floor co-op on Park Avenue filled with a glorious art collection and opulent furnishings. Likewise Marge Schott, chairman and majority owner of the Cincinnati Reds: She lives alone under a 110-ton slate roof in a 19-room stone mansion in Indian Hill, Ohio. The original owners devoted a room solely to flower arranging. "The Schotts liked to drink more than arrange flowers so we turned this into a bar," she says, with a hearty laugh. What a pleasure to find CEOs who take pride in elegant surroundings!

But what have we here? John Schwemm, the head of R. R. Donnelley, the world's largest printer, has lived in the same modest house in the Chicago suburbs since 1970, long before he became a CEO. And GenCorp chairman Bill Reynolds, too, has happily stayed put in his respectable 19th-century house behind its white picket fence in the village of Gates Mill, Ohio. He bought the house nearly two decades before becoming GenCorp's CEO. While he has purchased a few additional properties in the village over the years, he has never felt the need to trade up houses. And so you can find him from time to time near the potbellied stove in his "barn" room.

Barn room?

For every entrepreneur like Steinberg, who shouldered his way into the big leagues, or Schott, who was born into them, there are many more Schwemms or Reynoldses, CEOs who climbed the ladder to the top, hand over hand. They didn't get there by throwing money around and now that they're chairmen, they aren't about to develop a sudden fondness for ostentation. Their homes are pleasant and tidy and tend to reflect the same conservative spending habits that put shareholders so much at ease.

A corporate chief is in the marvelous position of being able to do anything he wants, housing-wise—even if, as in the case of John Schwemm—he chooses to do nothing.

Money is rarely a problem, and neither is status. So the CEO can create his own ideal environment for escaping the daily executive grind. Some go for privacy, some for comfort, some for grandeur, some for animals, some for haute decor, some for tennis, some for the view. Anything goes.

Some CEOs like to recognize their new-found rank by trading up. When Edwin Jefferson ascended to the chairmanship of Du Pont he bought the magnificent Centerville, Delaware, estate belonging to former chairman Charles B. "Brel" Mc-Coy—putting green and all—claiming he needed a bigger home in which to entertain.

Others stay rooted in abodes they purchased on the way up. When Jefferson's successor, Richard Heckert, took over, he was content to remain in his existing home, which happens to be a 300-acre farm in Kennett Square, Pennsylvania.

Is it better to move *before* or *after* becoming CEO? There's no easy answer.

It may also be up to the wife. More than likely it has been she all along who banked the home fires while he was setting the corporate world ablaze. She may be the same little home-body he married 30 years ago, with no desire to sever her roots in the community. (Or to part with the shower tile she so lovingly selected. Most CEOs don't get to be CEOs by worrying whether the shower curtain goes with the tiles or by picking out the everyday silver.) On the other hand, she may think she has paid her middle-class dues and be chafing for opulence.

And, even if a CEO does move, it may be for reasons unrelated to his new status. When he was offered the top job at Ryland Homes, Ted Peck had little choice. Ryland was based in Columbia, Maryland. He was living in Toledo. And Les Coleman's promotion to chairman of Lubrizol had less to do with his move than did a second marriage. In selecting a wooded retreat in the Chagrin Valley east of Cleveland, privacy was a primary objective.

One theory holds that aspiring CEOs don't invest much energy in dreaming about acquiring the perfect home. Wrote William H. Whyte in his 1956 classic, *The Organization Man:* "No dreams of gothic castles or liveried footmen seize his imagination. His house will never be a monument, an end in itself. It is purely functional, a place to salve the wounds and store up energy for what's ahead. And that, he knows full well, is battle."

A notable exception is Saul Steinberg, who carried a life-long desire to reside among world-class furnishings. So he bought an old Rockefeller place on Park Avenue. And his passion for art requires space, which proves useful for another of his priorities: philanthropic entertaining.

Bill and Jo Reynolds found they wanted more space in which to house visiting guests, but they didn't want to abandon a town they loved. So they bought a guest house. The Schwemms, too, felt at home in their suburb, Downers Grove, Illinois, on the outskirts of Chicago. So they stayed there, feeling no need to add rooms or buy nearby properties. (They did, however, pick up a Windy City pied-à-terre and a Florida condo.)

Which leads us to another issue. To preserve his image as a prudent caretaker of corporate revenues, a CEO may find it advisable not to flaunt his good fortune with an extravagant change of venue. Hence, the existence of second, third, and even fourth homes tucked away in attractive corners of the country, to supplement a primary residence that doesn't draw too much undue attention. Our *Wall Street Journal* survey of CEOs found that 69.5% own two or more homes.

But for this chapter, we concentrate our reporting on chief executives' main residences. Our tour takes us inside five CEO homes, each of which reveals a different CEO style.

Looking for an Escape   The main thing to know about Lester Coleman as it relates to his home is that he is a Boy Scout. Still. Not only is he on the National Executive Board of the Boy Scouts of America, but in 1988 he received the William S. Spurgeon Award, the Pulitzer Prize of Scoutdom, which has been awarded to more than a hundred organizations but only to three individuals. Coleman, age 58, is also an ardent conservationist and nature photographer.

Each day he trades the honking of horns on a 25-minute commute from the headquarters of Lubrizol near Cleveland for the honking of geese on a miniature five-acre preserve he calls home. For Coleman, mere privacy is not enough. Indeed his modest two-story beige house on a cul de sac is easily visible from the road. More important is the wooded setting that allows him to commune with the nature he came to revere as a Boy Scout.

In the office, Coleman is a low-key, approachable man but no one ever forgets that he's the boss. "Here," he says, speaking of home, "it's sort of nice to put on my blue jeans and my old clothes and go out and work in the yard or walk up and down the street with the dog, and just be somebody nobody worries about."

Coleman's house is not elaborate, and the $350,000 price tag reflects the lot on which it sits more than the structure itself. He and his wife, Cathy, spotted the then three-year-old, four-bedroom home two years ago in a Realtor's magazine. Leafing through separately, both were drawn by the same picture of a duck pond and a hammock.

Today, Coleman sits next to a large window in the living room that commands that view—absent the hammock, which belonged to the former owner—his chair angled toward the pond where he can watch nature's unending show. Deer parade across his view. Rabbits skitter through the grass. Hawks swoop down, seeking a mouthful of dove. Geese engage in territorial squabbles. And then there are the ducks, steaming purposefully across the pond or languidly coasting from bank to bank. At any given time there are as few as 4 or as many as 120. Coleman particularly likes to watch them land.

The show continues all year long. An aerator keeps the pond from freezing, and there is an all-you-can eat (if you're a duck) corn bin. Bird feeders draw additional feathered friends. "I can watch the seasons change by the color of the bullfinches," he says.

There are more ducks inside. Colorfully painted decoys roost atop kitchen cabinets and perch on shelves in every room. Ducks adorn the walls in paintings by naturalists or in photographs Coleman has taken. His only hunting is "with a camera." And it includes not only wildlife but flowers as well. He is a strong supporter of Ducks Unlimited, an organization devoted to preserving duck habitats.

He is an inveterate collector. Indeed, it seems that if Coleman happens to acquire more than one of something, he begins to collect it. His acquisitions have taken over his basement, which is large and extraordinarily neat. Along one wall are the caps, perhaps 100, from Lubrizol and Lubrizol customers, Boy Scouts, assorted concerns like America's Cup and, of course, Ducks Unlimited. His buckle collection is down here, and so are the ornamental walking sticks—the one he used when he climbed Mt. Fuji and another from China's Great Wall. Shelves house his books. A Boy Scout series (example: *Boy Scouts in the Maine Woods*). Tomes on fishing and wildlife. He's read them all. He's also kept his college chemistry books. Coleman holds a Ph.D. in chemistry from the University of Illinois and started with Lubrizol in 1955 as a chemist. Upstairs is more current reading by some basic he-man writers: Robert Ludlum, James Clavell, Louis Lamour. James Michener is another favorite.

Down here each morning amid his paraphernalia, Lubrizol's chairman begins his day with simulated outdoor activities: rowing and running as he watches the news. He gets to the office early, but he's generally home shortly after five, preferring to continue his work there if need be. "I would much rather bring stuff home and do it than stay at the office and impress people," he says.

When this getaway isn't enough, he has yet another, more rustic retreat: a place on a lake near Hanover, New Hampshire, for skiing, hiking, canoeing, golfing, tennis and sailing.

He says his wife consulted a department store decorator in furnishing the house. Since then, they've been winging it. "Decorators are great, but I really don't want someone telling me what I like and don't like in the way of the extras," he says. A decorator might not have understood the ducks, nor appreciated the stuffed animals that he's given Cathy, or even the Cabbage Patch doll, factory-named Coleman Lester (can you believe it?), that Lester Coleman had to have after a friend spotted it in a department store.

Although Coleman has a well-equipped shop in the basement, he puts more time into outdoor than indoor maintenance. "I love to mess around in the woods," he says. He planted 300 seedlings—flowering shrubs and some conifers to break up the monotony of the prevailing beech, maple and hickory trees—and is attempting to create a garden of delicate wildflowers. But even as he speaks, there are grapevines out there with a stranglehold on trees. The top of a beech that fell off the other day awaits the ax. He regards his property with the mixed emotions of a housewife, who likes to clean but is never satisfied. "The nice thing about this property is you can do as much or as little as you want," he says, revealing a nonperfectionist side that is unusual among CEOs. "But anytime you get woods, believe me woods creep and if you don't keep after them they'll take over."

Stepping Back in Time The year 1967 was the one in which Bill and Joanne Reynolds's furniture seemed to spend as much time on the road as it did with them. They owned four houses that year, but the last was the one in which they reside today, a 19th-century white frame house in the charming little village of Gates Mills, Ohio, not far from Coleman's home.

It happened this way: They were living in Detroit, where they had sold one house and bought another, their dream house, when Reynolds's employer dispatched him to Cleveland. There they moved into a home in staid, well-to-do Shaker Heights, bought in haste so their three children could start school in September. But Jo Reynolds was not entirely satisfied. "It was a big old barn of a place that was too formal as far as I was concerned. It was fine if that was what you like, but I had three little kids at the time who were playing soccer in the big old front hall, and it had a little postage-stamp backyard, and the whole thing was just awful for me."

One day an acquaintance in real estate called her and took her to see yet another home. Jo loved it. "So Bill came home that night and I said, 'Well, I really just happened to see this really darling house.' And he said, 'There's no way.' " Safe to say, this was a man who had come to view an agreement of sale as an instrument of torture. Under his protests, they drove out to see it the following Sunday, and bought it the next day.

Why? you might ask. It kind of "fit our values," they say. These are not moral values, like honesty or courage. Nor financial values, in the sense of a good investment. These are life-style values. Gates Mills, with 322 households, a post office, a grocery and a school, offered "a little more space" (Bill); "freedom" as in to "let a dog run" (Bill); "more casual life-style" (both). The dog's freedom has since been snatched away by the government. Dogs must be leashed.

So at day's end, A. William Reynolds leaves GenCorp, a high-tech company which derives half its income from missile systems, drives 40 miles into another century and the simple life of a country squire, albeit it one with a Harvard undergraduate degree and an MBA from Stanford. Although a friendly, relaxed man, he possesses an air of reserve not unusual among CEOs. His home has the same air about it. There is casual—as in a ski lodge, where you'd take off your shoes, flop down in front of the fire and scatter magazines and papers all over the floor. And then there is the Reynoldses' version of casual—a home with a simple but elegant country decor.

In 1985 when Reynolds ascended to the top post at GenCorp, he saw no need to go elsewhere. He and his wife chose instead to prepare for a future filled with visiting children and grandchildren by purchasing the town's onetime barbershop—which had fallen on hard times—and renovating it into a cheery, two-bedroom, fully equipped guest house. Should a child want to settle in Gates Mills and run into a housing shortage, no problem. The Reynoldses also bought another house which they are currently leasing out.

Like many of the village residents, the houses in Gates Mills have pedigrees. Next door to the Reynoldses' is the one

built in 1837 by the Gates family, who came from Connecticut and started a lumber mill. The Reynoldses' house, which
also dates from that era, acquired an interesting addition in
1920 when the woman who owned it converted to Catholi-
cism. There was no Catholic church in the area, so Cleveland
church authorities were willing to send out a priest to say
mass in her house. The woman had misgivings, however,
when she realized that her fellow worshipers were the hired
help of Gates Mills. "She had become a Catholic but not a
Democrat," Reynolds says. She didn't want the lower-class
Catholics tromping through her house. So she added a room
with a separate entrance.

Today the onetime chapel serves as the Reynoldses' living
room. As rooms go, it is handsome, with a fireplace, book-
laden shelves, chairs and a sofa in a cheery floral print, and
a white Yamaha grand piano anchoring one end. But they
don't spend much time there, preferring the informality of
the "barn room"—an enclosed porch with shingled walls and
a potbellied stove and a large portrait of a pig commissioned
by Jo, to Bill's dismay. Or they're in the kitchen, with its
floor-to-ceiling bookshelves lined with cookbooks and its six-
burner professional range and double-door freezer big
enough for a small restaurant. Jo is an accomplished cook,
known for throwing complete Chinese banquets. Jo Reynolds
also worked professionally as a decorator for more than 10
years. So the home reflects her taste. An elegant 1760 high-
boy stands in the foyer. It's from the town of Exeter, New
Hampshire, where Reynolds prepped. But most of the furnishings are of the more roughhewn country variety. And
some of the chests and tables are graced with two- to three-
inch-high porcelain reproductions of authentic English homes.

The house is larger than it looks. Upstairs are four tiny
bedrooms—daughters Mary and Morgan, now grown, each
had two—plus the master bedroom. Son Timothy's room on
the first floor is a guest room.

At the rear of a backyard filled with pachysandra, a pool
sparkles beneath hundred-year-old maples and elms. Reynolds says this is his favorite place when the weather permits. Beyond the yard is a right-of-way where an interurban
railroad once clattered into Gates Mills, bringing wealthy
families from the city to weekend retreats. It has been gone

for 70 years. And beyond that is a wide grassy expanse—the polo grounds of the Gates Mills Hunt Club. They aren't big enough for polo, however. Members play on a public field. Because they prefer golf clubs to horses, the Reynoldses for years resisted joining the club. Finally, they succumbed to destiny. Jo pointed out, "It's just silly. We have one of the best restaurants in Cleveland a football field away from us. Maybe it's time we joined. Now we can't understand what took us so long."

When Charles P. "Ted" Peck was recruited by Ryland *Feeling We've* Homes, he found himself with an interesting problem on his *Earned It* hands.

Ryland was in the forefront of the colonialization of the suburbs. In the 20 years after its founding in 1967, the company built 60,000 homes, many of them the shuttered, two-story models in vibrant colors that incorporated fireplaces, french doors and other stylistic touches reminiscent of the founding families. Where one such authentic house might have been home to a gentleman farmer with several hundred acres, now there were hundreds of reproductions on the same site. And nowhere was this more in evidence than the Howard County countryside around Columbia, Maryland, where Ryland had its corporate headquarters.

Nothing against Ryland, of course, but Ted and his wife "Dee," short for Delphine, did not want to live in a Ryland home. Nor did they have to. "If you're at the top," says Dee, a forthright, matter-of-fact woman, "no one's going to tell you what to do." So they commissioned an architect and hired an independent builder.

The result is a rustic $700,000 Tudoresque nook in the woods, that incorporates some of the things they liked best from the other houses they have lived in as Ted worked his way up the corporate ladder of Owens-Corning to the post of executive vice-president. Explains Dee Peck, "A lot of people said, 'Did Ryland build your home?' And I said 'No,' and they said 'Why not?' And I said, 'Because Ryland doesn't build custom homes.' "

To be sure, there isn't much to suggest that first little house they lived in more than 30 years ago, when Owens-Corning sent him to Newark, Ohio, for a year of training. Peck rented it in a summer recreation area called Buckeye Lake for himself and his bride, whom he had met at the University of Pennsylvania.

When winter rolled around, silencing the nearby roller coaster, the couple made a startling discovery. The only heat was a single-burner stove. "That was our honeymoon house," recalls Dee with a laugh. "Not only did I spend the winter there, I got pregnant there and had morning sickness there, in the chill. But when you're young, who cares?"

When Peck served a stint in Pennsylvania, they bought a somewhat larger house in Levittown, a name that would become synonymous with tract development and the "ticky, tacky houses" of the post–World War II era. They took a loss when they sold a year and a half later because buyers could still buy new homes at the price the Pecks had paid. Even before that, Ted Peck had an experience with a development home. Growing up in Lancaster, Pennsylvania, he lived in a subdivision that failed after just two homes were built. "That does have some significance," his wife says. "Even at a young age, he was aware that the builder could go broke."

Before taking the post at Ryland, 63-year-old Peck and his family of four children lived in Toledo, where Owens-Corning was headquartered, for 27 years. There they had three houses, the last, the one they cherished most, on the Maumee River.

When they got to Howard County, located between Washington and Baltimore, they thought they might like one of the old gracious historic homes that had survived the onslaught of suburban development. But all the old gracious historic homes were occupied.

Peck didn't want to move to either city and commute an hour each way. So they decided to build. They found a lot on a knoll sloping down to a creek and bordered by county parkland, and commissioned an architect.

From the entrance, there is a view straight through the living room that captures a tranquil expanse of woods. Throughout the house, windows frame outdoor vistas. No other homes are in sight. Beneath a cathedral ceiling, bookshelves line the living room and a collection of comfortable couches and chairs occupies the center. A Tudor feeling suggested by the ceiling is a nod toward Dee's English extraction and also the Tudoresque central Pennsylvania home Ted's family traded up to, as his father rose in another corporation, Armstrong.

In addition, he says, "The high ceiling lets large crowds feel not so constrained. We wanted a place that allowed us to do both social and business entertainment." There is yet another reason, perhaps more important. One of their favorite houses in Toledo also had a cathedral ceiling, and each Christmas they filled it with a huge Christmas tree that was the centerpiece of two parties, one social and one business. Cutting and raising the tree was a great family tradition lost when they moved to a home with a lower ceiling. Once again the Pecks are able to have large trees.

The living room separates the two main floor wings. One wing is occupied by the dining room, kitchen, and eating area; the other by the Pecks' master bedroom suite, which includes his and her dressing rooms and a laundry room, plus a bath with a Jacuzzi. A large rear deck overlooking the yard and woods stretches from the living room to the kitchen. Below, the basic layout is repeated, with a family room and kitchenette in the center that doubles as a meeting room or a play space for little visitors. Four bedrooms house returning children and grandchildren.

As well-heeled veterans of a lot of homes, they were able to have things tailor-made. In the kitchen, the dishwasher is raised, so its user needn't bend over. (Actually, there are two dishwashers, to ease the load when entertaining.)

"We're not art collectors, not antique furniture people," says Ted Peck. Indeed the one really old piece is from neither family, a grandfather's clock that a friend located for Dee. Most of their furniture runs to reproductions.

When it comes to home repairs, the head of a major home-building company has to line up just like anybody else. "The place is booming and any sort of trade person—they are so busy with new construction, that unless you're an old customer, they don't want to even mess with you," Dee says. Howard County doesn't have a service sector like older, urban areas. She had to beg a gardener to add her to his list of customers, pointing out that she was en route to other jobs. It's a region where maids get rich. A single example: Dee employs a cleaning service whose founder is doing so well she recently moved into a $300,000 house herself.

Dee says it annoys her to hear first-home buyers complain about the prices of today's housing. The Pecks certainly have paid their dues by living in small houses, so why not others? "None of the young people would deign to live in a house as small as the Levittown house," she says. (But if they did, maybe her husband would be out of work.)

Feeling at Home in an "Old Shoe" of a House

Rain pelts the cab as we head out the East-West Expressway from the center of Chicago. It's the morning rush hour in both directions, with the outbound lanes nearly as sluggish as the inbound. Thunderclaps, followed a nanosecond later by a bolt of lightning, and more thunder.

Eventually, the exit sign for Downers Grove looms through a curtain of rain. Guided only by a map with an "X" marking the site of the house of John Schwemm, our first task is to find a section of the suburb called Denburn Woods, then to locate a street named Turvey. As we eventually find our way onto one of several streets named Turvey, we round a bend—as detailed on the map—and before us sits a huge, freshly built, stylistically ambiguous home. Set back from the road behind a screen of trees, it has several peaks, multiple floors, and tiny windows. It certainly seems grand enough to house the CEO of America's largest printer. The lights are on in a small house adjacent to the driveway, and we pull over to confirm that the mansion does, indeed, belong to the Schwemms.

Our anticlimactic discovery? The Schwemms live in the equivalent of a gate house to the looming mansion.

As John Schwemm ("Call us 'Jack' and 'Nan' ") moved up the corporate ladder from attorney, to general counsel, to vice-president, and finally CEO and chairman of the firm that prints 450 phone books, 250 magazines, books for 900 publishers, plus catalogs, newspaper inserts and a fair proportion of the circulars that end up in American mailboxes, the couple could certainly have afforded to leave Downers Grove, where homes sell for/from $250,000 to $500,000 and a "handyman's special" can still be had for a bargain $80,000. They could have opted for a better address in Oak Park say, which is fairly close, or one of the affluent North Shore suburbs near Lake Michigan, like Winnetka or Kenilworth, where even homes as modest as theirs cost twice as much.

Schwemm, a tall, square-jawed man with dark hair, has a simple answer: "We're not pretentious people," he says, suddenly wincing at his own words, and quickly adding: "It sounds like I'm being pretentious using the word *pretentious.*"

So they never seriously considered leaving what Nan calls their "old shoe of a house" in an "old shoe of a town." They talk about both with great affection.

Downers Grove, they note, was the first official subdivision in the state of Illinois, and also contained the first official golf course west of the Alleghenies, albeit one with only nine holes.

The town is as all-American as the name suggests, both in appearance and history. The Downer for which it is named was the gentleman who stole—make that acquired—the future subdivision from the Indians in 1832. It has a main street called Main Street and a creek whose name hardly anyone knows. Everyone just calls it "the creek."

The Schwemms can walk to the center of town in 10 minutes, where there is their bank, hardware store, grocery, church and a Walgreen's, on whose board Schwemm sits, as well as the red-brick train station where he boards the train into the city, a 22-mile ride in 23 minutes. A waiting car picks him up at and delivers him 10 minutes later to the corporate headquarters.

The train is in fact *the* reason the Schwemms have lived in Downers Grove since they were newlyweds.

Both are from Barrington, Illinois, an hour away, where Nan grew up in a house Jack describes as "modest" and he in one that was "modest to good." After graduating magna cum laude from Amherst College, where he majored in religion, he went to the University of Michigan law school. Setting out to buy a home in 1960, he and Nan decided not to live too close to their families. But they wanted to be on a rail line. The Northwestern at that time was not as good as the Burlington. "We started in La Grange (where they had an apartment) and went as far out on this railroad as we could afford," he explains. "That's how we landed here." Schwemm was 26 years old.

Their first home was a three-bedroom split level. Their second, a four-bedroom Colonial. In 1970 they reverted to a three-bedroom home when they bought their present dwelling, which had started out in the post-war period as a modest two-bedroom, one-story house with a tiny living room.

Today it still has one story and isn't much grander, with just three bedrooms, three baths, an expanded living room and an enclosed porch. But it isn't just any-old-house, either, thanks to its previous owner, a man named Gordon Metcalf who was the chairman of Sears from 1968 to 1972. (Metcalf, who moved out of this house midway through his tenure as CEO, had other outlets for his Edifice Complex. He commissioned the 110-story Sears Tower.)

It isn't every house that can claim to have had two CEO owners, one right after the other, particularly in view of its modest dimensions. But perhaps the Sears chairman found Downers Grove in keeping with his store's humble image. "When we moved in they had every conceivable Sears appliance," Schwemm says. Over the years those have been replaced, although Nan's exercycle that sits stage center on the porch is prominently labeled with the retailer's name.

The Schwemms were enchanted by some of the home's custom features. The L-shaped living room is distinguished by a wall of handsome floor-to-ceiling maple cabinets and a brass-hooded fireplace that dominates one end. Another bank of cabinets sets off the dining room. Silverware drawers are lovingly lined with felt and there is a divided section for trays. Handmade tiles from Cuernavaca adorn the kitchen.

In showing us Metcalf's additions, Schwemm pulls aside drapes to reveal 12-inch wall speakers. "He put in things that in their day were extremely unusual, like built-in speakers. . . . The guy who did it died and we don't use them because nobody's been able to figure out the wiring," he says.

In 18 years the Schwemms have done little to the house, other than thermopane the porch to make it a year-round room and install a swimming pool shaped like the head of a tennis racket and a sauna in the side yard vacated by a large old tree.

Jack's home office consists of a desk at one end of their none-too-spacious bedroom. The desk however, commands views of the expansive, shady backyard and the pool. Although their lot is just five-sixths of an acre, they joined with four other families to buy three adjoining lots, to prevent builders from coming in.

The home is comfortably furnished with overstuffed chairs and sofas, where teddy bears have taken up residence. Nan professes a taste for simple furnishings. Not long ago she went on a tour of professionally decorated homes and returned declaring, "If I never see another swag, it will be too soon."

The house's cabinetry doesn't leave a lot of space for wall hangings. Antiques are not among their passions. Jack jokes that they are the oldest, most valuable things in the house. There is a small painting of note in the hallway, however, a work by Jack's grandfather, George O. Butler, of a couple sitting on a bench in the woods, as a puppy plays nearby. Butler's painting of an Indian maiden has adorned the Land O' Lakes butter box for the better part of this century.

The cleaning is done by a service, except when Nan is out of town and Jack tackles the house himself. "Those ladies," he sniffs, gesturing toward the top of the living room drapes, "never run a dust thing across that."

As the door to the Park Avenue apartment opens, a short, stocky man in a dark suit and tomato-red bow tie breaks ranks with a half dozen Rodin bronzes standing guard in the spacious foyer and extends his hand. "I'm Saul Steinberg," he says.

Feeling at Home in 34 Rooms

At his side is Gayfryd Steinberg, a slender, dark-haired Canadian who stands shoulder to shoulder with her husband in New York's nouvelle society. Their home shelters a multi-million-dollar art collection housed in a 34-room residence once owned by the Rockefellers.

"Are there really 34 rooms? Does that count bathrooms?"

"Yes," Gayfryd says.

"No," Saul says.

"Oh, Saul it counts closets and everything. I'm so sick of that statistic. I don't like to use it."

Suffice to say that on this floor there are two baths, a large drawing room, a dining room, a smaller dining room and a three-room kitchen complex. On the two upper floors there are bedrooms all round for the six children—three of whom still live at home and only one of whom is a product of the Saul-Gayfryd alliance—a master bedroom suite, a family room, a maid's quarters, assorted baths and dressing rooms, and, of course, the film projection room and the gym. Somehow it all adds up. It takes the work of three full-time maids to make all the crystal gleam and the silver shine.

Believe it or not, the Steinbergs insist they lead a perfectly normal life in these expansive art-laden environs, among porcelain and candelabras and wallpaper depicting French maidens and works bearing such names as "Plague at Athens." You can sit on the furniture, and the kids—two boys and a girl—do skate on the irresistible wooden expanse of the entrance hall, although, Gayfryd notes, matter-of-factly: "Their father doesn't like it." To accommodate him, they use skates with plastic wheels. Only the cat Felix was unable to handle all the space. (Or maybe it was the trips in a box to their Long Island retreat in Quogue.)

In any event, Felix retreated to the kitchen and wouldn't come out. Steinberg gave him to the chauffeur, whose apartment, as one might expect, is somewhat smaller than the boss's. Felix is happy now, Steinberg says. "He loves it."

Just like ordinary people, the Steinbergs struggle to balance their children's needs with their own. Even when a formal dinner party is on the schedule, both Saul and Gayfryd make it a point to sit down with the kids when they eat at 6:00 P.M. Sometimes Steinberg eats, too.

"Saul is a two-dinner person," Gayfryd says. He protests weakly. "I'm not always a two-dinner person."

Like other parents, they wrestle with how much TV is too much, although Saul jokes that the Spanish language network Telemundo is okay. It's his.

Saul Steinberg always knew he'd live somewhere like this. He grew up in a two-bedroom apartment in the East New York section of Brooklyn. Sometimes he would take the subway into Manhattan, to visit the Frick Museum, the former Fifth Avenue mansion of coal-and-steel baron Henry Clay Frick, which today houses the Frick art collection and is furnished in a grand manner. Once when he was no more than nine, Steinberg prevailed upon his parents to allow him to take along his six-year-old brother Robert, with whom he shared a room. (His sister bunked in with his parents.) "This is where we're going to live," he told the wide-eyed youngster.

As a youth, Steinberg displayed other tendencies that suggested he was not long for Brooklyn. It's not every pre-teen who reads *The Wall Street Journal* and subscribes to *For-*

tune. Skipping grades as he went along, he graduated at 19 from the Wharton School at the University of Pennsylvania.

The Frick wasn't for sale in 1970 when Steinberg, barely in his thirties, went looking for a place to live with pockets fattened by an adroit takeover of Reliance Insurance.

He did the next best thing. He bought the nearby home of another robber-baron's son, John D. Rockefeller, Jr., and then he stuffed it with the work of artists also represented in the Frick. Guys like Titian, Rembrandt and Rubens. (Brother Robert did him one better, geographically speaking. He actually moved to Fifth Avenue, just five blocks from the Frick.)

These days Steinberg is chairman and chief executive officer of Reliance Group Holdings, Inc., a diversified financial services company that employs 9,500, and his baby brother is second in command. Estimates of his worth run around half a billion dollars. Steinberg owns not only the Park Avenue digs, but the oceanfront home in Quogue, 90 miles away on Long Island, and a ski retreat in Vail. He dreams perhaps of a country home built from scratch with Gayfryd. But they both say their primary residence will be the one on Park Avenue.

Their building is at the intersection of 71st Street, just a short cab ride north of Reliance headquarters. On upper Park, though, the frantic pace of midtown yields to the more leisurely saunter of people who shop at Cartier and Saint Laurent Rive Gauche.

Four doormen monitor the traffic across the marble floor of the wood-paneled lobby, where there are fresh lilies on each of several tables. Children burst in after school lugging hockey sticks and jackets emblazoned with the names of New York's exclusive prep schools.

When they married in 1983, Gayfryd wanted to move. She thought the place was "too big, too much to do, too much upkeep." Saul resisted, thinking of his collection. And Gayfryd eventually came around to his point of view. "When it came down to it, where would you put all the things he really loved, which involved some large canvases? The answer was that there really wouldn't be another place to go."

The tour—there is no other name for a stroll through one of the world's major private collections of old masters—begins in the library, Steinberg's home office, where he often holds business meetings, particularly on weekends or Sundays. He does not share the reluctance of some CEOs to bring business into the home.

"That's a Hals right behind you," he says, casually waving toward Frans Hals's, "Portrait of a Man," a goateed Dutch squire in a white-collared smock and broad-brimmed black hat. Steinberg continues walking and talking at a dizzying pace. "Those three are Rembrandts . . . this is the first Cubist painting that Henry Moore did. This is a Francis Bacon. I guess he's the greatest living artist in England today. This is a Brueghel, this is van der Meer."

Steinberg made his first acquisitions when he was running Leasco Data Processing Equipment Corp., a company he founded in 1961 at the age of 22. "Around 1965, I sold some stock in Leasco . . . and I got $3,160,000. I promptly put $3 million into municipal bonds. They paid five percent interest and I thought, 'I'll have $150,000 a year after taxes. I'll never need more money than that.' I took the other $160,000 and I bought paintings. I bought a Giacometti sculpture, and a very bad Picasso painting . . . I bought that Barlach sculpture there, and Henry Moore, and that's when I started collecting."

At the moment his two favorite paintings are on loan to exhibitions: Rembrandt's "Portrait of an Old Man" and "Plague at Athens" by Flemish painter Michiel Sweerts. This is a sore spot for Gayfryd, who is in charge of decorating. Annoyance creeps into her voice. "A couple of things are always gone, and I'm the one that has to move them all around. I don't mind lending but after awhile we never have it all around. . . ." She gestures to empty spaces on the drawing room wall. "That's where the Sweerts was, that's where the Rembrandt was. What happens when you lend things—you have these little wires hanging off the walls."

After their marriage, Gayfryd redecorated the whole apartment to complement the period art. The paintings in the drawing room hang on walls of a deep rose Fortuny silk. Handpainted with portraits of French maidens, the wallpaper in the first floor powder room was left over from an order placed by Versailles.

When Steinberg makes an acquisition, Gayfryd's role is to find it a home.

"Saul is a true collector," she explains diplomatically. "He would have what he loved hanging on a string from the ceiling in the center of the room to look at it. He buys things without thinking about where to put them.

"He doesn't buy pretty pictures. He has an incredible eye. I'm not quite the purist that he is. I do worry about where something will go if we buy it. Not that I'm going to paint a room pink around a pink picture but I like a thing if we do buy it to be put up somewhere. Saul would really stack things up in closets, because he loves it. He would just kind of bring them out every now and again and look at them.... He sends them home and I find whatever spot that I can to put them up. Behind every picture are a thousand nail holes. We can never get rid of anything because we'd have to wallpaper every room in the house."

What *Town & Country* magazine termed a "Barony on Park Avenue" has been an asset for their philanthropic causes. As one might suppose, one of Steinberg's favorites is the Metropolitan Museum. Gayfryd's is PEN, the international writers' organization. The Steinbergs' fund-raising events are exceptionally well-attended. Says Gayfryd, "It's very easy to fund-raise. People want to come to see the art."

Then she adds, as an afterthought: "It makes you feel better about having all this space to yourself."

–MARY WALTON

DOMESTIC
REALITIES

The scene is idyllic: A young, prosperous executive realizes he needs to spend time with his family so he arranges an extravagant, extended vacation. Last year, they went skiing in Switzerland for two months; the year before on a two-month sail on the Baltic Sea. This year, the executive has decided, he'd show his children something really exciting: an African safari, where the only communication with the outside world is via messenger on camel-back.

All is going well. The husband is managing to rekindle his relationship with his wife. His children are happy to have their father with them for a change; the father, for his part, is happy to be able to share such an educational experience with his kids. They're just a typically affluent American family on vacation together.

A lovely scene, picture-perfect. Too perfect, as it turns out. One day that messenger on camel-back arrives to tell the man he's wanted back at the office. He rides off through the desert, back to the corporate jungle. His forlorn family waits anxiously for his return.

Sound like a script for a movie? Perhaps. But for Thomas Watson, Jr., that experience was all too real, and too frequent. "I realized I had an absolutely all-consuming job," says the former CEO of IBM, "and that if I didn't break big chunks of time out for my family, they would become strangers." So he'd often arrange trips like the above—only to have them cut short by pressing business at home or by unavoidable visits by IBM colleagues to his out-of-the-way hideaways. But inconvenient as such interruptions were, he says, he never considered changing his methods. "You just gotta do things like this or you lose track of your family. Or they lose track of you."

Nobody ever said a CEO's life is easy. Sure, the rewards are great: All the chiefs we interviewed made salaries of at least several hundred thousand. And the perks aren't bad either: stock in the company, lots of travel, membership in private clubs and plenty of special treatment. But getting to and staying at the top of a major corporation requires more than native ability; you have to be willing to play politics and able to handle people, too. But most of all, any CEO will tell you, you have to have a commitment to the job that goes well beyond that of a permanent middle manager. And such a commitment necessarily requires sacrifices. Often, the family is the first to go.

According to a poll of executives' wives conducted by *The Wall Street Journal* in 1981, "lack of time with husband" is the disadvantage corporate wives mention most. "One summer my husband was home forty hours to change clothing from Australia to France," one wife complained. "I have spent many, many days alone . . . when I would have liked to have been with my husband," says another. When children enter the picture, things get more complicated. "Our sons really didn't have an opportunity to learn what a father is," says one corporate wife in her forties. "My husband was rarely home, and when he was, he was too tired to make time for their needs. He rarely attended their school activities, nor was he aware of their particular interests."

Most CEOs, however, will tell you they try to make room for their families in their schedules, and some go to elaborate lengths to do so. There's Nolan Archibald, CEO of Black and Decker, for example, who has established Monday nights as Family Night for him, his wife and their eight children, ranging in age from 17 years to 18 months. As active members of the Mormon church, Archibald believes that "no other success can compensate for failure in the home," and this is a message he hopes to teach his children. "We try to arrange something the entire family can participate in," he says. Sometimes it's something recreational—a group swim or a trip to see a play—but often it's a presentation of a Biblical story or a discussion of a social issue. Each week, one child is the leader and each other child has a role to contribute. "We find this educational and a great challenge," Archibald says. "It's not easy to find something that will engage both a teenager and a two-year-old."

Does the Archibald Plan work? Of course, he says it does—and that his children are as well-adjusted as the next, and his marriage as strong. Whatever their particular method, most CEOs will tell you the same. But the fact is, some CEOs—whether by sensibility or design—create and maintain stronger family ties than others. "The most traditional structure of a CEO family," says Peter Davis, director of Division of Family Business at the University of Pennsylvania's Wharton School, "is one in which the husband does the business and the wife does the emotional work of the family." But some families are more traditional than others.

You could almost imagine J. R. Ewing dining here, in the opulent restaurant on the twelfth floor of the Fort Worth Club. With its high ceilings, large wood-paneled rooms, marble floors, and crystal chandeliers above the large, widely spaced tables, this members-only establishment is clearly the place for movers and shakers, Texas-style. Everything about the place is large—even the windows around which the tables are strategically placed to give diners a wide-angle view of the outsize Texas skyline.

But this is Fort Worth, not Dallas, and our dinner companion, John Roach, as his fellow Texan Lloyd Bentsen might say, is no J. R. Ewing. First of all, he's not an "awl" (read: oil) man, but the CEO of Tandy, also known as Radio Shack,

Old Think:
The Roaches

a manufacturer of electronic equipment from personal ste-
reos to computers. Despite his reported salary of over
$800,000 per annum, he's not in J. R.'s class. He doesn't own
a ranch—just a home inside the city limits, a lake house at
nearby Eagle Mountain, and a retreat in Destin, Florida.

And perhaps as important, his personal and family life don't
begin to compare to those of the fictional Mr. Ewing. Roach
has been married to the same woman for almost three decades and he has two adoring, pretty daughters, ages 22 and
16. And sure, they may be dressed and madeup and bejew-
eled in a manner that would make Sue Ellen proud, but John
Roach wants you to know that his family's life is so simple,
so normal, that it borrows more from *Leave It to Beaver* than
from *Dallas*. "We have the same problems as anybody else,"
says Papa John, his solid-gold cufflinks in the shape of the
Lone Star State gleaming even in the dim restaurant light.
"Everybody puts on their pants one leg at a time."

Still, when you've lived in Fort Worth most of your life,
gone to the local University (Texas Christian), and worked
for one of its largest companies for twenty-two years, you—
and your family—can't help but become part of the Old
Guard, and something of a celebrity. Tonight, at the club, the
Roaches are treated like royalty: Waiters hover about and
just about every other diner who walks in stops by for a
quick audience. "Why, hi," Jean Roach says to a couple being
shown to a table nearby. "Nice to see you." Then an aside
to us. "I'm sorry. I would have introduced you, but I can
never remember their name."

But there's not much Mrs. Roach is forgetful about. A classic corporate wife, the late-forty-something matriarch of the
Roach family looks not unlike Anne Richards, head of the
Texas Democratic Party, who got famous telling the world
that fellow Texan (and Roach family favorite) George Bush
had been born with a silver foot in his mouth. Exquisitely
coiffed in a matronly, I-spend-a-few-hours-at-the-beauty-
parlor-twice-a-week style, Jean Roach is her husband's help-
mate in the most traditional sense. Except for a few years at
the beginning of their 27-year marriage, she has not worked
outside the home, and her job now is to stay in touch with
the children while also standing by her husband's side at any
number of Tandy-related social functions. More talkative than
the CEO, she's the one who keeps the conversation going,

peppering her own revelations with polite questions to the interviewer. "Where are you from?" she wants to know. "What does your daddy do?"

Mostly, though, she and her elder daughter Amy talk—about a friend of Amy's one of them ran into on the street that day, or about some amusing family story. "Tell her about that report you did," Jean Roach coaxes. Needlessly it turns out, because Amy is only too happy to oblige: "I wrote a report for class on the computer business," she relates, as her father smiles, apparently knowing the punchline. "I interviewed a lot of executives at Tandy, and the teacher was like, 'How'd you get to those people? They're hard to get interviews with.' The whole class was laughing when she said that. . . ." And the whole family is laughing now.

Then there was the other time—oh, it was embarrassing—when the students in Amy's speech class were asked to give a talk on the person they most admired. The first speaker—a young man Amy didn't know personally—stood up and spoke about John Roach, the work he'd done at Tandy, and "all sorts of details" including a mention of his salary. When it came Amy's turn to talk—she was speaking about a lobbyist she'd met on one of her trips to Washington with her father—she introduced herself by saying, "I wish I could say my name was Amy Smith, but it's not. It's Amy Roach."

The other student's "face just about dropped," Amy says. Gol-lee, but it's hard to be the daughter of one of the most famous men in town, especially when you stay in that town and go to the same college your famous father attended. But there are also advantages, Amy says, and she doesn't mean just the giant gold-and-diamond ring that was her parents' gift to her from their recent trip to the Orient. She doesn't even necessarily mean the occasional, wonderful trips she's taken to places like New York or Europe. "The best thing about him is that he's just Dad," she says. "He's there for the family all the time."

At least he tries to be. "I spend as much time with them as other fathers," Roach says, not undefensively. "If it were up to me, I'd have dinner at home every night." But of course, it's not always up to him; business often intrudes, so it's usually Jean, not John, who shows up at younger daughter Lori's private high school for basketball games (she's the team manager), and it's Mom who plans the birthday parties. But John does try to stay in touch: He's installed a Tandy computer in the kitchen so that each week he, Jean, and Lori (Amy no longer lives at home, but in an apartment with another TCU coed) can type their schedules in and print them out so, the father says, they "always know where everybody is and what they're doing." And if he can't be where they are, at least everybody can always check in by phone. Car phone, that is. "We have four cars and four car phones," he says. "Other people might call that a luxury, but for the way we live it's more a necessity." Tonight, in fact, Lori—who has just gotten her driver's license and her first car—is going to have to skip out early on dinner to attend a birthday party with her friends, and before she leaves, her mother admonishes her to call from the car if she has any problems. Lori—who has barely spoken a word all evening—nods politely.

Of the two daughters, Amy Roach is clearly the more voluble, the more at ease, and the more in touch with her father. "I oughta give you a medal," Roach has said teasingly upon arriving to find that Amy—who drove over from school—has arrived before him. "You were on time for a change." "Well, Daddy," says his daughter, coyly affecting righteousness, "you said 7 o'clock and I was here at 7 o'clock." Obviously, Amy Roach knows her father. She's learned that the way to engage him in conversation is to develop interests similar to his and to bring them up. "Oh, Daddy, I'm sorry," she says at one point. "I forgot to tape that *20/20* segment on new televisions."

John Roach is clearly at his most comfortable talking about work, and when the conversation turns to more mundane concerns—like shopping, a favorite topic of his wife and daughters—he tends to tune out. But then, between his work and family commitments, he doesn't have time for many other interests. He admits that the last movie he saw was probably *Patton,* and that he rarely watches television. And though he gives generously to such cultural institutions as the ballet, he hasn't been to one in years. When would he have time? He works six days a week and his Sundays are taken up with family-related business like . . . "Well, let's face it," he says, looking around the table. "My family is all women. What do I do? Whatever the women arrange."

Jean Roach, in particular, arranges a lot. She may not work outside the home, but she is hardly a housewife in the traditional sense. (She does, after all, have help: a woman who comes in every day to cook and another who shows up to clean three times a week.) She may talk on the phone to her elder daughter at least once a day ("I think as she's ready to move away, she feels the need to be closer,") and she may, like other mothers, go out to buy paper plates and balloons for her younger daughter's sixteenth birthday party, but she has additional responsibilities. Almost every week there is work to be done for the number of social and charitable organizations with which she's involved. ("Are you familiar with the von Bülows?" she asks her guest, as a lead-in to a tale about her recent lunch with Claus von Bülow's stepchildren, Alexander and Anna Laurie von Auxersperg, who have become involved in a Fort Worth-based victims-services agency. "I just think they're lovely.") And just last month the Roaches sponsored an Arts Council benefit for which the entertainment was to be a performance by Jerry Lee Lewis. But Lewis canceled at the last minute, and Jean was left to find a substitute. She did—Chubby Checker—and "everyone had a wonderful time," though the Roaches were quite upset about the way the local paper—the *Star Telegram*—covered the event. "They didn't report that everybody was twisting," says Jean. "All they talked about was the people who didn't show."

"What do you expect from the Startle-gram?" her husband, who has been silent now that the conversation has turned away from business, asks angrily. He's not overly fond of the press, he explains as he pours himself another glass of wine. "Business reporters are always jealous and angry that they don't make as much money as you."

"Oh, John," Jean Roach says, trying, apparently to head off a tirade. "Not every reporter is like that."

Yes, well, it's not easy being royalty; just ask the Windsors or the Helmsleys; there are always those pesky press people snooping around. "We have the same problems as anyone else," John Roach says, as if repeating a mantra. "We have homework, basketball, and stolen cars."

Stolen cars?

"My mother's Fleetwood was stolen from the street right in front of my apartment," Amy laughs. "Remember that, mother?" And the two women are off again on a tale about the everyday problems of the First Family of Fort Worth. For another moment, the spotlight is off the King, and he sits quietly, pouring himself the last of the second bottle of wine.

New Think:
The Raticans

Diane Ratican is in what must properly be called a tizzy. She has agreed to let us see her suburban Los Angeles home and now she's nervous. "I have to share this with you," she says soon after opening the door. "When you said you wanted to see the house . . . I thought, oh, but it's being redone. I wish you could have waited." But after all, she promised, and immediately it becomes clear that Diane Ratican is a woman true to her word; she takes us on a tour of her four-bedroom home, introduces us to her three children (Michael, 16, Eric, 13, and Kimberly, 8) and even has us meet the contractor who will be doing the renovations. "Here, look at the plans," she says eagerly, unrolling page after page of blueprint. "Every year Pete tells me I have X to spend on the house."

This year's X may be a multiple of what it's been in the past—of course she won't say—because her husband Peter Ratican has just recently been called in to help ailing Maxi-care, one of the largest health-care systems in California. But even so, the plans are not extravagant; upstairs, the contractor will make the master bedroom suite a lot larger and one of the children's playrooms will be turned into a bathroom. There will be some changes downstairs as well, but they'll be mostly cosmetic, not structural. The Raticans already have a swimming pool (de rigueur in southern California) but it's not an imposing one, nor is much that is inside the house. Instead of the jade collections or antique lamps one might expect to find in the home of a prosperous businessman, the Ratican house is decorated in what might be called "Young Family": there's no expensive art or rare collectibles, just lots of serviceable furniture (in very California shades of mauve and pale green), many family photographs, and virtually every corner stuffed with the children's sports equipment or toys. Some of that will change, Diane says, with the renovation, but a cursory look at the plans suggests the renovations will not lift this casual suburban house into a Beverly Hills–type mansion. The biggest change, in fact, will be that Michael and Kimberly may switch rooms so that the little girl will have a private bath and no longer have to share with her two big brothers. The operative word here is "may" because Michael, two years shy of going off to college, has indicated that he's attached to the only bedroom he's ever had and he may not be ready to give it up. "You may get to see a sibling argument," Ratican laughs as she leads the tour.

But if Michael is upset—indeed, if any of the Ratican children are put out by the appearance of an unknown person in their midst—they don't show it. "Want to see my 'It's my ponies'?" asks Kimberly, referring to a collection of horse dolls. Michael sits on the sectional sofa, genially telling us all about his recent mock-senate exercise at school; as a congressman, his issue was whether to allow AIDS children into school and he lobbied hard for his colleagues to vote yes. Eric, a 13-year-old with the strongest handshake on record, is quieter, but completely at ease; he's an actor, you see, and has starred in a number of TV commercials, so he's used to dealing with all sorts of strange grown-ups.

It's only when their mother announces she's got to go—we have a dinner reservation—that the Ratican children suddenly have problems. "Mommy," says Kimberly, "we have to do my book report on *Stuart Little.*" Diane seems perturbed. "You know the rule about homework," she tells her daughter. "You knew we were going out tonight. . . . Okay, we'll get up early tomorrow and work on it, but you'll have to skip art time tomorrow." Kimberly is upset (art is her favorite thing; she is going to be an artist) but says to a visitor: "I don't like it when they go out."

But now Eric has a problem. "Mom," he yells, "where's the camera? I want to take the pictures to be developed now."

"Well, I don't know where it is. I could have sworn I put it in my briefcase when we left Park City." (The family has just come back from one of their thrice-yearly group vacations.)

"But where *is* it?" he asks, frantically opening the doors to the built-in cabinets in the living room.

"Honey, I don't know. You can tear up the house if you want, but it's not here. I've looked. But I've got to go. I'll ask Daddy about it at dinner. *"Buenas noches,"* she adds to the Mexican housekeeper Cecilia. "We won't be late."

Diane Ratican is less than 10 years younger than Jean Roach, but her manner and look suggest she was born in another century. In a black sweater, skirt and very-high-heeled black pumps, she looks more like someone who works in one of the glamour businesses L.A. is famous for than like a corporate wife. On the drive into town, to Ma Maison, one of L.A.'s tony but not too trendy restaurants, she is extremely open, "sharing" insights into her children and reflections on her 22-year marriage to "Pete," who was her high school sweetheart. When we meet him, Peter Ratican is similarly unimposing. An average-looking man with a laid-back California cadence, he seems less like a hotshot than like a typically successful L.A. businessman. Like the house we have just left, the Raticans are accessible and strikingly unpretentious. Maybe it's their relative youth, or maybe it's the California in them, but Peter and Diane Ratican are as unobtrusively successful as the Roaches are opulent.

The Raticans are an example of the new breed of CEO families: full of ambition, yes, but ambition tinged with memories and attitudes of the sixties through which they lived. They're not particularly acquisitive; despite Ratican's CEO status and his previous high-level jobs with Price Waterhouse, MCA and DEG Entertainment, they do not own a country house or a Mercedes. They do have Cecilia, but she only lives with them a few days a week. The eldest and youngest Ratican children go to public school and while the area in which they live is affluent, their schoolmates are not the sons and daughters of big names or movie stars but of successful, upper-middle-class businesspeople. (Eric, the middle child, goes to private school with some other child actors, because he needs a place that is "flexible" about his work schedule.) "You asked me if our kids live differently from other kids," Diane says. "They do," Pete interjects, "but we were always different parents. We've always tried to treat our kids as individuals and as adults, even though that isn't always realistic."

It probably helps that their parents are very much individuals as well. Although they've been together since their days at a local L.A. high school, Diane and Peter Ratican have always kept separate identities: When they first married, Diane taught at the 39th Street School, in a tough neighborhood of Los Angeles. "I really thought I could change the world," says the woman who apparently bought into the values she learned at liberal University of California at Berkeley. When she discovered that she couldn't, she moved on to teach a gifted program at a more middle-class public school. "That was probably the happiest time in her life," her husband says. Peter Ratican, for his part, was never the liberal hippie his wife was—"I was an athlete, but I did have long hair and once got into a fight with my father about growing a mustache"—but he's always admired his wife's independence. "She's a perfectionist," he says. "Whatever she'd want to do, I'd say, 'Just go to it, kid.'" About three years ago, Diane Ratican decided she wanted to go into her own business—importing children's clothes—and today, with her husband's blessing, she presides over her own company, Diane's Designs.

By his own admission, Peter Ratican always expected to be a leader—"I was always the catcher who called the pitches or the quarterback who called the plays"—so it comes as no surprise to him that he should be the chief of a major company. But Diane Ratican was not born to be a corporate wife—though she played the role when it was necessary, like when Ratican was on the partner-track at Price Waterhouse. "We gave a lot of parties for clients. We traveled on behalf of Price Waterhouse; we were in their brochure. I was involved, and I wanted to be," she says. She doesn't say so, but the relief in her voice makes it obvious that she's glad that period is over. While she'll still join her husband to entertain clients, she doesn't feel she must be involved with the workings of Maxicare, allowing her all the more time to devote her energies to her family and her job.

Despite his new job, Ratican maintains close ties to Diane and the children. "He always takes my calls, no matter how busy he is," Diane says. But more than that, he remains active in the affairs of his children, serving as soccer coach for the boys and as his daughter's companion at her Indian Princesses meetings once a month. In fact, when Ratican was offered the job at Maxicare, he didn't make the decision until he'd held a family conference. "The kids got a chance to voice their fears about it," Diane explains. "One of them might have said, 'Daddy, then you won't be able to come to my soccer games,' but they knew in the end that the person who had to make the decision was Pete."

Make no mistake: As atypical as the Raticans may be in some ways, there's no question that it's still Mr. Ratican who heads the household. It's just that now that Diane is working at something she loves, they have to be all the more careful about their family time. Planning ski vacations like the one they've just come back from helps; so do the few minutes of individual conversation each parent gives each child every night. But if the second career creates scheduling conflicts, it also gives family members new opportunities. Diane, for example, has just come back from a buying trip to France, on which she's taken her son Eric. Last year, older son Michael accompanied her and stayed a few weeks with the family of one of her French contacts. "We don't believe in sheltering the children," Ratican says. "The more experiences they have in life, the better able to deal with things they'll be."

Sometimes children of successful executives find their parent's example daunting: "My husband represents too much of an ideal to live up to," says one of the women surveyed by *The Wall Street Journal* in 1981. "The children will never achieve what their father has." But the Ratican children—though young—already seem set on their own paths. Eric, whose father initially hoped "he'd get this acting thing out of his system," seems committed to the idea of continuing his work on television. And Michael thinks he wants to be a doctor, "Partly, I think," admits Diane Ratican, "because it's something no one else in the family does." That Peter Ratican is in the health-care business apparently does not count.

But then, one wonders just how long Ratican will remain where he is. "I don't think this is the culmination of my career," says the forty-five-year-old CEO. And later, as an aside, "And let's see if it's a health-care business when I get done with it." No, the Raticans agree, the worst thing you can do is become complacent—that's something Peter Ratican says he learned from his baseball coach in high school. "He told me that if winning was more important than playing the game I had no right to be there in the first place."

It's a typical comment from Ratican, whose conversation is full of sports clichés and Vince Lombardi-isms, the perfect counterpart to his wife's tendency toward words such as "sharing." Maybe it's the California in them, but the Raticans seem remarkably unselfconscious about voicing platitudes: their religious beliefs (he was born Catholic, she Jewish) come down to "treating other people the way you would like to be treated" and their philosophy of childrearing is "encouraging each child to take risks and to be an individual." These things may sound jargony and unspecific to the outside observer, but to judge by the closeness the Raticans exhibit—each toasts the other and clinks glasses repeatedly throughout the meal—they believe in them and in each other. "There's nothing I wouldn't talk to Pete about," Diane says. There's no problem too small to bring to the attention of the CEO.

Not even that missing camera Eric was so upset about. "Pete," Diane asks, "do you know where it is?"

"Sure," replies the head of the household. "It's in my briefcase."

"Oh, thank God," Diane says as if they've solved a family mystery by locating the Canon Sure Shot. "I'm going to call Eric right now so he can get some sleep."

When Donald Weber was named CEO of Contel Corporation, his one concession to his new power was asking Contel chairman Charles Wohlstetter if he could trade up his company car. Today, instead of a run-of-the-mill sedan, he drives a black BMW—"I've always wanted to own one"—but other than that, his life hasn't changed much. He and his wife, Rosemary ("Rosie"), live in the same house they've lived in for 13 years; their children—Jennifer, 23, Steve, 21, and Christopher, 17—go to the same schools, work the same jobs and have the same friends. And while an observer might say such caution is wise under the circumstances—the telephone and communications company has had three CEOs in as many years—it is as much a reflection of Weber's personality as it is a conscious strategy. "I believe in building on what you've got."

The Webers

When CEOs talk about their personal lives, as a rule they like to present themselves as unpretentiously as possible. They're all just "regular guys." They have "normal families" who are just doing "what everybody else does." But sometimes these "ordinary folks" work so hard to seem unpretentious that the artifice is suffocating. Not so with the Webers. Dining with four of them—son Steve is off in the navy—at

THE CEO FAMILY

MARITAL STATUS*

Married	94%
Divorced	3%
Separated	1%

*two respondents were never married; one is a widower

TIMES MARRIED

Once	81%
Twice	16%
Three times	2%

NUMBER OF YEARS MARRIED

Fewer than 5	6%
5–10	6%
11–20	7%
More than 20	82%

Atlanta's Ashford Dunwoody Country Club one unseasonably warm March evening really is like having a meal with a run-of-the-mill "modern" family. There doesn't seem to be too much going on under the surface, and if nobody is particularly scintillating, well, that, perhaps, is the price of normalcy.

All this is not to say that the Webers are in line for a remake of *The Adventures of Ozzie & Harriet;* their lives are a bit more glamorous than that. Weber travels a lot on business (sometimes as much as three times a week within the country, a couple of times a year outside of it) and he makes a point of getting home pretty much every night when he's in the country—but, of course, he couldn't do that if he had to fly on commercial airlines. "That's one of the advantages of a company jet," he explains. When Chris mentions tickets to the Atlanta Hawks games, they're not just tickets, they're box seats, as are the seats with their names on them at just about every major sporting event they care to attend—from the Olympics to the U.S. Open. And when Jennifer marries in three weeks, there will be an elegant wedding with seven attendants and 200 or so of the family's most intimate friends as guests at a chic local country club. "We always have time to discuss political and world issues," says Weber, "but I've also tried to convey to my children that profit is not a dirty word."

If it were, one would have to call Donald Weber a bit foul-mouthed; the green stuff comes up a lot in his conversation. Without being asked, he allows as how he makes "five and a quarter, five and a half a year" but that his house payments (on the four-bedroom home he and Rosie bought when they first came to Atlanta) are about "$611 a month." He laughs when describing the Oriental breakfront a former Contel CEO purchased for what was, briefly, his office. "I think it cost 12 grand," he snorts. At dinner, he relates—with no little pride—the story of one of Christopher's friends discovering, via a magazine article, just "how much Chris's old man was worth." No, Donald Weber is definitely not of the old-money, never-talk-about-it school, but then he doesn't pretend to be; despite the acquired Southern lilt, the Pittsburgh native is forthright Midwestern.

He still speaks with some awe about "real New Yorkers" like Charles Wohlstetter, a "real fine gentleman" who lives on Fifth Avenue and "goes out every night." And while he, Weber, is often called upon to join the chairman at social functions there, he's never quite at home at places like the Metropolitan Opera, because "I'd never been to an opera in my life and I don't understand Italian"; still, he manages to enjoy the scenery and costumes and the fact that he can drink champagne during intermission.

When he mentions other places he visits as CEO—a subsidiary company in Europe, for example—he speaks of the experiences as special treats: "Rosie and I were fortunate enough to take a trip to Switzerland," he'll say. And like another famous Midwesterner, Ronald Reagan, Weber possesses what has come to be known as the common touch, greeting everyone from employees in the hallways of Contel to waiters at the club by their first names.

The family sitting around him tonight seems just as easygoing. "He doesn't even have a desk at home," volunteers Jennifer, who goes on to explain that when her father comes home at night, he joins them in the family room where they watch TV or talk. When he has to work, he peruses his papers there with the gang. Chris banters easily with his father, too, laughingly telling the story of the family trip they took to Barbados a few years back and the bets he and his dad make on sports. "Sometimes, I can even get this one up to two bucks a game," Weber jokes. Chris's goal, he says, is to get his father to try the sport for which he is fanatic: water skiing. "No way," says the CEO and the family laughs; it's a well-worn joke by now that Weber has a deathly fear of the water. But his son's obsession with it—he may want to become a professional water-ski instructor—doesn't faze the CEO father in the least. "I think they should all do whatever they want to do," Weber says, although he does have some expectations for them. "I think that the little daughter [sic] will pursue marketing and then have some children," he opined earlier. She is, after all, the offspring of a man who has said on at least two occasions that "God calls upon us in life to play many roles—citizen, Christian, parent. The one I wouldn't have missed is being a father."

How Rosemary Weber feels about her roles in life is less clear. Asked about the role of CEO wife, she'll say only that it's "a little more to do than before" and "kind of fun." And yes, she admits, when Jennifer is married and settled and

DOES SPOUSE WORK?	
Yes	6%
No	93%

NUMBER OF KIDS	
None	2%
One	4%
Two	25%
Three	33%
Four or more	36%

Chris is off at college, the senior Webers may kick up their heels a bit more, travel and spend. But in the meantime, she's content to be mother to her children and wife to the husband she says "probably has a little more pressure on him now," the husband who by his own admission "hasn't really changed" in the 25 years of their marriage.

"As I've made more money, instead of the cheapest scotch, I buy Chivas Regal," he says, back again on a favorite topic. "Instead of $395 suits, I now pay $795." So really now, can a house upgrade be far behind? "Well," Weber admits, "if all goes well, maybe next year we'll renovate the bathrooms."

—SARA NELSON

BASIC
TRAINING

Harvard turned you
down?

University of Cincinnati too dull to hang in
for four years?

Don't fret. Forget what your parents told
you—or what you tell your kids. You *can*
make it to the top without a college degree.

You don't have to be a publicly certified
genius on the order of William Gates III, the
whiz-brat who dropped out of Harvard after
one year and founded Microsoft. Or a publicly
recognized renegade à la R. E. (Ted) Turner,
who got booted out of Brown in his senior
year.

Although *The Wall Street Journal* Survey of
Executive Style reported that 93.4% of the nation's CEOs graduated from college—among
them, 35% had master's degrees and 12.5%

*Getting by Without
a Degree*

had earned doctorates—a college degree doesn't a CEO make.

True, an Ivy League credential on a résumé generally is regarded by management as something of a bonus. But in some circles, it's only slightly more of a bonus than is the ability to look good in a tux. For example, rank-and-filers who are laboring to reach the top in our nation's so-called hard industries, such as autos, chemicals and oil, have a better chance of getting there if they earned hard-industry-type degrees at a Big Ten, not Ivy League, university.

Lawrence Rawl rose to the top of Exxon with a bachelor's degree in engineering from Oklahoma and the determination of an ex-marine. General Motor's Roger Smith has both an engineering degree and MBA from Michigan. "I could hardly wait to get out," he now says. General Electric's John Welch has a Ph.D. in chemical engineering from University of Illinois. And no one in Wilmington, Delaware, can remember the last time Du Pont took seriously a CEO-contender from Harvard, Yale or Princeton.

But formal higher education, at any college or university, simply takes up too much time for hard-driving entrepreneurial types who may find it difficult enough to sit through a lengthy due-diligence meeting, let alone a lecture on postwar European labor theory. Maybe that's why Turner, who would have graduated from Brown as an economics major in 1960, once answered the exam question, "Give your picture of Alexander the Great," with a single phrase: "A courageous general on a black horse."

Indeed, many of those who became CEOs-without-degrees get there by founding a company—a feat that may be less traumatic than enduring pledge week on an average campus. (Ted Turner, by the way, spent some of *his* fraternity pledge week hitchhiking in a dress, wig and makeup to Smith College.) Among the entrepreneurs on our list of non-degree'ers: Amerada Hess founder Leon Hess, Browning-Ferris Industries founder Harry J. Phillips, Giant Food founder Israel Cohen, Toys "Я" Us founder Charles Lazarus, and Subaru of America co-founder Harvey H. Lamm.

It goes without saying that you may be in a position to skip the college route if the company you join bears your name. That's what CEOs August A. Busch III, Barron Hilton, and countless other family business heirs have done.

What's far more impressive, though, is to rise to the top of someone *else's* corporation. Which brings us to the career path of Lawrence O. Kitchen, the degreeless, recently retired CEO of $11 billion Lockheed Corporation.

Kitchen was the eldest of six children of textile-mill working parents in depression-racked Shelby, North Carolina. He graduated from Shelby High School in June 1941 and spent the summer working in a cotton mill. "That job," he said later, "taught me what I didn't want to do."

So he joined the marines, an organization that, in a few months' time, needed all the few good men it could get. It was in World War II, and by serving in an engineering squadron of a marine aviation group—eventually supporting the Bouganville campaign—that Kitchen figured out what he wanted to do with his life. "The marines gave me a totally new perspective on the world. And I fell in love with aviation," he said.

Other important discoveries? "I learned to be disciplined in my work habits and, as a result, I started to become impatient with people who don't work hard. I learned that the success of any organization is not a one-man show, it's a team effort. And I learned that life is tough." What better qualifications, you might add, for a CEO.

After four years as a marine, Kitchen "knew I didn't want to go back to Shelby and work in a textile mill," he said. Instead he took a job with the Naval Bureau of Aeronautics in Washington, D.C., as a clerk/typist. He did that until he found a job opening in maintenance engineering into which he could maneuver.

"It was obvious to me that I had to have a lot more education if I were to advance in the field of aviation. So that's what I did," said Kitchen. Thus began what was to be an obsession over the subsequent decades: a dedication to night school.

So a succession of night-school courses and training programs (and, yes, devotion to his job) propelled his government service career. And after 12 years, at the rank of GS-13, he "saw the challenges slipping away," he said. He turned his back on civil servant retirement benefits and took a job offer at Lockheed to start a logistics organization for the Polaris missile program. The year was 1958.

Kitchen's strategy for advancing had two unique elements.

First, of course, there was the education. He enrolled himself in "every training course that the corporation had," from finance to general management. "Anything that could help my career," he says. On top of that he studied nights at whatever local institutions were available wherever he was posted. For instance, Kitchen recalled that while employed at Lockheed's Sunnyvale, California, operation, he took courses at a small college in Los Altos Hills. (He couldn't remember the name but his résumé lists it: Foothill College.) He attended a management program for executives at University of Pittsburgh.

Second, once he tackled a particular assignment, he would train a replacement and request management to move him elsewhere. What's so unusual about that, you ask? "I said I didn't want any pay increase, I just wanted an opportunity to do more," he said. "[I told them] if I made it, fine. If I didn't, they could move me somewhere else. I was trying to branch out from a specialty to learn more about the total operations so I could become more of a generalist manager."

Nobody but a CEO's mother would want to read a blow-by-blow account of every step up the Lockheed corporate ladder. It's enough to say that the ascent was steep and swift. And the only question to ask Kitchen is how he endured all those obnoxious comments from competitors who graduated from Harvard, Yale or Princeton (or, for that matter, Illinois, Michigan and Ohio) along the way.

"You know," says Kitchen, "that sort of thing is an issue only when you first start out, only when you're in a first-line management or supervisor position. And I can hardly remember that far back."

If your fortunes ever call for incarceration, please take note of the Number One rule of prison etiquette, a rule that applies to all types of prisons throughout the criminal world: Never ask a fellow inmate what crime landed him. If he wants to tell you, he'll tell you. If he doesn't, he won't.

We raise this little bit of advice because it's apparently one common feature shared by prisons and the upper echelons of corporations. The old where-did-you-go-to-school game isn't played in executive suites. "Once guys reach this position [CEO], whether they went to an Ivy League school or a West Coast school doesn't matter," says Kitchen. "It doesn't enter in anymore. People look at your achievements. Not

THE LARGEST CORPORATIONS HEADED BY CEOS WITHOUT COLLEGE DEGREES

COMPANY	CEO
Kroger	Lyle Everingham
American Stores	L. S. Skaggs
NYNEX	Delbert C. Staley
Anheuser-Busch	August A. Busch III
F. W. Woolworth	Howard E. Sells
Archer-Daniels	Dwayne O. Andreas
Gulf & Western	Martin S. Davis
Amerada Hess	Leon Hess
Dana	Gerald B. Mitchell
United Brands	Carl H. Lindner
Toys " Я " Us	Charles Lazarus
Giant Food	Israel Cohen
Greyhound	John W. Teets
Castle & Cooke	David H. Murdock
Subaru of America	Harvey H. Lamm
Crown Cork & Seal	John F. Connelly
Square D	Dalton L. Knauss
Fleetwood Enterprises	John C. Crean

once since I've been chairman of the board has anyone asked me where I went to school. In fact, I think it goes below the CEO level. Once you get into the middle-management level, where you either perform or you don't, nobody cares about your education."

For some folks at the top of an $11 billion corporation, it would be a point of pride to have ascended above the better-educated masses. But the former chairman of Lockheed never took that stand; he never considered himself superior to those who went to college. In fact, he sounds something like a radio public service announcement when he offers advice on the topic:

UNEXPECTED ALMA MATERS OF CEOS

CEO	COMPANY	SCHOOL
August Busch (Certified Brewmaster)	Anheuser-Busch	Sibel Institute of Technology
Thomas A. Holmes	Ingersoll Rand	Missouri School of Mines
Thomas G. Plaskett	Pan Am	GMI Engineering & Management Institute
John H. Gutfreund	Salomon Brothers	Oberlin College

"Get yourself a college degree if you can. It'll make your life a lot easier. It's tough performing a job, raising a family and going to night school. Sure, you probably work harder to make up for not having gotten your college degree, but it's also a tough route." Then he adds: "And you should never stop educating yourself. If you do, you're dead."

–DAVID DIAMOND

The Truth About Military Preparedness When General Brehon Somervell was named president of Koppers Company, shortly after World War II, he reportedly was asked how he intended to succeed in a high-level corporate position without a corporate background. His legendary reply: "I can't lay an egg, but I sure as hell can smell a rotten one."

Fact is, chief executives who've done military stints are often in a better position to take leadership roles than are their counterparts who've never served. Harvard can teach you to chart cash flow. The U.S. Marines can teach you—at a particularly impressionable age—how to feel comfortable telling a subordinate he's a goof-off (Or, if you're not an officer, how to live with the news that you're goofing off and better shape up.) It can teach you that unless you gather support among your subordinates, you can expect them to screw you over the first chance they get. (Or, if you're not an officer, how to screw over your superior first chance you get.) These are abilities it can take decades to develop properly in the corporate sphere.

Considering when they grew up, it's no surprise that many of today's chief executives were military men. Most of them came of age during World War II or the Korean War, when avoiding the military was difficult as well as unseemly. The next generation of CEOs will be from a different kind of era. While young men of moderate means and education marched off to battle in the rice paddies of Vietnam, the wealthier and better-educated ones stayed at home attending graduate school, or like Vice-President Quayle, writing press releases for the national guard.

Thus, while Vietnam has produced a large number of thriving entrepreneurs—the most visible of whom is Federal Express chairman Fred Smith—the future crop of more conventional CEOs with combat training is likely to be pretty thin. And this could make a big difference in the executive suites of tomorrow. Texaco chairman James Kinnear's 30 months of Korean combat may have helped him fend off Carl Icahn (who served in the army but not in a war). But what's going to happen to similarly ambushed chief executives who lack any military experience at all? And will we lose touch with such military-corporate phraseology as "pulling rank," "strategic planning," and "recruiting officer"?

(It's a good thing former USX chairman David Roderick, who was a marine sergeant, achieved equal rank with Exxon chairman Lawrence Rawl. Otherwise, you could picture them in a typical corporate deal: "Maggot, you can lower your price on fuel for our Southworks mill or you can give me a hundred push-ups!" But one suspects that, all other considerations being equal, Roderick did feel a bit more at ease dealing with Exxon's Rawl than with other oil industry CEOs, such as Amoco's Richard M. Morrow, Mobil's Allen Murray or Texaco's Kinnear, all of whom were Navy men, not Marines.)

Would-be chief executives miss out on a great deal of education by learning the ropes at First Boston instead of at Fort Bragg. When Ross Webber, a management professor at the Wharton School, recalls his hitch in the navy, he reminisces not about the adventure but about the management training.

"The strongest lesson you learn from the military is that you're not alone, that survival in a military situation depends upon accepting the interdependence with your platoon or

WHERE THEY SERVED	
About 75% served in the U.S. Armed Forces and 2.4% saw combat:	
Army	28%
Navy	25%
Air Force	15%
Marines	3%
National Guard	3%

whatever unit you're involved in," he says. "When I look at people who move up the management ladder, one of the most difficult things for them to learn is how dependent they are downward. Because your subordinates can really screw you anytime they really want, if they get angry enough, because you can't possibly monitor closely enough to control all of their behavior. And that's one thing that you learn in the military. That you need the people below you and that you need to be in their good graces."

He adds that contrary to popular mythology, the overwhelming majority of decisions made in a military setting are made by consensus, not by direct order. The military, he explains, teaches the subtleties of knowing when to make a unilateral decision and when to make a decision that draws on consultation with the people who report to you. The fact is, unless it's in a crisis situation, most decisions are not of the top-down variety; they're done after an officer builds coalitions. "It's exactly like in business," Webber points out. Another lesson learned quickly in the military: the risks you run by ignoring your subordinates.

Officers in the early days of the Vietnam War marched into jungle battles while their alienated men stayed behind. The officers who survived quickly adopted a more acceptable management strategy. Would-be CEOs run similar risks in countless corporate scenarios. Trouble is: Unless a manager is already a CEO, there isn't much likelihood that, like some of his Vietnam counterparts, he'll get a second chance. After all, Business Is Hell.

The ultimate business of the military is war. What could possibly be more stressful? So the stress of war, even the stress of boot camp, trains CEOs unlike anything else—including business school statistics courses.

When Icahn goes in for the kill and the epinephrine starts to gush through the CEO's body, he can say to himself: "This was nothing compared to being ambushed by the Chinese back in Korea." (Advice: But you can't spend too much time dwelling in the past or you'll rapidly become a part of it.)

Many navy veterans sentimentalize endlessly about drunken shore leaves and such, but Webber preferred a different memory. "One of the great experiences in the military at a young age is learning how to look at somebody directly and tell them that their performance is inadequate and they've got to shape up," he says.

For a young officer, that sense of authority, that feeling of autonomy, and that freedom to get things done might result in culture shock when he eventually finds himself stationed at IBM. Those CEOs who went into the military immediately after college achieved a strong sense of job satisfaction and challenge. One expert suspects that "most of them found it a difficult transition to the first job in a corporation. They probably resented the fact that the corporation didn't provide enough of a sense of challenge and satisfaction in task performance."

Did that dissatisfaction somehow propel them up the corporate ladder? "I think the frustration of an early job where the organization seemed to be telling them that if they just paid their dues in a quasi-training job that they'd be rewarded with a challenging one made them eager. I would imagine that many of them fought and tried to do whatever they could to get visibility to move up the organization faster in order to get into some meaty position," says Webber.

None of this academic speculation immediately leaps to mind for Inland Steel chairman Frank Luerssen, who spent the years 1945 and 1946 in the Navy. He says, tersely: "I think it gave me a pause to mature a bit." So, yes, in addition to all of the above, the recruiters are right. The military does build men (if they happen to be of that gender). And when those men work at it feverishly enough, sometimes they become CEOs.

And just think: They get to see the world.

The election year of 1948 brought a slew of U.S. presidential *Looking* hopefuls to New Hampshire. And in the town of Exeter, stu- *Good on* dents at the venerable Phillips Exeter Academy campaigned *Paper* for the prep school's mock election. Among the more popular contenders were Dewey, Thurmond, Truman, Vandenberg, Wallace and Scatelli.

Scatelli?

Even revisionist historians aren't likely to recall Nick Scatelli, the presidential candidate who ran on the teetotaler platform with the slogan: "Cleanse your belly with Nick Scatelli." That's because Scatelli was the brainchild of Howard ("Toga") Love, who 41 years ago was the managing editor of *The Exonian* student newspaper.

"The mock election was taken very seriously at the school. Delegates were nominated and so forth, and a group of us decided that we would create a fictional candidate, make him a Navy war hero, and get him nominated," says Love, who went on to become CEO of National Intergroup, a $4.5-billion-in-sales conglomerate based in Pittsburgh. "I can't even remember the political party he was associated with. But we got that silly bugger nominated. Then the school didn't know whether to let it out or not let it out," recalls Love. "We thought it was the greatest thing we'd ever done. We thought it was the absolute cat's meow."

The particular brand of prank described here by Love is a prep school classic. Visit any campus or talk to any alumnus, and you are likely to hear a similar story. At Ivy League colleges, slightly older preppies are similarly in the habit of creating fictional freshman students, falsifying their records for four years, then cheering their names when they are announced at the commencement ceremony.

According to figures compiled by Boston University sociologist and dean Michael Useem in 1984, approximately 10% of the directors of large American corporations were educated at 1 of 13 elite boarding schools, even though these institutions' combined enrollment totals less than 1% of the high school population. According to our survey of 351 corporate CEOs, 19% got their undergraduate degrees from an Ivy League college.

So, what is it about these velvet-padded, tradition-bound reformatories that they turn out so many successful graduates?

Is it that they enroll people already destined to succeed? A quick flip through old Exeter yearbooks reveals names such as William K. ("Kissie," "Willie-Willie") Coors, Exeter '38 and retired CEO of Adolph Coors; Richard C. ("Tex") Marcus, Exeter '56, and CEO of Neiman-Marcus; and H. John ("H-Bomb") Heinz III, Exeter '56, U.S. Senator and heir to a pickle fortune.

Is it that they take in kids who already have the advantage of rich and powerful parents and give them rich and powerful friends as well? CEO Love, for example, is the son of

HOW EDUCATED ARE CEOS?

Highest level of education

High School	6%
College	46%
Master's Degree	35%
Doctorate	13%

former Chrysler chairman George Love. His Exeter school-mates included A. William Reynolds (nickname: "State"), who graduated with the Class of '51 and now is chairman of Gencorp. If Love had been a few years older, he would have prepped with young men who went on to head Drexel Burnham, Cheeseborough Ponds, and Bankers Trust.

Or is it something else? Are rituals such as the phantom-person practical joke really training tools to demonstrate the rewards of manipulating the system? Is it possible that these schools really *have* found a way to teach arrogant adolescents some real-life practical lessons?

We chose a warm spring day to visit Exeter to see what we could find out.

Kendra Stearns O'Donnell, Exeter's thirteenth principal in 207 years, walks along a campus path more or less oblivious to the "Clash Day" participant in front of her. Clash Day is a weekly ritual that encourages students to don unconventional apparel—within the confines of the school's dress code. One young man is wearing a standard navy-blue blazer, but with the hairy pants of an ape costume. Another wears a foulard tie around his neck and a "Real Skiers Don't Have Real Jobs" T-shirt. "Something interesting happens in places like this," O'Donnell remarks. "Kids begin to believe that those leadership positions are theirs for the asking. And I think that you have to believe you can do it. . . . Those who don't aren't going to end up at the top." O'Donnell continues: "Of course, that translates into 'when I graduate from college I'll make $200,000 in my first year' and we think 'Oh, how naive they are,' but when they realize they must start at the bottom, they'll make that adjustment. These aren't the kind of kids who would go off to be carpenters in Vermont. And what reinforces that is that once they get here, they see that adults take them seriously."

When you ask Howard Love how prep school prepared him for life at the top, he first replies in terms of academics and the curriculum. "I didn't have any gaps to fill when I got out," he says. But when he thinks a few moments longer, he declares that it was his editorship of the school paper that made the real difference.

He says, in effect, that he was taken seriously. "They gave you a wide latitude on how you handled your affairs. If we got carried away on one event, we were called in and talked

THE SIX HOTTEST COLLEGES FOR CEOs	
Where CEOs Got Their Undergraduate Degrees	
Yale	6%
Princeton	4%
Cornell	3%
Wisconsin	3%
Harvard	2%
Illinois	2%

to by the principal who would say, 'Look, you've got a responsibility here. These are the kinds of things you should give some thought to,' not, 'Hey, we're shutting the paper down, you guys have done a lousy job.' " As a profit-making venture, *The Exonian,* "awakened a latent sense in the free-market system," he explains. "It was my first exposure to that type of thing. I enjoyed it. I thrived on it."

Thomas C. Hayden, an Exeter counselor, says that he thinks prep schools give students both a healthy interest in success and some of the means to achieve it. "The first ethic of these kinds of places, these independent boarding schools, is success. The students are told about success stories of one sort or another and they're taught to savor success in the culture."

In addition, Hayden adds, "They acquire social skills that are very real and profound. And at places like this, and at the colleges these people go to, they develop networks that are very, very helpful at proceeding in the business world."

They also seem to pick up the subtle tricks that are so beneficial in leadership positions. In fact, here's a typical scenario designed to bring out the primordial CEO in your average preppie:

You are the dorm student proctor. One of the kids in the dorm tells you he's going to sneak out for a date. Your options are to let him do it or not. You tell him he can't go.

He says, "What do you mean? We grew up together, we came here together. I helped you with math for four years, every night. You wouldn't be graduating from this school if I hadn't helped you."

But you respond: "You saved me from math, I'm saving you your Exeter diploma." It's not easy to overcome the impulse to be a nice guy, but, after you've done that twenty times you realize it's right, because the kid's not going out and you don't feel guilty about it.

Such actions comprise a rite of passage, according to sociologists Peter W. Cookson, Jr., and Caroline Hodges Persell. In their book, *Preparing for Power: America's Elite Boarding Schools,* they explain how prep-school rigors are no less harrowing than comparable rites of passage hosted by more primitive cultures—and no less indoctrinating. So while a bush tribe's rite may prepare an adolescent for wilderness survival, for instance, the prep school's rite may produce an equally valuable skill. What could that be? Write Cookson and Persell: "A key component of the prep rite of passage is the acquisition of the moral authority to exercise power without remorse."

Hayden concurs that if the dorm proctor in the above example is learning anything, it's how to exercise power without feeling the slightest twinge of remorse. What's more, he adds: "That sort of situation is just not available in the home or high school all that often."

And then there's something else that's not available in most high schools. The traditional centerpiece of most Exeter classrooms is an the oval-shaped 16-place table, known as the Harkness Table, around which students and faculty sit and debate the great issues—much in the manner that a board of directors would discuss the merits of a management pay hike. With the Harkness (named after a benefactor, Edward L. Harkness) Table, and the 15 kids around it, a teacher can assume the role of a provoker of conversation.

It probably gives more oomph to the task of teaching and makes it more fun, but the major rewards are reaped by the students. They develop the ability to think quickly and properly out loud. In the Harkness classroom, they are often called upon to solve a problem by dealing with a set of facts, and do it before the bell rings. "Much the way company executives do," says Hayden.

He's right. And when we sit in on a ninth-grade English class taught by Russell D. Weatherspoon, we catch a glimpse of a board meeting of the future. The students have been reading *A Midsummer Night's Dream* and Weatherspoon throws open the class to a general discussion on the topic of gender roles—one of the play's subthemes. What better possible subject for a bunch of 14-year-olds who, away from their parents' nests, are eagerly beginning to discover the opposite sex?

A slightly-advanced-for-her-age girl with embryonic feminist ideals voices criticism of the subservient role many women are forced to play. A clean-cut young guy nonchalantly issues a defense of macho rights. "... But enough women had to *agree* with the system," he says at one point. "If they all disagreed, it wouldn't be like this." As he speaks, he works hard at trying to flatten down his cowlick without drawing undue attention. There is the class joker, a short boy who tries to make everyone laugh while he negotiates a compromise between debaters on either side of the issue.

Around the Harkness Table, as students defend their 14-year-old-style rhetoric, they seem to know the discussion's hidden agenda: They are scoring points. Each one is coming to the priceless realization that a person must think before speaking. Each one is learning—if only subliminally—to become articulate.

That Exeter training ultimately produces someone like Wole Coaxum. A healthy-looking and easy-going young black man from Cleveland Heights, Wole was 18 years old when we spoke with him in a student lounge on the eve of his prep-school graduation. His goals are clearly defined: By age 60 he wants to "have a chair on Wall Street." (The first step is an education at Williams College.)

Why Wall Street? "Over the spring vacation I had a job interview with Morgan Stanley for a summer internship," he explains with poise, as if our discussion were a job interview. "And just walking in that area and having the knowledge that I have about Wall Street, I enjoyed it. I felt that if I were in that work situation, I would just thrive. I remember calling my mom. I was in front of the Bank of Tokyo and I just felt things are happening, just going on that I could be a part . . ." He looks up and stops talking, as if he has realized he must have gotten carried away and that he probably isn't communicating or even making much sense. Then he blurts out: ". . . it's dollars!"

His buddy and crew-team mate, Andrew Ambruoso, 18, who hails from Long Island, wants eventually to be some sort of CEO, but he hasn't determined which industry he prefers. By way of elimination, he says to Coaxum: "People on Wall Street are driving, driving, driving. Doesn't that get, like, crazy?"

To which his pal replies: "Oh, but I would get a summer place on Martha's Vineyard where I could go for the weekend. You couldn't do that [Wall Street] all the time." The he thinks for a brief moment and says: "Either that or politics."

As our discussion draws to a close, the Economics Group, a club of budding venture-capitalist types, wanders into our meeting space; they have reserved the lounge we are occupying. Nearby, members of the Asian Society are gathered for a meeting.

A striking difference between, say, Exeter '48 and Exeter '88 is the diversity of the student body. The Exeter of Howard Love was comprised almost exclusively of young WASP men. Today, 42% of the students are women, 13.7% are Asian, 5% are Black, 2% are Hispanic. On top of that, some 18% of the student body are on scholarships (a figure that does not include scholarships given to the children of faculty or staff members).

Miraculously, by graduation time most of the students appear to be cast from the same mold. Does Exeter take kindly to free thinkers? While administrators and faculty members at Exeter repeatedly speak in glowing terms of one particular student who they say has become widely respected for his animal-rights activism, a different story is revealed on a dining room bulletin board notice. The notice reads:

EXETER'S VOICE FOR ANIMALS MEETS

TONITE, 7 PM, MAYER AUDITORIUM.

Handwritten below it are the words:

RELAX, CHARLES

Students at Exeter are articulate, bright, and, if they survive the four years' rigors, they are confident. (Another thing that distinguishes places like this from public high schools is how frequently you hear the word "burnout.") And that confidence can launch a nonstop corporate career.

It can also teach a bunch of smirking fellows that it's possible to sit around an oval table, summon their collective power to invent a political candidate, and convince a population to elect him president. Now that's not meant as nostalgia for the days of Nick Scatelli. Isn't that roughly how it works in the real world?

–DAVID DIAMOND

GETTING BY ON $875,000 A YEAR

"F

rankly, I'm a lousy money manager," says Ron Naples, the 44-year-old chairman and CEO of Philadelphia-based Hunt Manufacturing. "If I managed a company like I manage my own affairs—boy, I'd be in trouble."

Fortunately for its shareholders, Naples has done a swell job of keeping Hunt's bottom line in tip-top shape. (The maker of Boston pencil sharpeners and X-Acto knives saw profits of $26 million on sales of $179 million in 1988.) Naples didn't do so badly himself. His total compensation in 1988 was $374,667, and $1 million in 1987, when he exercised some stock options.

But his admitted inability to handle his personal finances as well as he handles those of the company makes him somewhat typical

A CEO and His Money

among CEOs. Financial advisers have long known that a guy who spends a lot of time focusing on his company's business is likely to neglect his own. "It's frustrating," admits Naples, "but on the scale of things to complain about, not having time for my personal money management is probably one of the better things."

There's also a big consolation prize, of sorts: With stock incentives that enable a CEO to buy shares in his company's stock at a reduced rate, a CEO may be doing his personal portfolio a favor by devoting his energy to his company's—not his household's—fortunes. Stock incentives generally are tied to company performance and often far outweigh a CEO's salary. For example, Jim Manzi, the 36-year-old newsman-turned-marketer who runs Lotus Software earned $26.3 million in 1987; the lion's share of that came in the form of stock options he exercised; his salary was a paltry $941,000. Excluding such stock incentives, chief executives of the 500 largest U.S. public companies took home between $528,000 and $1 million in salary and cash bonuses last year, according to Hay Management Consultants, which specializes in executive compensation.

Does money like that change your life? "My wife and I often look at one another," says one $1-million-a-year executive. "It might be after we've bought something expensive that we never would have thought about buying a few years ago. And we'll just look at one another and say, 'Can you believe we just did this?'"

We should note here here that while public-company chief execs are very well paid these days, the CEOs themselves invariably mention that the *real* money comes from *owning* a company—or at least being the one to take it public. In 1988, Texan Michael Dell went public with the company he founded, Dell Computer. He's now worth $10 million and change—and he hasn't yet celebrated his 25th birthday. Then, of course, there's Bill Gates at Microsoft, barely 30 years old, who became a *billionaire* a few short years ago when his software company sold stock.

While the high-tech whiz kids are becoming overnight moguls, there's still plenty to go around for the well-compensated wage slaves (if that's the proper term) at the top of the corporate ladder. After the welcome shock of knowing he's got a lot of money wears off—and these zillionaires tell us it eventually does—a CEO has to put up with some hassles that most people don't. For one thing, most of us have the relative serenity of knowing that our salaries are known to only a select few. Think of what it must have been like for Lotus's Manzi when he became a business magazine cover boy—and subsequently had his eight-digit income reported in just about every publication in America except *My Weekly Reader*.

Even Ron Naples, a corporate pauper by comparison to the software CEOs, has seen his compensation listed in the Philadelphia newspapers and *Forbes*.

"I must admit that when they come out with the lists of the highest paid CEOs I always look at it," Naples says. "It's a strange thing. In one sense you hate to be on it. But in another sense you hate not to be on it. I don't think we'd be human if we weren't interested in it—almost in a voyeur sense."

Across town from Naples is First Pennsylvania Bank's George Butler, a young-looking bank chairman, albeit one with graying hair and the old-fogey habit of relaxing by lighting up a big cigar.

"It annoys my wife that everybody in the world—or at least everybody locally—knows how old I am and how much money I make," Butler says. (For those who haven't committed it to memory, he's 61 years old and had cash compensation in 1988 of $675,000.) The banker himself is not so thin-skinned, although he says, leaning back in his chairman's chair in a corner office that affords perhaps the best view in Philadelphia: "I'm not going to run around and tell people how much I have in my checking account or shelters or other stocks or that sort of thing."

Financial planners who work with CEOs report that an executive who even *knows* how much he's got in the bank and shelters and stocks and that sort of thing is a rare animal.

"There are really three distinct types of CEO," says Earl L. Wright, president of the Englewood, Colorado-based Asset Management Group, a financial planning firm that works with a number of chief executives throughout the country. "Thirty to 40% are pretty much on top of their personal affairs, but don't feel they're adequately managing their assets. Another 30 or 40% control things pretty loosely. They can find things if they need to, but they really have no control."

Then there's what Wright calls the "Frenzy" group. "Invariably they never have enough time for personal affairs. They don't see enough of the value in it. They figure if the company prospers, so will they. But their personal affairs are in such a state of disarray that they're really dangerous," he explains. (Dangerous to *what,* you might ask? Having the water service turned off because they never bothered to pay the water-sewer bill?)

What's more, says Wright, some CEOs become so accustomed to dealing with the big numbers of their corporate balance sheets, that their personal finances seem measly and boring in comparison—and foster neglect. In 20 years in the business of advising top executives, Wright has learned that "it's sometimes difficult to get them to pay attention to any number that doesn't have six more zeroes after it.

"I've actually had guys who talked *millions* when what they meant was *thousands,*" he says. "It's really hard to focus down on personal affairs for these people, when the magnitude of what they deal with all the time is so high."

And while these are men who have to have all the answers when it comes to company business, they seldom are that well-prepared with their own money.

Take our friend Ron Naples. Naples comes from a working-class New Jersey family and attended public schools there before being appointed to West Point. After 10 years in the military (including a tour as combat commander in Vietnam), he got an MBA from Harvard. For most of his twenties he and his wife lived on army lieutenants' pay—$303 a month. "In all that time," he remembers, "we never really thought about money. We just lived on what we had."

Now that he makes $303 every hour or so, he still can't take much time to think about it. So, he says: "You end up doing the easiest thing."

The Easiest Thing **M**ore and more, chief executives are being awarded the perk of having a company-paid personal financial planner at their service. (According to a survey by Heidrick & Struggles, the venerable executive recruiting firm, 52.7% of CEOs get such a perk.) How much of the steering a planner does depends on the executive. Some require only some practical, impartial advice on estate planning or taxes. Others want that and much more. Asset Management Group lately has developed software to handle a CEO's financial life down to nitty-gritty details like paying the electric bill. The company will even train someone in the executive's company (usually the administrative assistant) to handle the computer work involved. "It's become a profit center for us," reports Earl Wright.

A planner might be someone like Rick Helberg, who works for CIGNA Corporation as executive vice-president for corporate financial services. He's got a client roster that includes nearly a dozen CEOs. At 37, he is usually at least a decade younger than the men whom he advises.

Helberg enters their lives when they're "really starting to make some money." But since his clients are usually distracted by business, he usually has to force them to think about their money. What's his trick? "I have to make myself a real pain in the ass," he says.

Helberg remembers sitting with a CEO, explaining various savings plans, delving into the intracacies of trusts, only to have the executive lean across the desk and whisper, like some sort of 12-year-old with his heart set on expensive video games: "I'll save next year, I promise. But please let me have the Porsche this year."

On the other hand, Helberg has on occasion had to tell CEOs to spend more money. Just as there are CEOs who try to live on 110% of what they make, there are some who spend money as if it were just coming into fashion. Although they're paid like Croesus, they still feel like trainees. "Sure," says Helberg, "I've recommended to clients that they spend more. 'C'mon,' I'll tell them, 'Take your wife on a cruise or something.' "

Ask a dozen CEOs about how they spend money and if they're willing to open their mouths, you'll hear 12 different scenarios. So we relied on some financial planners to spot the patterns. "As a general rule," says one planner, "these guys live on their salary, bank their cash bonus, and whatever stock incentives they get they hold on to, because that's where they're really building their wealth."

Where Does the Money Go?

Within that broad generality there is plenty of room to accommodate variations in life-styles. When it comes to spending their fat salaries, executives are all over the map—figuratively and literally. Where a CEO lives will not only

GETTING BY ON $875,000

What would a typical CEO do with a gross pay of $875,000? We asked Rick Helberg to supply us with the budget for one of his clients. The following is the actual spending of a 48-year-old chief executive for the year 1988. Numbers are rounded.

INCOME: $875,000

	AMOUNT	PERCENTAGE OF INCOME	USE
Expenses	$ 26,500	(3%)	Mortgage, main home
	$245,000	(28%)	Cash purchase of vacation home
	$ 17,500	(2%)	College tuition, two children
	$ 17,500	(2%)	Charitable contributions
	$ 78,750	(9%)	Living expenses (includes: food, entertainment, clothing, clubs, vacations, etc.)
	$227,500	(26%)	Taxes (federal, state, social security)
	$262,500	(30%)	Investments (most are long-term and weighted: about 60% in stocks, bonds, and cash, and 40% in real estate, equipment leasing, and similar investments)

—JOHN MARCHESE

force very practical life-style decisions (a 14-room mansion is a little cheaper in Shaker Heights than Stamford), but more qualitative differences in style as well. And there are industry-to-industry norms as to how money should be spent.

For instance, if you're a CEO in, say, Bartlesville, Oklahoma, chances are nobody will notice if your home lacks a screening room. But in Los Angeles, among entertainment-industry CEOs, screening rooms are de rigueur. So are fancy cars, says Joe Smith, CEO of Capitol Industries-EMI, the Hollywood entertainment company. Other obligatory acquisitions for entertainment-industry CEOs in LALA land? "The house at the beach is mandatory and a lot of people go for a ski place in Aspen or Deer Valley," he says. (And season tickets on the floor for the Lakers, another near-necessity, cost $10,500, or $250 per game.) Smith adds that, even in Babylon, insurance-industry CEOs and bankers are not expected to spend money on such frills.

Meanwhile, on the East Coast, in Quaker-influenced Philadelphia, top-banker George Butler typifies the local style. Contrary to Joe Smith at Capital Industries-EMI, who rattles off his "wish" list, Butler keeps a list of things he *won't* spend money on.

"I would never buy a Rolls-Royce," says Butler. "To me that's ludicrous." The list continues . . .

". . . To have a big, *huge,* vacation place—an eight-bedroom, four-bath place on the beach or in the mountains. . . . For my wife to wear a five-carat diamond. . . . For her to have six different fur coats. To own a huge, huge, huge house. . . ."

Butler likes to tell the story of driving to work one morning—in the company-issue Buick—and waiting at a stop light when a shiny red Mercedes convertible pulled up beside him. The driver was a spiffy young man, perfectly coiffed and expensively suited, and as he draped his arm over the sports car's steering wheel, Butler noticed a giant gold Rolex watch.

"Jeez," Butler reports. "Right then I thought to myself, 'Where did I go wrong?' "

Some executives believe there is a generational difference in the spending habits of CEOs. Basically, they say, it comes down to who remembers the Depression and who doesn't. Those old enough to have bad times etched in their memories are more conservative with money. They shy away from using a lot of financial leverage. They live unostentatiously (albeit very well). Younger CEOs are often quite different.

"No question about it," observes one financial planner. "If they're relatively young and they're making a lot of money, *boy* do they spend it."

"I've never been afraid to use leverage to get what I wanted," says Christopher Whittle, chairman of Whittle Communications, who is young and making a lot of money. When *Time* bought a piece of Whittle's Knoxville, Tennessee-based media company in 1988, the founder pocketed between $40 million and $60 million. For the 43-year-old Whittle, leading his particular executive life-style includes a five-room apart-

NUMBER OF VEHICLES OWNED OR LEASED BY CEO'S	
One	17.1%
Two	32.5%
Three	21.7%
Four	13.4%
Five	5.1%
Six or more	4.0%
None (specified)	4.0%
No answer	2.3%

FAVORITE CEO CARS	
DOMESTIC	50.1%
Cadillac	19.7%
Lincoln Continental	10.0%
Oldsmobile	8.5%
VS.	
IMPORT	41.9%
Mercedes Benz	19.1%
BMW	5.1%
Jaguar	4.6%

ment in the Dakota on Central Park West. Add to that a home in Tennessee and a vacation retreat in Vermont and mortgage payments alone start adding up.

Then there's Whittle's little hobby of collecting 19th-century art, which virtually chokes his expensively redecorated New York apartment and costs millions to keep up. "Let me make one thing clear," Whittle says. "My company [revenues in 1988 topped $100 million] is not in debt. But I personally see nothing wrong with debt."

Isadore Sharp, the 57-year-old chairman of the Toronto-based Four Seasons Hotels, also sees nothing wrong with spending money on hobbies, although his large stake in the company he founded leaves him free to spend without incurring debt.

"I'd say that the biggest expense my wife and I have is buying antiques," Sharp says. "It's a hobby. My wife is a decorator and very knowledgeable. She's got a collection of oriental carpets that keeps growing. We don't even have a place to put them now. We have a lot of rolled-up carpets."

Unlike the Philadelphia banker, the Canadian hotel executive does not have an anti-wish list. "I've learned never to say never," Sharp says. "I don't live lavishly, but I've found that what we say we would never do at one point in life, we consider a necessity at others." For instance? "Would I buy a private jet now?" Sharp asks, then answers: "No."

"But," he qualifies, "I may change my opinion."

Who Handles the Money

Regardless of how lavishly or plainly a CEO lives, someone's got to handle the mundane details of daily life—paying the telephone bill and various mortgages, handling invoices from the dry cleaner, paying off club memberships. Again, there can be quite a range of styles, but executives seem to break down into three groups. Some, like George Butler, handle their own money. "My wife will admit that handling money is not one of her strong suits," Butler says. "And I consider that sort of thing too personal to give to my assistant."

Isadore Sharp, on the other hand, gives all day-to-day work over to his longtime secretary. "I'll look at every bill once," he says. "Then I pass it on to her. I'm not really concerned with the question of privacy. When you've worked very closely with somebody for that long," he says, "there are very few secrets anyway."

Ron Naples takes a third tack.

"I spend very little money myself," Naples says. "Almost everything we spend revolves around a decision my wife Suzanne makes. She doesn't work and is in the home environment all day, so she knows better than I do what's needed."

"She handles all the money," he continues. "She writes all the checks. If I want to join a club or something, I have to ask her for a check. I don't even have my own."

The Napleses' money management system developed over many years, starting in those days when Lt. Naples brought home $303 a month and the family shopped at the PX. Nowadays Chairman Naples brings home a check every two weeks (he's paid just like everybody else in the company—second and fourth Thursday of the month) that totals about $7000, after taxes.

He'll drive home to the four-bedroom contemporary house they've recently purchased on Philadelphia's Main Line ("We don't have a mortgage," he says, "just a demand note with a bank. It's a truism that banks love to lend money to people who don't really need it.") and unceremoniously present this check to his wife.

"I'll say 'Look, I've got this $7000 check. Do we need it for anything?' " he reports.

"And she'll say, 'No,' so I'll send it off to fund somewhere.

"Or sometimes she'll say, 'Well, you'd better put it in the checking account.' And that's how those decisions get made."

Forget those ad campaigns that feature successful-looking people forever waving credit cards. Every executive contacted said that for day-to-day living, cash is the medium of exchange. In cases where credit cards *are* used, it's only for convenience and all bills are paid in full monthly. As Naples puts it, "I just assume that we have the money to buy anything we want." George Butler goes so far as to never carry a wallet. "I have cash in my pocket and a pen in my coat," the banker says. "That's all I've ever needed."

Adding it all up, financial planners see a wide range of spending habits among CEOs. "I have one guy who is burning $45,000 a month," says a vice-president at Asset Management Group. "And I've got another who is worth maybe $500 million who gives his wife about $1000 a month to take care of everything."

When Ron Naples's wife doesn't need any money for the household, he is faced with what CEOs like to characterize as the bane of their existence. (And CEOs, remember, have lots to choose from. Gadfly shareholders, for example). The Investment Decision.

Where
They Invest

"The way I figure it," says the publisher Chris Whittle, "if I spent the time necessary to figure out if some company out there is being run right"—here he sweeps his arm toward a wall of windows in his Park Avenue office that looks out toward most of Manhattan and many of the nation's corporate headquarters—"it would take away a lot of time that I need to make sure *my* company is being run right." Consequently, Whittle has no money in company stocks, and what money is left over after debt service and his art purchases is in money funds.

George Butler has made what he calls "run of the mill" investments. He's bought a "substantial" amount of life insurance, and he defers income, but otherwise just some real estate partnerships for the tax benefits.

"What you end up doing for investment is the easiest thing," says Ron Naples. "I would bet that 75% of my cash resources right now is sitting in money market funds. Now any intelligent investor would say, 'What, are you crazy?! You should be doing blah, blah, blah.' But I don't have the time or the inclination to worry much about it.

"What investments I do have," Naples adds, "haven't happened because I've made a lot of rational decisions, like I ought to have X amount in this and X amount in that. This thing will just come along"—Naples currently has real estate "things" and oil exploration "things" and a leveraged buyout fund "thing" among other "things"—"and I'll say, 'All right, I'll put my money there.'

"All of a sudden I've got an investment portfolio and I don't even know what shape it is, whether it's an elephant or a mouse."

One noted marketing whiz, Franklin Mint founder Joseph Segal, who is now chairman of the home shopping network QVC, admits that his investment of $20 million in a piece of real estate on Lake Geneva called La Mirador, which started as a simple pension and is now a luxury resort, started off simply and has grown and grown, with no returns in sight.

"I would like to turn this into a profitable enterprise some day," Segal says. "If we weren't treating it as a labor of love it could be done." In any case, it's a real estate investment. "Some people may own a $20 million piece of art," Segal adds. "This is sort of in the same category."

Even though the old saw, "Nothing's certain except death *Taxes* . . . and taxes," seems like it was handed down on Mount Sinai, it has only been since 1913 that Americans have paid a tax on personal income. That doesn't stop people who earn as much as CEOs from thinking they've made up for lag time. It is not unheard of in the executive suite (where there is no doubt much grumbling) for the tax bill to equal salary.

Ron Naples was hit with such a tax bill in 1987, when he exercised his options on a substantial block of his company's stock. Because the stock award was counted as income, and because he was in the top tax bracket, he ended up having to borrow money to pay taxes that year.

"In fact," he says, "in the last couple of years it has not been unusual for my income taxes to be as high or greater than my income. So I have to make up for that by borrowing money."

Most of the time, though, CEOs don't have it so tough. As a general rule, financial planners say, a top executive can expect to pay a third of his income in taxes. CIGNA's Rick Helberg keeps a sample financial plan around in a sumptuous leather folder. In it, he figures that on an income of $700,000 you're going to wind up paying at least $280,000 in taxes, if you itemize deductions.

On one hand, that leaves $420,000 to spend. On the other, and to put these figures in perspective (which CEOs often find themselves trying to do), $270,000 would have paid the salary of a hundred George Butlers when he started working for First Pennsylvania Bank fresh out of Wharton back in 1950.

"I don't think it's unreasonable for me to pay taxes," Butler deadpans. "A *reasonable* level of taxes."

So, does he try to make that level a bit more reasonable with tax shelters? "Yes," Butler admits. "But not to the extent that some other people might.

"The reason for that is, one, I'm head of a public company, so something that might be borderline I would be reluctant to do because of the adverse publicity and reflection on my company.

"Secondly, because my company is a bank I have to lean over even more not to get into outlandish tax shelters."

With changes from the tax revisions of 1986, financial planners say that even the standard-issue real estate syndication deal, which had for years drawn lots of CEO income, is no longer so attractive. "A lot of guys are getting killed from those things," says one planner who works with chief executives. "The tax benefits of a lot of them are nil these days and meanwhile they're holding the bag on some bad investments. A lot of smart people made investment decisions for their own money that they never would have justified if it were their company's money."

But if taxes are hard to live with for an active CEO, they become downright onerous for one who's planning to die.

"You see," says Rick Helberg, "the way it works is totally opposite of how people *think* it works. When we're making a financial plan, I have to confront the CEO with the facts of estate taxes and the taxes on heirs. If he doesn't make a careful plan, Uncle Sam will be the main beneficiary of his estate."

Now, this is not the sort of talk CEOs like to have. "I think some of them truly think they're immortal," Helberg has noticed.

He's exaggerating, of course, but there are indications that CEOs at least like to consider the idea. Asked if he had a financial plan for when he was gone, the banker George Butler snapped, "No, I'm immortal."

Of course he was joking. (It seemed . . . probably.) In fact, Butler says, "My wife and I have always had the philosophy that we're not going to live our lives so we can leave money to our children. Our kids will get a reasonable amount of money when we die. But I think my kids ought to work hard. They ought to be able to say, 'My parents were a help to me, but I did this on my own.' "

At least one chief executive, the legendary investor Warren Buffett, chairman of Berkshire Hathaway, has decided that none of his estimated $2 billion personal fortune will go to the kids. "When a very rich child is born he's handed a lifetime supply of food stamps," Buffett has said. "They have a welfare officer, only he's called the trust department officer, and the food stamps are little stocks and bonds."

"Yes, it's a big question with these guys," says Tom Zanecchia, an Asset Management vice president who works with a number of retired CEOs. "There are usually three stages that people go through.

"Most people spend their lives building an estate for themselves for retirement. And they spend most of that estate during their retirement years.

"The second level," Zanecchia continues, "comes when a CEO has locked up a couple or three, four or five million bucks. Then he starts structuring his investments so that his heirs are receiving something even before he's gone. He starts thinking about the grandchildren—education trusts, that sort of thing."

But there's even another level.

"Once you get into estates of more than 10 or 15 million dollars," the planner says, "the thinking gets even more philanthropic. Those guys are much more interested in leaving a legacy. This sort of thing is real popular with chairmen about to retire. The first thing is usually a chair with their name on it at a university." (At a top business school like Wharton, such a legacy sells for at least $1 million.) "Anything in excess of $15 million or so, and people start wanting to have an impact on society like the Rockefellers and Fords."

On a more humble level is Ron Naples, who theoretically has two decades of work left, and is in no great rush to, as he prefers to put it, "fall on my sword." In fact, it is only recently that he wrote a will. (CIGNA's Rick Helberg says he's seen a number of CEOs, some with huge estates, who had not written a will.) For Naples, the simple act of making out his will led to the first fight with his wife over money that he can remember.

"It was probably one of the major differences we've had in the last 10 years," he recalls. "I had to assume that I was dead, and that my wishes would have to be stated explicitly, so I had the lawyers draw it up so that I would leave her enough money to live comfortably for the rest of her life—she would get all the income from the assets—but the assets themselves would pass to the kids.

A GOLDEN
PARACHUTE BEDTIME
STORY

Although the preferred route for getting your big payoff is by toiling years with a company, finally accepting the top job and then making all around you prosper, there's still a quicker way to get rich in the corporate sweepstakes. Get to the top and then get fired.

Much of the furor over so-called golden parachutes—lucrative severance agreements for executives who are dismissed in a takeover, leveraged buyout, or merger—has died of the past few years. Still, tales of CEOs getting rich because they've hit the bricks did prompt columnist Calvin Trillin to write, "Occasionally, I muse a bit about how much I might like being fired from a high-level position in a major American corporation."

Surely the best-known golden parachutist is Chicagoan Donald Kelly, the former meat-packing-company accountant who became, in *Forbes*'s estimation, "the stuff of corporate fantasy and business legend." By his early sixties, Kelly was doing fine, making $900,000 a year as CEO of Esmark.

When the food-and-packaged-goods giant Beatrice took over Esmark in 1984, Kelly got a severance agreement of three times his annual salary—roughly $2.7 million. And he made an estimated $14.6 million from his Esmark stock holdings. You might think that would be enough for Kelly to kick back and work on his backhand.

Nope. Two years later, Kelly joined with New York investment firm Kohlberg, Kravis, Roberts and Company and raised $6.2 billion for a leveraged buyout of Beatrice, which they took private. Not only did he become chairman of the company that fired him, Kelly netted almost $7 million in advisory fees from Kohlberg, Kravis. His next project was to sell Beatrice back to the public, making his stake in the company worth around $400 million.

Don't think there wasn't hardship along the way. It was reported that for a while there, when he was a CEO-without-a-company, he missed his corporate jet.

JOHN MARCHESE

"She was aghast," Naples says. " 'How can you do that?' she asked. 'It says you don't trust me.' "

"Yes," says Rick Helberg, "when you start talking about the great beyond, you get past the intellectual stuff and you find out what in his guts he's feeling."

Financial If ever you'd wish to test the hypothesis that looks could kill,
Goals try asking an executive, "You're really in it for the money, aren't you?" If ever you would like to study the true art of rationalization, ask a very highly paid CEO, "Does money make you successful?"

"Absolutely not" was the answer one CEO gave to both questions, although he elaborated on the second. "Material success doesn't mean you're a successful person. I know a lot of people who are successful when it comes to money, who are not really very good people as people."

So, now that CEOs are often making that mythical measure of financial success—a million dollars—every year, you would think that they've satisfied their financial goals. Nope.

"If money satisfied all your wants," says the banker George Butler, "then why are people driven—after they've made $50 million—to make *another* $50 million? It's just human nature to want more than you have. Not everybody is like that, but it's a fairly general human characteristic."

"It's true," agrees the Four Seasons' Isadore Sharp, who, although he has yet to buy the personal jet, *has* bought four houses and what seems like acres of oriental carpets.

Sharp reasons that most corporate chiefs quickly get used to the perks that come with their office. But when it comes to financial goals, are they really all that different from everybody else?

"At the heart of it," says a planner who has worked with many, "I would say no. They have goals—financial goals— that are about the same as everyone else's, just like you or me. The difference is, their goals have a lot more zeros after them."

–JOHN MARCHESE

COUNTRY
SQUIRES

Sign above the bar:
MONEY ISN'T EVERYTHING, BUT IT DOES TEND TO KEEP THE CHILDREN IN TOUCH.

A Weekend at Flying "M" Ranch

To report that Barron Hilton and his pal Arthur are engaged in a game of gin rummy would be inaccurate; the guys appear to be consumed by their cards, barely aware of the California landscape outside the corporate jet windows or their convivial comrades or the anticipatory energy that permeates this salon-in-the-sky. When the Macanudo that perpetually sticks out of Barron's mouth needs a light, the Hilton chief executive gropes around for his lighter—never glancing away from his cards—and if he finds it he relights the cigar; if he doesn't, he doesn't.

Reluctantly, Barron pulls a jack of diamonds from his hand and slaps it on the fold-down table. "I gotta help you," he moans.

"Hep me. Hep me," responds Arthur.

Barron is losing, but we've still got a good half hour to go. Once, on a flight from Europe, Barron and Arthur played gin rummy for 12 straight hours. This flight is scheduled to land in Nevada 40 minutes after it began, but one gets the odd impression that if Barron looked up from his losing hand and sent the appropriate message to the pilot, our magic carpet ride would end in, say, Djibouti instead of at Hilton's isolated vacation ranch—merely to keep the card game in progress. And what's more, no one would quibble with The Baron's decision.

Picture couches in a private jet and an assortment of women sipping morning coffee, chattering about jewelry and tea. At the opposite end of the cabin, a few husbands recline in easy chairs, reading the *Oakland Tribune* and occasionally blurting out regretful comments about Dan Quayle or the San Diego Chargers. But the real action is at the fold-down table, where Barron and Los Angeles restaurateur Arthur J. Simms are like a pair of playful kids. When Arthur (alternately called "Arturo" and "Arthur J.") wins a hand, he starts saying things like, "Now, what hotel do I want?" When he loses, he tries to figure which of his "Mimi's" restaurants he'll have to fork over.

Eric Hilton, a Hilton executive vice-president, looks up from a newspaper just long enough to predict that his older brother's luck will change. And sure enough, somewhere over the Sierras, it does. Suddenly, The Baron is winning.

He isn't a real baron. "Barron" was his mother's maiden name. But he's got an aloof, quiet, regal quality (that's been attributed to shyness), and he's rolling in money, so the title sort of fits, enough that it's easy to slip up and say "Will you be joining The Baron in his balloon tomorrow morning?" or, fifteen minutes before the jet reaches the ranch landing strip, looking down at the sage-blanketed mountains, "Does all of *this* belong to The Baron?"

Yes, it does. Five hundred thousand acres (but hey, who's counting?). What doesn't fit in Nevada laps over into California. And although most of those acres actually are leased from the federal government in a long-term lease deal, the

Flying "M" Ranch could probably make a bid for statehood; it's bigger than Rhode Island.

For a reporter working the CEO circuit, a weekend at the Hilton ranch offers the definitive peek at chief executives on vacation. In the interest of accuracy, we've got to admit, though, that Barron Hilton and his bistate retreat are in a class above vacation homes belonging to such working stiffs as Union Pacific chairman Andrew L. (Drew) Lewis, Jr., and SmithKline Beckman chief Henry Wendt (whose getaways are featured later in this chapter). Hilton is different from those guys—and the majority of CEOs—because he owns a sizable chunk of the company. But his ranch does typify the sorts of places that hired-hand chief execs tend to daydream about from their pedestrian condos in Florida.

The weekend begins with a rendezvous with Barron, his wife, Marilyn, and eight other upper-upper-income types at the San Francisco Hilton (you know a better place?). From there, a wagon train of limos glides you to the Oakland airport. That's right, to get the true picture, you've simply *got* to fly into Flying "M," although support staffers have been known to get there by negotiating the county road leading from Yerington, Nevada, 30 miles away.

Without a flight attendant on board, one must rely on Barron to signal the jet's descent. So as he folds his cards and tabulates the score, it's time to buckle up. And outside, Eden unfolds: smogless blue skies and so much postcard greenery that true Nevadans probably shake in hallucinatory disbelief. We pass over a field of yellow sunflowers and carefully cultivated rows of orange and red marigolds.

One by one, the guests step from the jet and into the warm Nevada sun. As they do, and as the ranch compound comes into focus, respectable Republican workaday attire becomes instantly inappropriate to the surroundings.

Let's survey the property.

We can see the gray-stained-wood-sided, red-shingle-roofed ranch house and a courtyard of adjacent guest cabin-suites. There's the refurbished stone-and-adobe stagehouse (built in 1854–1872), with its first-floor recreation room and second-floor dormitory for Reno Hilton staffers on duty for a Flying "M" weekend. There are the hangars for Barron's menagerie of aircraft. There are the cages that house thousands of quail, pheasant, and chukar (a partridge varient) that will grow up to be released for hunter-guests; there are kennels of spaniels and Labrador retrievers to take those guests hunting. There are the pool, tennis court and putting green. Not one but two satellite dishes pull in sports programming (sans commercials) from network feeds. There's the East Walker River for German and rainbow trout, and the ranch fishing pond into which are dumped young bass, perch and trout for angler-guests.

All of this, needless to say, is a heck of a lot of adventureland for one CEO family alone. So on weekdays, while Barron labors at corporate headquarters in Beverly Hills, high-rolling regulars from the Las Vegas and Reno Hiltons are entertained as Flying "M" guests. Occasionally, Hilton execs use the facilities for business/pleasure meetings. Also, despite the fact that the working ranch's link to outsiders is by a tenuous radio-phone, there's been an earnest movement to attract non-Hilton corporate conferences.

But during weekends when the boss plays host, unstructured pleasure is the order of the day. And to make it onto the guest list is to find the likes of Cliff Robertson or John Denver climbing aboard Barron's biplanes or chowing down at breakfast. As *this* weekend's visitors stride from landing strip to living room, let's see who's here:

Arthur J. and his chatty, British-born wife, Joy Simms. Eric M. Hilton, in from his Hong-Kong base of operations. Jan Knab (wife of a former Prudential executive) and old family friend. Gregory R. Dillon, Hilton executive vice-president, and his wife, Nancy. Hilton public relations executive James R. Galbraith and his wife, Mary.

Many of the guests have known each other for years and have a nice way of sharing memories of, say, the silly outfit the white-haired Arthur J. once wore to the Bel Air Country Club or the sad marital plight of mutual friends. Off-color jokes, too, were heard echoing off the dark-hued walls. Did you hear the one about the nun and a camel?

But let's start this weekend at the top, as Barron Hilton gives these privileged guests their sleeping assignments, and as everybody waits for ranch hands to arrive with the luggage.

9:45 A.M., Saturday: The ranch house is decorated in Ethan

Allen-goes-West. Barron and Marilyn's private suite is at one end; at the opposite end are two guest bedrooms. Overflow guests sleep in nearby cabin-suites. Everyone washes with little bars of Hilton Hotel soap. With the possible exception of the big-screen TV, the most conspicuous living room fixture is a no-quarters-necessary slot machine that registers a jackpot when three likenesses of Barron Hilton spin in a row.

As a guest tries her luck, Barron emerges from his suite. He has shed his dark suit and now wears pale jeans, white T-shirt, a Barron Hilton Soaring Cup windbreaker and a funky white sun hat that will be atop his head throught the weekend. On his round, genial face sit a pair of sunglasses. A cigar is alight. And after lowering his average build into an easy chair that faces the big-screen TV, he quickly examines an issue of *Satellite TV Week* and then makes his way into the informal dining room for sausage, toast and coffee. One by one, the others join him at the round table, where the talk is of the new 10-station "shooting clay" range that's been crafted onto the Flying "M" desert. And then, after the victuals, Barron calls out the order to play with the first of what he jokingly calls his "toys." Even now, his voice rarely rises much above a mumble when he says, as only a member of royalty properly can: "Let's go shooting."

11:00 A.M., Saturday. It's walking distance to the shooting range. But why not let a pair of four-wheel-drive vehicles do the work? Besides, there's too much baggage: In addition to the five of us, there's a cooler full of beer and soft drinks, half-a-dozen 12-gauge shotguns and enough ammunition to win a war against the next couple of counties. Scorekeeper Jack Hedger, the bespectacled, jovial ranch manager, trains dogs to hunt so he's pretty good with guests who couldn't hit the broad side of a billboard let along outsmart clay birds. "There you go," he says, when a virgin clay shooter finally connects with one of a pair of clay doves at the "Passing Doves" station. Barron (whom Jack calls "Mr. Hilton") and Eric (whom Jack calls "Eric") don't need such encouragement, since they're blasting virtually everything to bits.

In this upgraded version of skeet, each of the stations is elaborately designed to replicate the special flight patterns of a different pair of game birds. When each shooter is ready to fire he yells "pull," and a caddy hidden somewhere in the shrub pulls a lever that sends the targets flying. (Occasionally, when a machine jams, he is heard to yell, "Just a minute, sir.") Each shooter gets 10 shots per station. Our favorite of the stations is called "Rabbit and Quail," at which participants are required to shoot first a clay "rabbit" that races along the desert floor, then, within seconds, a clay "quail" that soars across the sky.

It's a sport that's been popular in England for years, but which is just starting to catch on here—there are only 64 such shooting clay courses in the U.S.

When Barron finishes shooting at a station, Jack looks over his boss's scorecard and says something like, "You hit nine of them, Mr. Hilton. Great going." Then, the first sentence out of our host's mouth is: "How did Eric do on this one?" Yes, as we shoot and hump from station to station, there's clearly a minor, albeit good-natured undercurrent of sibling competition. And why not? Unlike the rest of us novices, only these Hilton brothers have been sniping at flying things since they were born.

At the final station, the most ingenious of them all, you find yourself sitting in a little wooden rowboat (this is desert, remember) that's built atop springs. You sit in the rocking boat and aim at overhead "geese."

After the last of the group has sniped at the last of the ersatz prey, Jack announces that Barron is our winner. Then, as we head back to the ranch house, someone turns around to ask Eric a question, but he has disappeared. He's back at "Driven Pheasant," practicing up for tomorrow's rematch with his brother.

1:00 P.M., Saturday. It's chow-time! We're all seated in captain's chairs around a long, board-of-directors-style table. There's something unusual about this room. On the one hand, a thick stone wall suggests rustication and an earlier century; framed color photographs of gliders add a modern touch. But there's also a photocopier machine, a personal computer and a facsimile machine. Our formal dining room doubles as a conference meeting room.

Barron and Marilyn are skipping this meal. But the rest of us gormandize on fried chicken brought out by a pair of superb waiters whose T-shirts read: "Reno Razzle, Hilton Dazzle." We drink iced tea and share airline horror stories.

5:00 P.M., Saturday. American cliché: A man sits in his living room, smoking a cigar, a Bud Light at his side, watching preseason football on TV. When a friend walks into the room, the man says, "We're supposed to be the underdog but we're ahead by 10 points." No, this isn't Mr. Sixpack in Peoria, it's Barron Hilton, and he has a special right to use the first-person plural when talking about the team. It's the San Diego Chargers, which Barron happened to found and of which he still owns 15%. What's more, he's not munching on chips. A waiter brings out a bowlful of fried quail appetizers, with sauce. "Try this stuff, it's great," says Barron. "Did you see that interception?"

The waiters, still in crisp white T-shirts, stand a respectable few feet behind Barron Hilton, hands clasped in back, their eyes riveted to the game. How nice to have servants who know enough to wait until a particular play is completed before interrupting to ask, "Mr. Hilton, do you want to wait until after the game to eat?"

"No, no. Whenever it's ready. I'm going to tape this."

Somewhere within the workings of each weekend guest, an internal clock signals a gland that transmits a message to the brain: It's cocktail time, the formal, daily ritual that separates daytime leisure activities from those of the evening. It's time for fresh clothes; more to the point, it's time to drink.

Guests amble in from the rooms and cabin-suites and begin milling about, playing the slot machine or its neighboring electronic poker device, sitting on a couch to catch a bit of the football, gathering at the swivel captains' chair-stools at the bar to exchange idle—yet, frequently, pensive—conversation. Among the men, there's an abundance of country-club wear (taupe shirts, crimson pants, white shoes—that sort of thing). When the women arrive, they are newly scrubbed, freshly painted, and they greet each other with encouraging comments regarding each others' apparel and accessories. When Barron changes into dinner clothes, he somehow manages to do it smoothly enough that no one notices he's left the room.

A waiter makes the rounds, discreetly asking each guest his or her cooking-time preference for the forthcoming filets. And he addresses everybody by name, giving the impression that he spent the predawn hours memorizing the guest list.

Then the waiters, too, are ready to clean up for dinner. Off go the "Reno Razzle, Hilton Dazzle" T-shirts; on come ruffled shirts and black ties.

8:00 P.M., Saturday. Along with the promised petit filets come lobster tails.

Maybe Barron is too shy for the task, so Greg Dillon takes it upon himself to coordinate the boy/girl/boy/girl seating. And even though he's taping the event, Barron repeatedly springs up from the table to check the status of the game. The Chargers, sadly, have fallen behind.

Now the big goal is to come out ahead on a point-spread bet he's made with Eric. Somewhat oblivious to their attractive meals, the fans perform a relay between their plates and the TV in the other room. When one is sneaking a bit of the game, he yells out: "Hey, come in here and see this pass." Then the other races to catch the replay. Then, when Barron runs back to the dining room and announces: "An interception!" Arthur, with whom the Hilton CEO has *another* bet, leaps from his seat and makes a dash for the living room. Would TV tray tables have been a better move?

Football fans would probably be astonished to learn that Barron Hilton doesn't react to a faulty Chargers play by rushing to a phone, conferring with majority owner Alex Spanos, and ordering up the dismissal of coaches and players. Instead, he is remarkably philosophical about the whole affair, focusing on the successes of the first quarter instead of the failures of the rest of the game. Actually, he appears more concerned about his side bets than he does with the team he brought into being.

Over dessert, Joy tells us that when she first married Arthur (it was a second marriage for both), she couldn't quite understand his mid-game telephone conversations with Barron, with all of their talk of wagering mere nickels and dimes. That is, until she came to understand that a "nickel" is $500, and a "dime" is $1000. And then comes the story about how Arthur, to get his new bride hooked on *Monday Night Football*, routinely paid her $100 for each football game she watched with him that his team won.

We'd been warned that early-rising Barron has been known to "turn on his heels" at 8:30 P.M. Sure enough, within minutes after dinner, he makes the announcement that ballooning is to commence at 6:00 A.M. He wishes everbody "good night," then he retreats to bed. A few of the guests step outside to identify constellations in the jeweled skies. But after about 10 minutes, all of the guests retire, leaving the staff to stay up and watch movies on tape.

6:00 A.M., Sunday. Could anything be finer than a balloon ride in Nevada in the morning? (Answer: a cup of coffee.) First, it should be mentioned that Barron isn't some sort of sadist to pick such an early hour to begin the day's activities; it's simply the only time the winds are sufficiently cooperative. Only three of us have risen early enough to fly with Barron this morning. And as we drive over to the hangar area, we catch a glimpse of it: Lying on its side on the landing strip like a sleeping animal is the magnificent, multicolored balloon. Barron and a three-member ground crew work to inflate the balloon with a fan mechanism, grabbing hold of the magical aircraft as it enlarges and then guiding it as it is ready to be set upright.

At the appropriate moment, Barron climbs aboard a basket that is so small it holds only pilot and one passenger. Then, a guest jumps in. Immediately, the balloon drifts up and into the crisp morning air; and one can make out the word HILTON, in giant letters, emblazoned across its belly. Barron takes each of the three guests on private rides, explaining the altitude meter, occasionally adjusting a blast of gas-fueled fire into the balloon to increase the hot air. Quietly, after the balloon has reached the proper altitude, Barron lets it float, pointing out the 11,000-ft. Mt. Grant, 20 miles away. There's a long, silent pause, then he points out a trio of deer along the river below; he becomes animated, like a youngster. Another pause, after which he explains theories of flight and spiraling columns of air.

In his final balloon ride, Barron and a guest find themselves trapped, mid-air, by unobliging air currents. Unable to make it back to the landing strip, he eventually brings it down on a rocky hillside, far from the dirt road that cuts across Flying "M" Ranch. We traverse boulders and brush in a pair of four-wheel-drive vehicles to retrieve them. And after the rescue is accomplished, the ground crew remains to deflate and remove the balloon, as Barron and guests head back for breakfast.

A few words about this ground crew are in order. It consists of ranch manager Jack; the "clay shoot" caddy; and one of the waiters. Each of them has a special talent for helping Barron get the most out of any of his self-described "toys." Jack, for instance, seems to know as much about training dogs as he does about wind patterns. These men seem to appear out of nowhere when their services are required for a particular pastime. Perhaps Barron is in electronic communication with them. But more likely they can read his mind.

And after they perform a necessary task—deflate Barron's balloon, stow away his shotguns, replace his beer—they somehow silently vanish, only to appear at the next toy, ready to go.

11:00 A.M., Sunday. After a breakfast that couldn't be beat (fried trout, homemade sausage, home fries, toast), Barron sits us down in the living room so we can watch a taped documentary about his biennial Barron Hilton Soaring Cup competition. In the half-hour film, which is narrated by John Denver, we see world-champion gliders in action, soaring 1,000 feet above the ground. Barron owned the ranch for years (first with several partners, then on his own) before learning that its "thermals," columns of air that keep gliders up and going, are among the world's best for soaring. It's a sport that Barron says "relaxes me."

Alas, the plane that tows Barron's gliders—he owns three—is undergoing some sort of annual checkup, so we won't get to participate this weekend. While Barron and Arthur settle down at a living room table for a few hours of gin rummy, Hilton exec Greg Dillon takes us on a tour of the aircraft. What we see are a two-seater, decathlon stunt plane in which Barron takes pleasure in flying upside down; an open-cockpit, 450-horsepower Stearman bi-plane; a Beechcraft Staggerwing from World War II (only a few still exist), with all-leather interior and Barron's name on the side; a Hughes 500D jet chopper; and, of course, his three sleek gliders, one of which boasts a 36-foot wingspan.

On the walk back to the ranch house, someone mentions a few of Barron's other properties. In addition to his lavish house in the Holmby Hills section of Los Angeles (featured on the television show *The Colbys*), he owns a home in the Palm Springs desert in which he and Marilyn spend many of the winter weekends. And he is a founding partner of a duck-hunting club near Stockton, California. It's apparently a club with a colorful past. Among its members was the late Clark Gable, who was reputed to have maintained a bottle of bourbon under his bed there. (When the legendary actor died, his fellow club members enshrined the last unfinished bottle.) We encounter another museum item as we enter the ranch house foyer: Hilton Hotels founder (Barron's father) Conrad Hilton's favorite saddle, with an identifying plaque.

12:15 P.M., Sunday. Back at the ranch, Barron is still playing cards and smoking cigars. A walky-talky by his side, he makes arrangements for this afternoon's shooting clay rematch. A few of the women watch tennis on TV. Some of the room's furnishings include a chess set poised on its own stand, a hefty salmon mounted above a mantle, decorative pillows that depict gliders, duck-decoys. Not the sort of furnishings that make jeans-clad guests feel the least bit out of place.

Lunch today consists of fried fish and fried onion rings. Barron, who sits at the head of the table, first declines then accepts the pecan pie dessert. Later, there's a repeat of Saturday's shooting match. Once again, Barron is high gun, with a score of 79 to his brother's 72 (out of a possible 100). The other shooters score too low to mention.

3:30 P.M., Sunday. In the living room, the women are watching *Empire of the Sun* on tape. Barron sits in his white easy chair, drinking Bud Light, paging through *Satellite TV Week,* looking for a sporting event. When the film's action is intense and unavoidable—say the young protagonist is fighting mercilessly for a scrap of food—Barron, who was a naval photographer's mate in 1946, looks up and says, "Boy, this is a serious movie," then he pages through his magazine some more, seeking an alternative.

Now ranch manager Jack takes many of us out to visit the birds. Each year Flying "M" Ranch brings to life as many as 18,000 pheasant, chukar and quail. In huge coops not far from the cabin-suites, we witness armies of tiny birds. Proudly, Jack points out an incubator in which 6,000 to 7,000 quail eggs are prepped for life. Next, there's the hatcher in which the eggs, after three days, emerge as full-fledged chicks. Pheasants, we learn, take 18 days in a "rocking" incubator and 6 days in a hatcher.

What happens to all of these feathery creatures? They're released for hunting, although many of them escape unscathed.

5:30 P.M., Sunday. Whenever Barron Hilton gets an anthropological urge, he can hop in a vehicle and head over to the petroglyphs. After about a five-minute drive and ten-minute uphill hike, one discovers a series of ancient Indian carvings on the surfaces of rocks. Ordinary folks would spend days hiking in the West without ever encountering such a wonder. But here they are, for Barron and guests, whenever they want them. We spend some time trying to make sense of the sunbursts, animals, and crude human figures.

The aura of the Old West truly is everywhere. The ranch property is dotted with seven full-fledged ghost towns from the Gold Rush days (one of which is a California Registered Historical Landmark). But this is a working ranch, too. And somewhere up in the hills, 1,200 head of cattle graze away.

8:00 P.M., Sunday. We had salmon hors d'oeuvres, and it seems as if some guacamolé was floating around. Dinner involved, among other items, Veal Oscar and ice cream with blackberries. For a brief moment, when Hilton Corporation business enters into the conversation, Barron asks Greg a quick question about how well a particular division head is doing at his job. Again, there's football on TV, and at one point when someone reported the score, Arthur was heard to say, "Another quarter and I'll own this ranch." But mostly there was joking, story telling and the distinct feeling that this would be our final meal together, so why not linger a bit longer and trade a few more quips.

9:00 P.M., Sunday. We've gathered in the living room for a few moments of football. Barron sits in his easy chair, Marilyn is beside him. We all laugh as Arthur responds to a bad play by sticking out his tongue and waving his fingers voodoo style at the screen. We amble about, sharing yet another final joke, exchanging business cards. It becomes clear that there won't be much time for such levity tomorrow morning. Word circulates that Barron wants to depart at precisely 8:00 A.M., and, as one guest puts it: "He's so generous with everything he has, the least we can do is be prompt when he wants us to be prompt."

8:05 A.M., Monday. Ranch hands want to know if our bags are ready; the chef wants to know what we want for breakfast. Everyone's in a rush. The word is now that "wheel's up" (the corporate jet's) is at 8:30. And we walk out to the landing strip in pretty much the same attire in which we arrived: dark business suits for the men, sensibly attractive outfits for the women.

9:10 A.M., Monday. Somewhere above Greater Yosemite, as our flight carries us toward Hilton headquarters in Beverly Hills, Barron—featuring gray suit, open collar, tassle shoes, shades, cigar—is back in gin rummy position with Arthur. The other men have started working on Hilton business, sifting through papers, jotting notes. The women are discussing employment issues and already referring to the pleasant weekend in the past tense. The business week is at hand.

About an hour after we begin, as the scenery below us becomes dotted with swimming pools, Barron makes some tabulations on a notebook. The weekend's final score from all the football and gin rummy? Barron owes Arthur $1045. Arthur owes Barron $10. Barron reaches into a pocket and passes his buddy a prewritten check for $950, then, under Arthur's protests of "we can settle up later," he fetches a hundred-dollar bill from his wallet and hands it over.

So much for the which-hotel-do-I-want business.

And Arthur gives Barron a ten-dollar bill.

Then we land.

9:45 A.M., Monday. Five gleaming limousines, some white, some black, all with trunks open, all with uniformed drivers poised to retrieve luggage, await us within inches of our jet, which has landed at the Van Nuys Airport.

There are hugs, kisses, handshakes and thank-yous. In pairs, we climb into assigned limos. Then the convoy sweeps out of the airport and disperses onto a maze of different freeways. Our limo ferries us toward LAX for the next leg on the CEO circuit.

H enry Wendt's oenological leanings are relatively new.

He's not someone who's dreamed for decades of growing prized grapes or of seeing his finest Zinfandel on the wine list at Le Cirque or of—and this gets pretty crass—getting on nationally televised commercials touting the loving care with which his pulp is fermented. No, the chairman of SmithKline Beckman's first notion was to embark on the leisure enterprise of cheese-making, but the numbers didn't crunch right.

*Henry
(SmithKline
Beckman)
Wendt and His
Vineyard/Winery*

So here he is, in crisp jeans and a Western shirt, looking a lot more down-to-earth than the wine lords on *Falcon Crest* look, but sounding surprisingly Californian when he explains that he bought 90 prime acres of Sonoma County with the hopes of preparing for his next "life stage." Still, you can't take the corporation out of the CEO. He adds: "And the economics of the business can be pretty good."

Wendt doesn't aspire to be Eric de Rothschild, nor does he ooze the cautious elegance of a prosperous American who's trying his darndest to purchase the undeserved trappings of European royalty. No sinister ambitions appear to be fermenting here, just to retire busily, profitably in a nice locale.

The vineyard, purchased in 1980, has already broken even, but the winery, in operation for five years, won't see black ink until 1991. Meanwhile, the 56-year-old Wendt toils away at SmithKline headquarters, some 3,000 miles east in Philadelphia, and comes here for holidays or as a stopover when he does business in Japan or Southern California. If his projections hold, this One Smart CEO should retire into his Quivera Winery and vineyard when the return on investment starts to really ripen—to something like 15% after taxes.

The SmithKline chairman, who never before owned a "so-called vacation home," started preparing for his little retirement enterprise about a decade ago. As we mentioned, his first fantasy was to make cheese, soft cheese, to be specific. "The more I looked at it as a business, the less attractive it appeared, so I started looking at vineyards, somewhat skeptically, feeling it would be hard to find really good property," he says.

But unlike the Spanish explorers who searched in vain for the rich, mythical North American kingdom of Quivera—for which this winery is named—Wendt and his wife, Holly, did find their little patch of paradise. It's a verdant hillside, teeming with yuccas and figs and eucalypti, bathed in the scent of flourishing California bay leaf, and steeped in local history (it's near the site of an Indian burial ground, and beneath its overgrowth are the tombstones of early Anglo explorers).

The misnamed Dry Creek flows past and each afternoon the Wendts maneuver their jeep (not just any jeep, mind you, but one of those spunky little buggers that won World War II) down to take a dip in the 60-degree water. "It's pretty darn refreshing," he says.

Today, Wendt steers past a vine of ripe Cabernet Sauvignon grapes and stops to pluck a few. "You know, one of the fun things is tasting the grapes," he says. "By tasting, you judge whether or not to pick. Then, when you taste the wine, you remember the grapes. Yes, you have to taste a lot of grapes and a lot of wine." When he drives by one of the 18 employees who work the Quivera harvest, he waves and says brightly, "Hello, Manuel." There's something delightful about all this Management by Driving Around.

"It's a great deal of fun and it's also very healthy," he says. "I'm still a manager, there's still a long-term strategy to implement, there's a team to keep motivated and directed. But I'm close to people working with their hands. I go out and work with [names an employee], pruning together."

He adds: "As a place to live, this is more than just a house at the beach, or cabin in the mountains, more than merely a reflective retreat. [It's an] active, busy, interesting place with a lot of vitality." So there are meetings aplenty, but they seem to exist outside of the realm of the dreadful. Imagine entertaining a pack of wine writers in an immaculate, Oriental-carpeted visitors' room that overlooks gleaming, stainless-steel fermenters.

Outside the winery, we find his son, Chip, and two others as they cull vine debris from a harvest that's being dumped into a crusher. Inside, in huge tubs, wine-in-the-making ferments away, and Wendt proudly encourages a visitor to take a whiff.

There's a less-is-more philosophy that permeates this enterprise. From its beginning, Wendt decided that his winery would concentrate on only a few varieties of wine: Sauvignon, Blanc, Zinfandel, and Cabernet Sauvignon. So as wineries go, this is on the small side. Wendt's goal is to produce an annual 25,000 cases by 1993, and to level off at that size.

Already, the wine has, in words this CEO doesn't favor, a "cult following." In Pennsylvania, for instance, followers are known to hoard the meager Quivera shipments the moment they arrive at the state-controlled liquor stores. Here in California wine country, Quivera's mystique is enhanced by the fact that the winery doesn't open its doors to any old passersby. Wine tasters must make appointments first.

Without getting too technical, it's great wine.

And such a life is the stuff of dreams, no? Most everybody

enjoys the rewards of wine consumption, but only a few other corporate chiefs have discovered the special pleasures of its production. Venture capitalist William Hambrecht invested in a neighboring place, the Bellvedere Winery and Vineyard, seven years ago. Times Mirror Chairman Robert F. Erburu relaxes at his 100-acre vineyard over in competing Napa County.

As each newcomer buys into the dream, there grows a mild local bias against vineyard gentrification, a variation of the "in come the rich folk, there goes the neighborhood" theme. But California wine country has seen a great many changes in the centuries since this region served as the northernmost point of the Spanish empire, and Wendt, who has a strong sense of history, seems to know them all.

So he relates a few local legends as he wends the jeep up to his vacation home, a contemporary, stained-cedar structure with salt-box angles that overlooks both vineyards and redwood forests. Inside the sparsely furnished home, Holly Wendt steps from a black leather chair and wanders over to a refrigerator to fetch Henry a Coors. There's some banter about Philadelphia politics. Then Henry, who runs three miles each day, makes the suggestion that we run together, something like 6:00 A.M. the following morning.

Even when they relax, these guys never quit.

Drew (Union Pacific) Lewis and His Farm From the road that winds up to Andrew L. (Drew) Lewis's 230-acre Lilliput Farm, we first catch glimpse of a small fish pond, and, along its banks, a fisherman waiting for a catch. The fisherman, clothed in outdoor gear inappropriate to the balmy June weather, is perfectly still, doesn't even look up to follow a flock of geese that flies by. On closer inspection, the fisherman turns out to be an obsessively realistic sculpture.

Is this what farmers are using for scarecrows these days?

But then, when a visitor pulls into the small parking area up between an antique barn and the much-modernized 18th-century farmhouse, it becomes obvious that a scarecrow is the last thing needed on this, the world's tidiest farm. A trio of large dogs will scare off any interloper, friend or foe. That's one of the reasons why Lewis, the former U.S. Transportation Secretary, felt so darn secure here after arousing the wrath of the nation's air traffic controllers, when he fired them all nearly a decade ago.

Sure, there are some CEOs who have adopted the rural life as a romantic ideal, playing the role of gentleman farmer. But Lewis, who bought this farm near the Pennsylvania crossroads of Lederach in 1958, is not one of them. The Union Pacific chairman is a member of a Pennsylvania Dutch Protestant sect known as the Schwenkfelders and grew up on a nearby farm that his father leased. As a youth, he was something of a fixture at many of the local farms, where he was hired to milk cows, bale hay, shovel manure.

Nor is Lewis a CEO who made good in the city and who prefers to spend weekends among the serenity of the cornfields or pastures or horses. That's basically what American Express chairman James D. Robinson III does when he retreats to his farm near Kent, Connecticut, or Usher Control Data's Robert McCollum Price visits his 470-acre farm in southern Minnesota for weekends.

Actually, Lewis is someone who never really left the farm.

For the first year he headed Union Pacific—while corporate headquarters were in New York and not an hour's drive away in Bethlehem, Pennsylvania—Lewis generally would spend a few weeknights, in addition to weekends, at the self-sustaining farm. He commuted to Manhattan by car or on the corporate helicopter. (He reimbursed the company for the cost.) When he absolutely *had* to, he stayed at the company's three-and-a-half-room Manhattan apartment (again, paying for it himself), but it's clear he harbors a distaste for the big city. In the farm's guest suite (where the guest list has included former Attorney General Edwin Meese), there's a bizarre, framed anti-New York collage. It features a knife mounted on an "I (heart) N.Y." bumper sticker: memorabilia from the time his wife, Marilyn, was mugged in a New York elevator.

The borders between Lewis's life on the farm and his job as Union Pacific CEO are indistinct. Take, for example, his home office. It's a one-room schoolhouse from the 1880s, maybe a quarter mile from the farmhouse, renovated and stuffed with antiques, a fax machine, a copier and, despite the fact that it's Saturday morning and Lewis has been baling hay for hours, a pair of busy secretaries. "I usually end up spending a few hours a weekend here," says Lewis.

CEOS ON HOLIDAY

For the decades he ran Triangle Publications, Walter H. Annenberg was renowned for the New Year's bashes he threw for high-ranking Republicans and others at Sunnylands, his winter home in Rancho Mirage, California. Question is: Now that Annenberg has sold his vast publishing empire, which corporate chief is likely to carry on the partying tradition?

Will the celebrating move over to the vacation dwelling of Ford chairman Donald Peterson, who also retreats to Rancho Mirage? Probably not, since he's rarely at his California desert home and it's an even rarer occasion when he makes it into the gossip columns. Or maybe the Palm Springs area social nexus will shift to Palm Desert, where Atlantic Richfield chairman Lodwrick Cook keeps a retreat. And there's always the community of Indian Wells, where Wells Fargo chief Carl Reichardt slips away for a break now and again.

One thing's pretty certain, though. Whoever takes over as the number-one CEO host is likely to do the hosting in one of the prime power-vacation locales. Fact is, when they want to get away from it all, CEOs tend to stick together. So celebrities of all stripes aren't about to converge on, say, Sun Company chairman Robert McClements, Jr.'s place at the Jersey shore next New Year's Eve, or even next Fourth of July.

The Palm Springs area is one resort region that's teeming with CEOs. The postcard-perfect island of Nantucket is another. Its former whaling village is the home-away-from home for IBM's John Akers, who bought and fixed up the whitewashed, widow-walked, two-story house on Pleasant Street. But with its clean black shutters, its bright-purple window-box flowers, its orderly white picket fence, and its dill and tarragon growing so neatly in the side yard, the model village house looks as if it couldn't take a bunch of rowdy Fourth-of-July revelers. And it's nowhere near the water.

He is wearing khaki pants and a checkerboard farm shirt and he takes us upstairs to show off what he calls his "ego wall," collections of photographs and such. (One noteworthy item that harks back to the firing of air traffic controllers: a British newspaper cartoon that depicts a control-tower washwoman saying, "All right, the one with the green and white stripes, and you're the last one. I have my own goddamn job to do.")

Next, Lewis maneuvers his mobile-phone-equipped pickup truck (complete with National Rifle Association bumper sticker) past a cornfield and we make stops at a succession of neat, modern structures that house an item of farm equipment here, a Model A there. On the ride back to the farm-

For CEOs in search of a place to party next summer, maybe the Nantucket house recently built by General Electric's John Welch, Jr., would be a workable option. The unmarked, cedar-shingled dwelling is cheek-to-jowl against the Sankaty Head Golf Course. So perhaps the festivities could be combined with a golf outing. Think of the fun guests could have fiddling with Welch's electric window covers or running down to take a dip in the Atlantic (although the currents get a bit too rough on this end of the island). The swimming's generally safer over by Cliff Road, where Texas Air chief Frank Lorenzo summers. But it's doubtful that Lorenzo could draw much of a high-echelon crowd. He hasn't quite been Mr. Popularity on Nantucket since he cut air service to the island in 1988.

If the timing were right, CEO party-goers could drop in at the pleasantly modest Nantucket village home of Kathy and Ned Hentz on Fair Street. They're the daughter and son-in-law of Lee Iacocca. The Chrysler chief visits them a few times each summer, sleeping in an upstairs bedroom, slipping into town for ice cream, driving cross-island for seafood, and generally trying—as CEOs tend to do at Nantucket—to blend into the regulation cedar woodwork. And he gets to play with granddaughter Katy, too. This is where Iacocca escapes when he tires of his digs in Bloomfield Hills, Michigan; Boca Raton, Florida; and his Tuscany villa, where he typically spends five weeks each summer.

Naples, Florida, on the Gulf of Mexico coast, and the Lost Tree Village enclave near Vero Beach, Florida, on the Atlantic, are two other CEO-heavy resorts. Actually, why not try something totally different? Why not throw CEO-watchers for a loop and hit up Inland Steel chairman Frank Luerssen to stage the next power affair at his refuge in Lakeside, Michigan. Then, after the party, everyone can do something *really* outrageous: Take his grandchildren fishing out on Lake Michigan.

—DAVID DIAMOND

house, the swimming pool and tennis court come into view. Lewis estimates he entertains guests here about eight weekends a year.

At the large vegetable patch, one of the farm helpers, a young woman wearing a clean, "Lilliput Farm" T-shirt, stops Lewis to say something involving cabbage, peas and string beans. A table is being delivered and Lewis lifts one end as it is taken into the farmhouse. Saturday stuff.

The house itself is crammed with tasteful, mostly antique furnishings, and Lewis scans a collection of autographed photographs that sit atop a grand piano. "Hey, Marilyn, what happened to that picture of Henry Kissinger and me on the tractor?" he asks. Lewis once advised Kissinger on the purchase of a used tractor for the former secretary of state's Connecticut farm. The picture is located. Henry's inscription reads: "I would definitely buy a used tractor from this man."

And so this is life down on the CEO farm. Lewis can rattle off the names of several other chief executives who own farms—they include T. Boone Pickens and his 2B Ranch in Texas—and it becomes obvious that the members of the community of CEO farmers have been weekend guests at each others' spreads. For Lewis, this kind of life not only is an extension of his childhood, but is an activity in which he doesn't necessarily have to "win." When he golfs and plays tennis, which he does on occasion, he hates to lose. "But when I mow the grass, I win every time," he says.

For the record, Lewis also skis, hunts and fishes. And just when it's starting to sound as if he truly knows how to live, and as we walk over to a barn, he says, unprompted: "Sure CEOs live differently, we make more money."

And then, he takes us to meet the nicest animals money can buy. We're standing at a neat barnyard fence.

"C'mon Batey," says Lewis.

No response.

"Hey, Batey. C'mon get up (whistles)."

No response.

The chairman and chief executive officer of Union Pacific is trying, with little success, to coax Beethoven, the black Great Pyrenees that keeps other dogs out of a sheep pen, to stand up on its four legs. But the dog was recently clipped and is still one razor-burned, sunburned, hurting animal.

"Boy, it really looks like he's stiff," Lewis tells us when the canine finally musters the strength to stand and saunter over to us.

"We better get him checked," he says. Then he turns his attention to the dog and asks, "You all right Batey? You don't look like you're walking very good."

Just then a Sicilian donkey struts past Batey and Lewis introduces her as Geraldine (born the evening when a Queens, New York, congresswoman was nominated to run for Vice-President). Lewis appears to have developed a splendid rapport with the many creatures here.

But there's a downside risk to all this palling around with everything from hogs to chickens. "The only problem you have," says Lewis, "is you've got to not get too friendly with the animals or you don't want to butcher them. You try to have an impersonal relationship."

We're looking for parallels, so we ask: "I guess it's probably like running a company. If you're a CEO you don't want to get too friendly with the employees, huh?"

"It's not quite the same," he answers, letting go of a brief laugh, "We don't butcher *them.*"

–DAVID DIAMOND

NEVER A WASTED MOMENT

For the most part, they come in before the hired help and if they leave early, it's probably to host a reception or dine with a client or have drinks with a member of the board—not, as is widely believed, to gallivant. The majority of CEOs (83%) responding to our survey put in between 10 and 12 hours on a typical workday. Add to that weekend duty (92% routinely work on weekends).

What remains is not a heck of a lot of quality time. But chief executives, we've learned, devour free time in the same efficient manner with which they manage their corporations. So whether it's bird shooting in Scotland or bridge at the club, their approach tends to be the same: The leisure activity has been carefully scheduled and often is designed to accomplish more than one objective. The reasoning is simple. Yes, it would be swell to break par, but why not entertain a potential acquisition candidate at the same time?

No, CEOs don't tend to hang around the paddle-tennis court waiting to help novices with their backhands; rare is the CEO who spends an early summer evening strolling in Central Park, ambling over to see who's playing in the band shell. By and large, one doesn't become the boss by soaking away crucial leisure time in a hot tub.

That's not to say corporate chiefs don't like to goof off. Truth is, they do. They just don't want to waste time doing it. This may explain the popularity among CEOs of bird-hunting clubs that hatch and release game fowl for their members, or private fishing clubs that control access to the best streams. The CEOs who flock to April Point Lodge, an upscale salmon fishing retreat in British Columbia (not a private club), are the type who want to catch a big fish, not merely sun themselves out on a boat and polish off some brews. To help them, the lodge provides first-class guides who do everything humanly possible—from negotiating the tricky inland passage waters to selecting, cutting, and hooking the appropriate bait—to increase those odds. And if a CEO wants to be even more confident that he won't waste his time in unyielding water, helicopter transportation is available to the best and most remote fishing spots, for $2000 a day.

With a limited amount of time to spend, and, for the most part, an abundance of discretionary income, chief executives increasingly are attaching the prefix *heli-* to the names of their favorite sports. For instance, at Utah's Snowbird ski resort, CEOs charter helicopters and guides to quiet, backcountry areas, such as the virginal Mineral Basin, which can be reached no other way. And after their helicopter guide takes them for a morning of heli-skiing, and if it's March or April, he may chopper them directly over the mountain to Wasatch State Park's 18-hole golf course for an afternoon round of heli-golf, with golf carts and cocktails provided.

The image of the workaholic CEO is the product of fiction. In *The Wall Street Journal* survey of 351 heads of large U.S. corporations, a mere 2.8% reported taking no vacation in 1986. More than half (65.7%) took three or more weeks. And that doesn't necessarily count weekend escapes or so-called meetings that combine business with pleasure. Such outings are practically the raison d'être for places like the Ocean Reef Club in Key Largo, Florida, or the Pointe resorts in Phoenix. And then there are company-owned retreats, such as Remington Farms, a huge wildlife management preserve on Maryland's Eastern Shore that's often used for business/ duck hunting meetings by managers at Du Pont, parent of Remington Arms.

Even though these corporate heads may not be workaholics in a literal sense, it's easy to see how they project a workaholic image. That's because when they do play, these can't-sit-still execs tend to play hard. Moreover, corporate leaders who are accustomed to relying on cash-flow projections, per-share earnings estimates and the like tend to be the type who want to do things they can quantify. Rare is the CEO who doesn't keep score.

There are exceptions, of course. Sun Company's Robert McClements, Jr., is a weekend carpenter. He built a house in Philadelphia for his family, and one for his parents. When his job as CEO demanded too much time for him to hammer nails into a new house he wanted to build in the Philadelphia suburbs, he opted to design the project and oversee its construction.

For Martin Marietta's Norman Augustine, it's dollhouses he prefers to construct, and as a family affair. Father and son do the design, building and electrical work; his wife and daughter are in charge of decorations. For Disney's Michael Eisner, a neat Saturday morning is spent watching his sons' soccer match. And Campbell Soup's R. Gordon McGovern, who, it might be noted, drives a Ford Taurus and flies in coach, likes to grow oversized vegetables in his Connecticut garden. (Since his company is in the business, maybe this *does* count as keeping score.)

Then there's Benjamin Jones, the former head of Monarch Capital, a Springfield, Massachusetts-based insurance company. He spends leisure hours as an emergency medical technician and paramedic. (He's also quiet about it. He was reportedly quite embarrassed when a photo of him performing that good deed at a major accident made its way into the local paper.) Jones, 66, is also the holder of a black belt in karate and enjoys running in marathons, two slightly more competitive activities.

SUITE HARMONY

Only 19.7% of CEOs play a musical instrument.

Most popular instruments are:

Piano	(played by 6.3% of CEOs)
Trumpet	3.4%
Guitar	2.3%
Clarinet	2.0%

By and large, however, our CEO survey suggests that America's business chieftains spend their time at more common leisure pursuit. Asked to name their two favorite sports, nearly 40% listed tennis, 15.1% preferred skiing, and 8% opted for sailing or boating. Racquetball or squash are among the favorite sports of 5.4% of our respondents; swimming was cited by 4.6%; fishing and hunting each are the choices of 3.4% of the chief executives surveyed.

So what about golf and jogging? A whopping 59.3% reported having played golf in the past year, making it the most indulged-in after-hours activity, but only 6% cited it as a favorite sport. (In response to another question, 14% did list it as a favorite hobby. But even if you assume that nobody listed it in both places, that's still less than half the people playing.) Similarly, nearly 28% of the respondents said they run or jog regularly, while only 1.4% of them claimed it as a favorite sport.

When it comes to card games, only 16.8% of the corporate chiefs reported that they don't play. Bridge, the most popular, is the preferred game of 29.1% of those surveyed. Gin rummy, particularly popular with Barron Hilton and among Detroit CEOs, was favored by 23.1% (the survey was blind, so we had to get the geographical info elsewhere), while poker was the favorite of 17.1% of the CEOs. The other card games registered too few players to mention. And we failed to ask about dominoes, which is a traditional passion among San Francisco CEOs, but not too popular among chief execs in other U.S. cities.

There aren't many couch potatoes among our nation's chief executives. Only 6.6% of the respondents watch more than 10 hours of TV a week. Do they read, then? Only one quarter of our respondents, 24.8%, reported reading fewer than 6 books a year; 41.9% read 6 to 15 books a year; 18.8% read 16 to 25 books, 13.4% read more than 25 books a year.

When asked the title of the most important books they read, our CEOs cited a wide range of biographies and business books, but their list was topped by David Halberstam's *The Reckoning,* about the battle between U.S. and Japanese auto companies, and thrillers of *The Cardinal of the Kremlin* genre. The *New Testament,* it should be noted, came in fourth.

Florida won hands down as the favorite CEO vacation area.

Next in popularity were Europe, the Caribbean/Bermuda, California, Colorado, Hawaii and New England.

Now. What's life really like in CEO Leisureland? Here's the field report.

If you ask a CEO why he golfs he'll probably rhapsodize ***Power*** about how it gets him outdoors, away from ringing tele- ***Golf*** phones and demanding subordinates. But so, by the way, does an afternoon of mowing the lawn. Or maybe he'll go on about the exercise of it all. (When Mark Twain called golf "a good walk spoiled," he probably was responding to some corporate type who praised the sport's physical require- ments.) And then there's the omnipresent competition. A golfer competes against the course, against his opponents, and, ultimately against himself. So golf offers some of the challenges of the corporate world. And landscaping, too. But after a week of going head-to-head against rival companies, you'd think a rational corporate chief would want to find solace in an isolation tank, not in a foursome on the links.

True to CEO form, Hertz chairman Frank Olson rattles off these and other reasons for golf's widespread appeal as he plays 18 holes at the Arcola Country Club in Paramus, New Jersey. Then, at the ninth hole, in response to a direct ques- tion, he does what successful corporate chiefs often do, he cuts right to the heart of the matter.

"There's no question that golf gives you great exposure," he explains.

Olson confirms that golf is, indeed, "the leisure activity of CEOs." Then, he briefly raises his gray golf cap (a souvenir from the course in Turnberry, Scotland), and adds: "So if you're in a corporation, you are more likely to be exposed [to the boss and other important folks] than is someone who fishes. That doesn't mean to say that you have an advantage, you just get more exposure." So maybe *that's* the main rea- son why so many corporate animals, scrabbling to become king of the beasts, take up this sport.

For the CEO, golf may be the ultimate multipurpose rec- reation. For one thing, it serves as a bonding ritual between business leaders. For another, it offers the chance to conduct quasi-business in a private and often neutral setting. At the end of 18 holes, a supplier and a customer might be inextricably connected in a new deal. On the links, a pair of members of a corporate board might forge a united front against rival members.

There are clear-cut guidelines to this business of golf. If a particular business matter needs to be discussed, the guts of the discussion should take place either before or after the golf—say, during lunch at the clubhouse—explains Olson, who plays frequently with customers and other executives. But CEOs know how to be smooth, how to get in those all-important, subtle comments during the round of golf itself. And with the four hours it typically takes to go 18 holes, there's ample time.

"Sometimes something will come up when you're on the golf course, about an issue. And if you have to wait at a hole for somebody, in an idle moment, you might bring it up," says Olson. Of course, only a fool would turn on the hard-sell during a round of golf.

Meanwhile, a CEO is likely to use a golf outing to study potential business partners or subordinates. "I can learn an awful lot about a person on the golf course. About his personality, about what kind of standards he has, about his courtesies to other people, or lack thereof. The golf course tells you a lot about a person," says Olson.

Just as a middle-rung manager uses golf as a chance to be exposed to the boss, the boss is using it as a chance to scrutinize the middle-rung manager. And after driving a ball into the sand, Olson tells the parable about a sales manager he once hired who lasted about a month, long enough to exhibit some inappropriate golf behavior.

"We were playing golf at a customer outing and this fellow was more interested in his own game than he was in other people," he says. "For example, he'd be closer to the hole than somebody behind him, but he'd go on and hit his shot without giving the courtesy to the other fellow, which is the etiquette of the game. And he knew better, but he was just interested in his own shot."

The story continues. "Then, later in the round, he did the cardinal sin. He said that he had a five, when in fact he had a six. And later on he did it *again*. I talked to him about it, [told him] I thought he had made an error."

At such a point, many a CEO wouldn't have gotten as far as the clubhouse without reading the employee his rights. But Olson managed to maintain a temporary cool. The employee was gone in two weeks, "as soon as I had a chance to get organized," says the Hertz chairman, "because the guy just absolutely didn't have any character."

Yes, yes, yes. There's the gentility of it all. The general exclusivity of country clubs, the luxurious tradition of caddies, the lack of perspiration, the cashmere sweaters. (On the autumn day we talked, Olson was wearing a yellow sweater over a plaid wool shirt, green cordoroy slacks, black-and-white golf shoes.) Something about the dress gives the impression that life is still as simple as it was, say, in the year 1457. That was when King James of Scotland prevailed upon Parliament to enact a rule making it unlawful for anyone to play golf. He wanted the populace to practice something useful, like archery, instead.

"I like the cleanliness of golf," says Olson, looking around for an example, then finding one. "The lawn is mowed." It's a decorous sport. Whereas in ice hockey, for example, pros routinely break into fistfights during the course of the game, golf calls for a heck of a lot more restraint. "You never say to somebody who's your opponent that you hope he doesn't make it," says Olson. It also calls for diplomacy. "And the great thing about this game is that when an opponent hits a good shot, you compliment him on it."

It's a tradition that is closely observed by Olson and a trio of others as they compete at Arcola. For example, whenever Olson's partner, "Jimmy," a furniture company CEO, hits a good shot, the opposing players are instinctive in their response.

"Great shot, Jimmy!" one says.

"Hey, that looked like a great shot!" the other adds.

The compliments are repeated even after Jimmy hits a "birdie" (one under par), securing the lead for the Olson-Jimmy alliance. And how do the winners respond to the success? Jimmy jubilantly waves his club, en-garde style, and then he and Olson slap each other with a "high-five."

(After each good shot he makes—and there are many this morning—Jimmy shouts the words: "Miller Lite!" Eventually, Olson explains that Jimmy attributes his superb golf performance to the fact that he drank only one beer the night before, a Miller Lite. His previous game, after a two-martini evening, was a disaster.)

Bad shots, by the way, require no comments at all. "You would never say to your partner, 'that was the dumbest shot I've ever seen . . .'" Olson explains. Then he glances over at a member of the opposing team, his personal attorney, and with mischievous glee, adds, "unless you happen to be a lawyer."

This foursome (the remaining member is a publishing CEO) are among the regulars who play each weekend day at Arcola. Olson, for example, comes to the club at 9:15 A.M. on Saturdays and Sundays. (On Sundays he attends 8:00 A.M. mass before playing golf.) Foursomes are formed pickup-style; partnerships are based on an even mix of handicaps. Olson's handicap is 10. He notes that there's no protocol among employees of different rank within a particular company, "about not wanting to play with somebody or wanting to."

There is an abundance of good-ol'-boy joshing among the guys. For example, one of them mentioned that Olson is the only member of Arcola to have a pond named after him—for hitting so many balls into it. "We really get on each other, constantly putting each other down and kidding," says Olson, pausing for a moment before adding: "It comes out of real affection." Walking from hole to hole, one of these male bonders sometimes tosses an arm around another's shoulders.

When Olson is asked how many golf clubs he belongs to, a couple of the guys crack up.

"You just asked the right question," says one.

"There's really two questions," says another. "How many clubs does he belong to and how many clubs does he belong to where the members like him."

The answer to the original question is that Frank Olson belongs to eight clubs. "But I'm embarrassed about that," he adds. In addition to Arcola, there's one in Florida, three in Maine (where Olson spends summer weekends), one in Virginia (near his wife's family home), one in California (near his family's home), and he belongs to Pine Valley Golf Club in southern New Jersey, which many consider the best in the world.

But Olson may be something of an anomaly among CEOs. He plays more often than most corporate chiefs and has

SHOP TALK

How much of a CEO's leisure time is spent with work colleagues?

Time	% of Respondents
None	20.2%
1–10%	59.5%
11–25%	14.2%
26–50%	2.8%
> 50%	1.1%
no ans	2.0%

managed to weave the sport into the tapestry of his life. For instance, through Arnold Palmer, who does advertising for Hertz, Olson has become acquainted with several pros. He regularly attends golf outings hosted by the publishers of *Time, Newsweek, Sports Illustrated,* and the like. Hertz, too, sponsors tournaments. Ordinarily, he plays with friends. But that doesn't stop him from calling up a fellow CEO golfer when he's in the same neighborhood. For example, if he's at his Maine retreat and wants to hit, he'll call up former Eaton Corporation Chairman E. Mandell DeWindt, who owns a home nearby in New Hampshire.

Olson took up golf when he outgrew baseball. He prefers it over such macho pursuits as hunting and fishing, he says, "because I don't enjoy killing things." Then he moves aside a red oak leaf with his club as he readies to make a putt, feet apart, knees slightly bent. It is a clear morning and the sunshine plays brilliantly on the expanse of tidy greenery that seems to stretch clear out to the Manhattan skyline. A swing. The ball travels smoothly and stops just short of the hole.

Fishing #1: Making the Fishing Scene at April Point

First let us say, there's fishing and then there's April Point. The former can be done in virtually any stream or pond, with a rod and reel, some bait, perhaps a rowboat. For the latter, we take a seaplane over evergreens and bays 100 miles north of Vancouver, British Columbia, to a place called Quathiaski Cove.

Still wearing our city clothes, we step out of the craft and onto a series of docks. The scene is idyllic; a collection of knotty-pine buildings with lots of windows meant to capture the abundant beauty: the pink sunset, the shimmering sea, the totem pole, zooming eagles, cavorting killer whales.

Around us is a wharf that feels more like a plaza, populated, as it is, by young fishing guides and corporate types who *look* like they're corporate types, even though they're dressed in the same fishing garb as the guides.

The plaza is bounded on one side by the room in which our catch will be registered, logged on computer, flash frozen and packaged. On another side is the dining room with its well-stocked bar, huge stone fireplace, requisite mounted salmon. Nearby are the suites and cabins, where the house-

"You don't have to touch it at all if you don't want to. Just reel it in."

–Dennis Washington, owner and chairman of Washington Corporations.

keeper will turn down our sheets and place a chocolate on our pillow each evening.

This is how CEOs prefer to fish for salmon.

The focal point of the April Point plaza is the fish scale. On any afternoon or early evening from April through October, proud executive fishermen and their low-key guides can be seen posing contentedly beside large, dead, tail-end-up chinook or spring salmon.

The Peterson family, which has owned and managed this place for 45 years, wants its guests to catch the biggest fish possible, or at least thoroughly enjoy the experience trying. So for an all-inclusive $395 per day, they provide the finest in everything.

Let us begin with the incidental. Say you're flying commercial into Campbell River, the town across the bay. April Point will send a limo to pick you up for the 15-minute ferry ride. Or, it's your birthday. The lodge will send a opera-performing waitress over to your table to sing "Happy Birthday." Or, you're a VIP, such as a corporate chief or a movie star. The lodge staff will do some detective work—discreetly ask your friends—to determine your preferred wine. Then, you're likely to do as Petersen Publications chairman Bob (no relation to April Point's Petersons) Petersen did after scanning the wine list. He looked up at his waitress and exclaimed: "Hey, how did you know William Hill Cabernet Sauvignon was my favorite wine?"

April Point president Eric Peterson, the easy-going son of the late founder Phil Peterson, gives the impression that he would stop at nothing to make his guests enjoy their stay. But he's also pretty darn modest. "My parents just established a good reputation and we're simply trying to enhance it," he says.

The real lure of April Point, of course, are the salmon that feed in the chilly local waters and spawn in the nearby Campbell River, establishing this locale as one of the best of several competing "Salmon Capitals of the World". Without those fish, this enchanted establishment would be just another waterfront escape. So to ensure that a healthy supply will be on hand for years to come (and to reverse some of the impact of pollution and commercial fishing nets), April Point will release 300,000 spring salmon this year.

More than that, though, the lodge offers its famous $50-an-hour guides, nearly 60 of them. Most are good-natured local young men (*Mademoiselle* magazine called this place the "Valley of the Men"). The best guides are booked up for a year in advance, and even an average one is proficient at navigating the tricky currents, explaining water depths, telling a fisherman client when to reel in, when to reel out, and cleaning the catch. After all, why should a CEO fisherman be expected to know such things?

"If you don't understand fishing, at least you'll catch a fish," testifies Dennis Washington, chairman of Washington Corporations, the Missoula, Montana–based conglomerate that bought Anaconda Copper's Butte mines. With the help of April Point's guides, he says, "You can be a good fisherman without being a good fisherman." Washington, it should be noted, likes this spot so much that he spends the majority of his summer weekends here, living on his 142-foot Atessa, docked in the April Point marina, shuttling in the corporate Falcon back to Montana on Monday mornings.

This is where former CBS chairman William Paley came for nearly four decades. Weyerhaeuser Corporation leases one of several waterfront houses on the property for the fishing season, which it uses to entertain customers, with chairman George Weyerhaeuser occasionally stopping up to make the fishing scene. James River Corporation usually leases seven suites here for the season. This was one of John Wayne's favorite haunts; the Duke was known for raising a characteristic ruckus. Bob Hope and Bing Crosby fished here. Actress Angela Lansbury fishes here, too. The guest list includes Zellerbachs and Kaisers and scores of others with important last names.

April Point keeps a computerized record of every catch made by its guests, high-powered or not. Generally, any spring salmon weighing less than 10 pounds is tossed back. But fishermen who catch springs weighing 30 pounds or more (while in a rowboat, with artificial lures, and with no more than a 20-pound test line) qualify for membership in the Tyee Club of British Columbia. Members of this elite, 55-year-old organization receive a small book—something on the order of the social register—that lists their names, addresses, the dates on which they caught their Tyee, and the name of the guide who assisted.The light-gray-haired, 50-year-old Eric Pe-terson, who worked as a guide in his youth, jokingly calls the Tyee Club of April Point "maybe the only club in Canada you can't buy your way into."

Technically speaking, he's right. But by paying for one of those guides, it could be argued, a CEO fisherman undoubt-edly increases his odds of getting in. "A good guide," says Canadian fishing columnist and author George Gruenfeld, "becomes a knowledgeable buddy, he's the friend that's been there before and now is taking you along." Sure, not *all* CEOs who are hooked on this sport let their guides do everything from baiting the hook to bonking the catch over the head with a little wooden club. But it's partly the possibility of delegating those generally unpleasant tasks, as well as the guides' expertise, that attracts CEOs to places such as April Point.

The day of fishing here typically begins with some coffee and muffins, home-baked by April Point matriarch Phyllis Peterson, age 79. The CEO guest (and, increasingly, his wife) steps into a 15- to 17-foot Boston Whaler with outboard ma-rine engine—April Point boasts the world's largest fleet of these fiberglass vessels.

A first-timer with visions of solitude will likely be surprised once he realizes that most of the boats—even those from neighboring lodges catering to the beer-and-pretzel clien-tele—all pretty much hang around together, wherever the fish are biting for the moment. Yes, it's practically gunwale-to-gunwale out on the passage, so much so that if guide or CEO wanted to, say, relieve himself without drawing undue attention, he'd have to make a little side trip to do it. Maybe there *is* something to be said for coughing up the $2000 a day to charter a helicopter to more remote spots. (After all, four fisherman can be squeezed in.)

But either way, whether one sticks with the crowd or forks over the dough for the seclusion, there's the unspeakable delight of getting a hit. First, feeling that little tug on the line. Then, excitedly matching wits with the fish of one's dreams. The joy of imagining the extensive proportions and later catching glimpses of even an average salmon as it dances frantically on the water. Fighting the fish. Landing it. It's a high.

And to commemorate a first April Point catch, guide instantly presents fisherman with a small lapel pin depicting a fish; then, if the CEO bothered to ask the lodge to pack some champagne in with the picnic lunch, a high-seas toast is in order.

It's amazing how a respectable 22-pounder can transform an otherwise droll corporate chief into something approaching an exuberant five-year-old. Back at the plaza, April Point staffers and others often gather at the scale to gawk and congratulate the lucky guest as he poses before the unlucky fish.

And the folks who run April Point have a solution to the age-old problem of what to do with a first-class catch, the old stuffing-versus-eating debate. Fishermen here can have their fish and eat it, too.

To preserve your catch for posterity, and in a method that is much more highbrow than regular old mounting, the lodge employs a Japanese artist who makes an elaborate, touched-up imprint of your fish according to the ancient Japanese art of Gyo Taku. So after the fish gets oohed-and-aahed over at the scale, it is carried to a small table near the gift shop, where the Japanese artist (who doubles as a guide) coats it with black ink, carefully spreads a stretch of fabric over it, later highlighting the fins, eyes and other parts with ink of various colors. The Gyo Taku mementos, suitable for framing, cost about $150.

Later, the fish will be either flash-frozen and shipped home or preserved in cans at a nearby cannery. April Point charges $1.05 a can for "fresh" salmon, $1.45 a can if you want it smoked first. Either way there's an added bonus: The labels bear the name of the guest who made the catch. Or they'll make lox out of your catch for about $1.35 a pound.

What a nice little souvenir for friends, subordinates, chauffeurs!

On the wall in the mahogany bar of the Pohoqualine Fish Association in Pennsylvania's Pocono mountains, there's an old cartoon. It depicts a geezer suited up and poised to fish in a trout stream, with his properly uniformed butler talking into a telephone mounted on a nearby tree. He says: "Hello, Upstream. You may release the trout now."

Fishing #2: Fly-fishing in High Style at Pohoqualine

The image sums up the atmosphere here at one of the nation's more exclusive, yet least known, private fishing clubs. The feeling one gets is that little has really changed since the 1890s, when a group of upper-crust Philadelphia lawyers formed the association by buying up nearly 5,000 acres, thereby controlling access to a large stretch of the trout-abundant McMichaels Creek. The private club has sold off more than half the acreage to the U.S. Department of Interior since then, but there are still eleven and a half miles of creek available only to the club's 60 members and their guests. Other changes can be counted on one hand: There are now plumbing, heating and women. Even the pancake recipe has been around since day one.

Pohoqualine permits only fly-fishing (although children may fish with barbless hooks on the spring-fed pond), and most of the members tie their own flies from deer hide, raccoon whiskers and feathers—with advice from the club's stream biologists, who know what particular insects are being consumed by the fish at any given time.

This place typifies the semi-secret private fishing clubs that are so popular among chief executive officers looking to get away from it all with only the right kind of people. The clubs are holdovers from the 19th century, and the one that's reputed to have the highest concentration of CEOs is the Restigouche Salmon Club, of Metapedia, Quebec.

With an undisclosed roster limited to only 29 members (generally about half of them American, half Canadian), Restigouche takes advantage of a Canadian law that bestows fishing rights to the pre-1884 owners of waterfront property. Since the Restigouche Salmon Club dates back to 1880, its extensive land holdings ensure that only its members and their guests (and nobody else, not even locals) can fish a 40-miles-plus stretch of the Restigouche River, which forms the border between the provinces of Quebec and New Brunswick. Members, who go there for Atlantic salmon, have their choice of three lodges in which to stay. They can sleep in either of the provinces.

Back at Pohoqualine, the lodge is a spanking clean, whitewashed, three-story building virtually inches from a country road. It had been a hotel since the 1830s and was a stagecoach stop before that. The original deed, from William Penn himself, is framed and hangs, somewhat informally, on a coat hook outside of the lodge dining room. There's a point to this loyalty to history: Pohoqualine's dedication to the past has helped it maintain an intoxicating bygone-era atmosphere, something that makes this place a clandestine haven for refugees from the complicated demands of the 20th century.

So when he was chairman of Scott Paper Company until 1983, Charles Dickey would come here to fly fish, because it "totally gets you away from everything," he says, "and it's a game of skill, too." The weekend after he announced plans to lay off 1,600 people as part of the restructuring of SmithKline Beckman, chairman Henry Wendt took his wife and daughter here. Out on the crystal-clear creek, among the mountain laurel and far from boisterous interlopers, a CEO can recharge in peace. (The fish? They're not biting like they once did, although the club hatches and releases annually.)

TO ARMS OR NOT TO ARMS
More than half of the CEOs responding own a firearm
Shotgun 41%
Rifle 32%

Inside the old-fashioned locker house, a separate white building with wide-plank floors, there are large painted-white, wooden lockers, many of which are adorned with long boots hanging upside down. Some of the lockers bear business cards that identify owners; for instance, there's a locker belonging to someone named Duffield Ashmead III, a Philadelphia attorney. There's a captain's chair in which members pull off their waders, and on the wall are a few framed memorials: the last fly cast by Charles Wetherill, the last cast of Wm. T. Elliot.

The members here tend to be on the elderly side (a bottle of antacid laxative is prominently on display in the bar men's room) and cultivate a great interest in memorializing each other's final fishing excursions. It doesn't take a visitor long to learn, for instance, that Joseph Wharton Lippincott's last cast took place in August, 1976, when the gentleman was 90 years old.

As an increasing number of these elderly members depart Pohoqualine, the club reportedly finds itself hurting for new blood (of members, not fish). But its people are unwilling to lower membership standards or to halt scrupulous background checks; they apparently reject many who try to join.

For his part, former Scott Paper chairman Dickey learned about Pohoqualine shortly after moving to Philadelphia. At a reception, he found himself discussing his fly-fishing hobby with a member of the club; five years later, he became a member. "The waiting list is quite long," he explains. (But maybe the club was waiting to see how he fared at Scott before receiving him.) Today, Dickey fishes at Pohoqualine two or three times a year. He also ventures out to other, nonprivate places to fish, depending on what he's looking to catch.

In the first 70 years of Pohoqualine's existence, women weren't routinely welcomed. (An exception was the time a member brought his bride here, probably off-season, for a weekend honeymoon. The room the newlyweds stayed in, the only one with a double bed, still is referred to as the "bridal suite.") Now, if a male member dies, and if his widow is generally well liked, she will be invited to join. Otherwise, the deceased member's initiation fee is turned over to his estate. (The amount required in initiation fee, annual dues and room rates are well-guarded secrets. If you have to ask, this place is probably not for you.)

Throughout the decades that this was a stag escape for well-connected Philadelphians, the men had a favorite Saturday night activity. They'd position their bodies on large metal serving trays and slide down the stairway, out the front door, across the porch and onto the road. Sometimes they'd toss small objects at an old, abandoned store that once existed across the road, hoping to break its windows.

Such shenanigans are rare now. On a typical weekend night these days, most folks will play cards in the bar or sit around reading in the low-ceilinged club room before retiring to bed. The 26 sleeping rooms are sparsely furnished, institution-style, with white-washed bureaus, simple green blankets folded at the foot of metal beds. Bathrooms, also of the bare-bones variety, are shared. It's hard to believe that this simple, charming retreat is in the same *county* as resorts that feature heart-shaped tubs, or, the latest in local decadence, Jacuzzis in the shape of champagne glasses.

Among the few nonfishing indulgences available are the elaborate meals. If the cook prepares, say, a leg of lamb for lunch, she'll have it delivered to Camp Alice, a little pavilion out in the woods. And members will stop, mid-fish, to eat. It's traditional for male members and guests to wear jackets and ties for dinner, except during the hottest days of summer. Air conditioning is a modern convenience Pohoqualine has yet to adopt.

"It's as much a social club as it is a fishing club," says one of the members. He wants to go off the record, and that's the only way most members are willing to tell an outsider about Pohoqualine.

There's a serving tray mounted near the bar that depicts a fish caught on a hook, with the words: "Even a fish wouldn't get into trouble if he kept his mouth shut."

What's Meritor Financial Group chairman Roger Hillas's idea of Sunday morning fun?

And a Few Words About Dogs

Chasing after a pack of yip-yapping beagle hounds over soggy fields, headlong through seven-foot-tall cornfields, into nasty, waist-high brush. The sport is called "beagling," and while it may not be the most popular of CEO pastimes, it's an example of a kinky sort of diversion that is considered quite acceptable in the chief-executive universe.

Beagling as it's practiced by the Little Prospect Foot Beagles, here in the Philadelphia suburbs, is a far cry from a sport by the same name that's common in the South and parts of the Midwest. "Beagling" in those territories generally involves staying up all night with a pack of dogs and some buddies and getting stone drunk. Nor should it be confused with a more formal and more demanding relation, "fox hunting" (which those in the know simply refer to as "hunting").

Fox hunting, a passion among the chronically moneyed, is conducted on horseback and the object is to actually do the fox in. Beagling, on the other hand, is performed on foot and the point is merely to chase down—not kill—a fox. The Little Prospect group, says one of its members, "hasn't killed a fox in three generations." Members settle for watching a fox retreat into a hole.

In England, where the sport has a substantial following, most beagle packs go after hares; in some parts of the United States where jackrabbits are plentiful, those annoying critters are the prey of choice.

"This is the kind of social stuff you have in a place like this," says Hillas, as we drive past some of the few remaining honest-to-goodness estates in Blue Bell, Pennsylvania, and he identifies who lives where, or, more to the point, who *lived* where. "This would be a get-together, you might have breakfast afterward, something like that. It's our way of socializing."

It's a mid-September morning, a few weeks before the true season, and the goal of the day's exercise is to get the dogs, not to mention the "field" of humans, back in shape after about five months of not hunting.

During the season, which runs from October 1 through April 1, participants dress in traditional outfits: dark-green jackets, white shirts, *ties,* etc. On this day, Hillas wears a Rossignol T-shirt ("I forgot who gave me this"), faded brown cordoroy slacks, an old pair of running shoes. He hasn't yet shaved. It's 6:45 A.M. and later in the day the chairman of the holding company for the nation's oldest savings institution will host the christening of his infant daughter, the product of a second, late-in-life marriage.

Hillas steers his pickup down a prolonged driveway belonging to the Master of the Hunt, a delightfully juvenescent septuagenarian named Anthony Nicholas Brady Garvin, who is the retired head of the American Civilization department at the University of Pennsylvania. Tony, as he's called, has been beagling since 1932. He keeps his 30-dog pack in kennels behind his magnificent estate (members of the association share the expense of maintaining the animals).

This sport traces roots back to the days of William the Conqueror, and so it seems, do most of the participants. Even the dogs are bred scrupulously from English bloodlines. The dogs, by the way, are counted in pairs as "couples," although the singular version of the term is generally used. So if you asked Tony how many dogs his pack contains, he'd say, "fifteen couple," instead of "thirty," if you asked how many would be running today, he'd say "seven couple," instead of (that's right) "fourteen."

One by one, the dozen or so human participants arrive, somewhat bleary-eyed, at Tony's kennel. Most of them are young men who learned the sport from their fathers and mothers. (This is a mixed-gender, multiage activity.) When they load the hounds into a container area grafted onto the back of a pickup, they lift the creatures as one would a sack of rubies, not, it should be noted, using the old LBJ ear-

grabbing technique. Next, our little caravan of vehicles heads
out the long driveway and over to a collection of estates on
which the beagling will take place.

Today, the Little Prospect Foot Beagles run over wooded
hills and green valleys owned by obliging local residents,
who are, for the most part, still asleep. "It's a fun way to get
to go through all the big estates," said Hillas. Indeed, there's
that exuberant feeling—lost to childhood for most—of running freely over someone's else's property. (We used to call
it "sneaking in.")

Hillas explains that it's not easy finding willing landown-
ers for the sport. "It's the new people who won't let you.
They think you're going to come and wreck the place. The
ones that have been around know you're not gonna hurt
anything," he says. And yes, as we chase after hounds who
themselves are chasing after eau de fox, it becomes clear
that part of the reason the "whips," as we're called, are
charged with keeping dogs within a certain perimeter is to
prevent them from wandering onto tennis courts, into swimming pools, or after a neighborhood cat.

It takes a heck of a lot of running to keep up. When the
dogs howl and congregate around a hole into which a fox
has retreated ("gone to ground,") hunt master Tony exclaims, "Woolywoolywooly." That's how he communicates
that this is the scent the dogs are supposed to follow, not the
scent of rabbit or deer or poodle, for instance. Tony toots on
a small horn when he wants to keep the dogs in one place;
whips lightly crack whips to make a noise that discourages
dogs from straying.

Tony points out a fox scent to a newcomer; it smells like
a delicate skunk. Then, when the dogs are momentarily finished trailing the aroma, he'll be gently congratulatory to the
beasts. "Archie, well done," he'll say to a particular dog.
When another dog won't stop yelping even though she
should, he'll say, "That's right, Esther, you're a big noisy
dog, yes you are." There's an irony to all of this: These dogs
are bred to chase foxes but they will never be allowed to
catch one.

The dogs are using the occasion to play king of the hill.
While running and yapping, they're constantly working to
reinforce their dog hierarchy, explains Tony. The humans,

on the other hand, don't appear to have any such concern. For them, it's a marvelous excuse for getting outdoors and romping through the woods on Sunday mornings. "It's definitely more process than product," says one of the beaglers. It's also an all-weather sport; these folks let neither rain, sleet, snow, etc., keep them from running with the dogs. "In the winter," says Hillas, as he pauses to catch his breath, "when you get out there in a cold day and they get in full cry, it's quite exciting." And afterward, a nice protracted breakfast. (That's when the dogs eat, too.)

–DAVID DIAMOND

HAS LIDO
LOST HIS
LUSTER?

**SJ** BOOK OF CHIEF EXECUTIVE STYLE: "... He's on his second book now ..."

NYNEX chairman Delbert C. Staley: "In fact I read the first two chapters."

WSJBOCES: "And what happened?'

Staley: "Well, the first chapter is devoted to how great a job he did on the Statue of Liberty project."

WSJBOCES: "And what about the second chapter?"

Staley (after laughing): "The second chapter about how much he loves his kids ..."

WSJBOCES: "Did you put it away and start reading *War and Peace* or something?"

Staley (doesn't reply but laughs again): ". . . It's how much he loves his two girls."

Poor Lee, superstar.

When it comes to fan mail, he's right up there with Bruce Springsteen, the other guy people call The Boss. For a period of time following the release of his first autobiography, Chrysler's very own LeBaron watched (gleefully, one suspects) as his LPW (letters per week) hit the 1,000 mark, forcing his overworked public relations staff to work even harder, returning calls from Hollywood moguls (what student of business will ever forget his performance on *Miami Vice?*), and making speeches to the Future Farmers of America. In fact, Motor City legend has it that one of the reasons he went out and hired a driver was so he could free up commuting time to read his mail. It's a story confirmed by Tony Cervone, one of his P.R. men, who added: "He reads it all, every last letter." As if you'd expect him to say anything else.

The cover of that first book, for those who may have blocked it out, featured him sitting at his desk in a very un-chief-executively position. His hands were clasped behind his head and he looked relaxed and vulnerable, pretty much how you'd want the boss to look if you decided to invite yourself in and ask for a raise. But he also bore a self-satisfied little grin.

Sure, Detroit's Main Man has a lot to grin about. But that's probably because he hasn't given much thought to what happens to CEOs who make themselves into heroes.

Other chief executives stop liking them.

Fact is, America's bestselling CEO can be a legend on the assembly line and a cynosure on any showroom floor he stoops to visit, but ask your above-average chief executive what he thinks of him and the response is likely to begin with the words: "Can we go off the record?"

"I guess you could intellectually argue that personifying a corporation works to sell product or build morale to create an image," says the painfully polite John H. Bryan, Jr., chairman of Sara Lee. Nevertheless, regarding America's Best-Known Fired Executive, Bryan adds: "He's bombastic. He has an opinion about everything, He's often wrong but never in doubt." But he goes on to praise the Chrysler head for "great presence" and "feeling for what he's saying."

"His recognition," says Hertz chairman Frank Olson, "far exceeds his contributions."

Jealousy, you suspect?

Maybe a CEO or two does secretly yearn to be a household word, which perhaps accounts for some of the behind-the-scenes cattiness. But chief executives are quick to point to members of their exclusive fraternity whose accomplishments should overshadow those of the Chrysler chief. That is, CEOs who deserve credit and yet are unknown to readers of *People* magazine.

For instance, Donald Peterson's spectacular turnaround of Ford is considered by many business leaders to be a far more impressive feat than You-Know-Who's government-assisted salvage of Chrysler. Yet no one, except perhaps Mrs. Peterson and a deserving few others, has access to a bare-bottomed baby photo of the Ford Motor Company chairman. (Come to think of it, Nicola and Antoinette's little nine-month-old does look kind of cute in that photo opposite page 174 of Book One.)

While Peterson himself agrees that it's next to impossible to run a company without public exposure, indicating that "Greta Garbo wouldn't make it as a CEO," by and large, chief execs are not easily impressed with those among them who take the publicity business to the hilt—or who start to believe their own press.

"There's a certain amount of visibility that comes with the territory. A CEO has to be accessible to the media, stockholders, customers, employees, and suppliers, and needs to participate in business, educational, civic and cultural events. It's all part of the job," reasons the Ford executive. But he's one auto chief who has never developed a taste for courting the paparazzi. "As for the hoopla," he says, "I can live without it—and do."

General Motors chairman Roger Smith explains that "even smaller companies can suddenly find themselves in the limelight. And since 'a company' is such a vague and abstract idea, it's the CEO who personifies the organization. It's the CEO who gets credit or blame for what the company does, regardless of whether or not those actions are the result of his or her decision." (Possible interpretation: Don't blame me that GM's had such a rocky time!) He adds that "the larger and more visible your company is, the more hoopla surrounds your activities."

But captains of industry are quick to distinguish between those who merely represent the company, promote the company and contribute to the betterment of humanity without trying to make themselves larger than life and those who do. And among corporate chiefs who were fortunate enough to enter the world sucking a silver spoon, there tends to be an "Oh God he's not gonna bring up that dreary son of poor immigrants business again, is he?" way of responding to the those who play up humble beginnings.

Needless to say, when a CEO reads a business autobiography, he is apt to be more critical, perhaps, than even the stiffest of reviewers. For example, one chief executive who asked to be "really off-the-record" calculated that Mr. Straight Talk's first book was two thirds ego and one third vindictiveness (to Henry Ford II). After all, who will ever forget that prized line from Book One: "You had to get Henry in those moments of sobriety."

Of course there are exceptions, corporate heads who found merit in Books One and Two and who, in general, support the burgeoning CEO-as-Hero trend. But they tend to sound as if they're competing for Miss Congeniality. The truly, truly amazing Dr. Armand Hammer, chairman of Occidental Petroleum and no slacker on the exposure front, enthuses himself into a dither about Book Two (even though it eclipsed Hammer's own autobiography on the charts).

"I just finished reading his second book. I just couldn't put it down," he says. "I was traveling, but every spare moment I had I picked up the book until I finished it. But I'm a great admirer of his. I think he's the kind of a CEO that's interested in the welfare of our country and I'm a great believer in what he says about various things and I think a lot can be learned by other CEOs by reading his book."

For the most part, though, the Big I example illustrates one of the major consequences of carrying on like a movie star. Even when a corporate chief's accomplishments are considerable and even when they do have good things to say (hey, what's wrong with motherhood, apple pie, baseball, working for a living, and the like?) self-promoters risk the admiration of their peers.

Consider retired Norton Simon chairman David Mahoney—who in the 1970s was referred to by *Business Week* magazine as "the Farah Fawcett of chief executives"—what's he doing these days?

Do you still want to hire that personal flack?

Okay, so the guy acts like a car salesman. You know the type with the late-night commercials. Every TV market in the country has one. In parts of California, it's Cal Worthington and his "dog" Spot; in Nashville, until his recent retirement, it was A. H. "George" Johnson, proprietor of Star Chrysler with his memorable line, "If George says it's so, it's so!" They don't evoke images of high-toned gentility. But if he's also the CEO of a very big corporation, how do other CEOs talk about him? Quite politely.

The Gentlemanly Art of Appraisal

That's right. While highly successful CEOs who would never think of indulging in self-huckstering may cackle at The Man Behind the Mustang's behavior, they are never brazenly critical. The unwritten CEO code dictates that unless it is a corporate raider who is the object of your remarks, you say things like: "I will say he's colorful. He's controversial. I guess he's doing what he wants to do and who am I to be critical?" These well-tempered words come from Amoco chairman Richard Morrow.

Hertz chairman Olson, an exceedingly likable guy, elaborates:

"He's widely off base in his pronouncements on the economy, past the point of what's productive." But to all of this Olson adds the obligatory "although I would never want to talk negatively about him."

To support this theory further, listen to what came out of NYNEX chairman Staley's mouth virtually nanoseconds after his little chuckle over the substance of those initial two chapters of The Sequel. He says: "I'm not being critical of him, but I think there are certain times when people get the spotlight and they love the spotlight and want more of the spotlight."

And Sara Lee chairman Bryan reasons that it wasn't the fault of Detroit's Biggest Wheel himself that all this public adulation came about. "And it doesn't bother me very much because I think he's probably being very natural," he says.

OTHER RISKS OF BEING A CEO HERO

1. Strangers from Terre Haute, Indiana, will write to you asking you to set them up in the muffler business.

2. Republicans will want to draft you for the U.S. Senate. (Henry Ford ran in 1918 and lost. The inimitable Frank Perdue, in perhaps his greatest contribution ever, turned down Maryland Republicans who urged him to run.)

3. You won't be able to get a quickie divorce (or a quickie, for that matter) without *People* magazine editors treating it as a major news event.

4. Obtrusive reporters will track down your mother and hound her for her pizza recipe.

5. You won't be able to nod off in a business meeting without it getting reported in another CEO Hero's book. (As T. Boone Pickens, Jr., detailed Armand Hammer's snooze in *Boone.)*

6. Nobody will ever be able to be your successor at the company. Who could ever match up?

7. Corporate gadflies will hound you at your company's annual meeting, insisting that you tell them how much time you actually spend on company business.

8. You may find yourself, as did Mister Lee, making the top ten of *Good Housekeeping* magazine's annual Most Admired Men poll, in the company of Jerry Falwell, Billy Graham, Pat Robertson and Tom Selleck.

—DAVID DIAMOND

These and similar remarks bear out a final reason why Our Hero isn't winning any popularity contests among CEOs. He's broken the gentlemanly ethic dictating that one corporate mugwump simply doesn't malign another.

–DAVID DIAMOND

A Few Words About (and Jokes by) a Self-made Hero

Waiting four hours to see Dr. Armand Hammer is a long time. Sitting in the Occidental Petroleum headquarters lobby, 15 floors above a Wilshire Boulevard backup, there is an urge to fake it. After all, we've been keeping company with a bronze-cast bust and an almost life-size portrait of the good man—as well as a driver waiting to chauffeur some Korean businessmen the two blocks to their hotel.

A shift has ended for one pair of security guards keeping

watch on the largely self-monumental works of art, and another shift begins. One of the guards, a former Los Angeles police officer, retreats down the hallway from which public relations staffers regularly emerge reciting apologies, and he returns with a cup of coffee. He settles down on an earth-toned sofa and talks fondly of hunting elk in Wyoming. Perhaps the conversation was sparked by a display of taxidermy on the wall behind a spiral staircase leading up to the doctor's office. It is a wild boar, head separated from skin, and the plaque reads: WILD BOAR SHOT BY DR. ARMAND HAMMER IN DECEMBER 1980 AT TELKI, HUNGARY, WHILE A GUEST OF FIRST SEC-RETARY JANOS KADAR AND DEPUTY PREMIER JOZSEF MARJAI.

Suddenly, simple arithmetic leaps to mind and the realization sets in: Hammer was 82 years old when he shot that thing!

There's something lovable about this CEO hero as he sits, like a Lilliputian giant, lost in his huge chair behind an oversized, curving desk, one side of which is lined with maybe a dozen clocks depicting the time in each of the world's capitals. He appears to be floating in a sea of autographed photographs from the century's primary political heroes: Lenin, Roosevelt, Kennedy, Gorbachev. There is even Prince Charles. . . . And there is what sounds like Muzak, with or without a subliminal message telling you you are in the presence of a great man.

You've got to admire Dr. Hammer for his amazing stamina. He got up at about 5:00 A.M. Spent a couple of hours on Occidental business. Swam laps for half an hour—the man is 91!—ate breakfast in bed. Made it to the office by 9:00 A.M. It's now closing in on 7:00 P.M. and the doctor isn't missing a beat—nor nearly finished his workday. It is a few weeks after the Moscow summit (at which, for the second time, he proposed to build Moscow's first golf course) and days before the tragic explosion of an Occidental oil rig in the North Sea.

For those who don't know the Hammer story, it would make a splendid TV mini-series. Raised on New York's Lower East Side and in a small town that has become the South Bronx, Hammer managed to complete his medical training while running—and making a substantial profit from—a small pharmaceuticals business that was started by his father, a physician who was a founding member of the American Communist party.

A self-made millionaire before the age when most men even start their first job, Hammer traveled in 1921 to revolution-tattered Russia to offer medical assistance to its famine victims. He was summoned to meet with Lenin, and in a fateful one-hour session with the communist hero, was offered the first American concession to do business in the Soviet Union. He spent nine years doing everything from importing Fordson tractors to opening asbestos mines to manufacturing pencils. And in the ensuing decades, he pursued countless passions that seemed to merge business with pleasure with global politics, whether as a dealer in highbrow art, a distiller of alcohol, a breeder of cattle, a driller of oil.

The reputation Dr. Hammer seems to have among today's CEOs is as someone with incredible capacities for work, accomplishments in global affairs, and self-promotion. Oh yes, and as a world-class nag. Regarding the last two of these, there's a sweet little story circulating among chief executives and other corporate types about how Hammer arranged his first sit-down meeting with President Ronald Reagan by persuading his barber to schedule them for the same time. It's a story Oxy denies.

Sara Lee chairman Bryan calls him "pushy and aggressive and always trying to get his name in front of everything," but adds that "It's hard to criticize him because he's making contributions."

But there is an abundance of criticism. For being too close to the commies, although he clearly is a die-hard capitalist. For his propensity to blow his own horn—to the point of creating his own mythology. And, among other things, for taking credit whether or not it's due. Does the criticism ever bother him?

(Author's note: Read the following quotes with a slight Miami Beach accent. Provide for occasional throat-clearings.)

"No. I don't say I like it. I've tried to fight back. A lot of people think that I should ignore it. I don't believe in that. I think anybody that attacks me unjustly—I think that I should respond. And I have done that all my life. Fought injustice and I'm still doing that," he says.

The criticism that hurt the most, he adds, was that surrounding his 1976 guilty plea for making illegal contributions to Nixon's 1972 campaign. "I think I was unjustly attacked. I did plead guilty to a misdemeanor because I was suffering from a heart condition and my doctors told me if I faced a trial I probably never would have survived." Regarding his $3000 fine and year of probation sentence, he explained: "My lawyer said that's not any worse than a ticket for speeding."

The man who dispatched a medical team to help the victims of Chernobyl, the man who worked behind the scenes to get journalist Nicholas Daniloff released from Soviet detention, has this bit of advice for any corporate chief who pursues goals that are loftier than a mere healthy dividend. "He can't satisfy everybody. He's always bound to get people who will oppose his views and he must be prepared to take a lot of abuse. But he's got to be determined that he's not going to be thin-skinned, that he's going to take it as long as his conscience tells him that what he's doing is right."

Armand Hammer makes no secret of his two grand life goals. "One goal is to try to bring peace between the East and West," he says, adding without pause: "On that I think I've been instrumental in bringing President Reagan and Mr. Gorbachev together." When the subject of his considerable influence is raised, he does demur, saying: "I don't know whether I have any influence." But then he adds, "But I feel that I can be a bridge. I am able to shuttle back and forth whenever there is a problem. As in the case of getting the Russians to leave Afghanistan. I was fortunate in being able to know [the late Pakistani leader] Zia so well that I could get him to agree to many things. And I have the goodwill of President Reagan and of course I have the goodwill of Mr. Gorbachev and I think I was able, because of that, to be instrumental in getting the problem solved."

His other major goal is to live to see a cure for cancer, and to that end he has contributed a minor fortune to cancer research; he also chairs the President's Cancer Panel.

"When I get those done and when I get Occidental stock up to $100 a share, I'll decide whether I should retire or whether I should still keep on until I reach 100," he said.

Where does he get such determination? "When I was a young student in college I used to read every book I could get my hands on that had to do with character building," says Dr. Hammer. "I read every Horatio Alger book." He laughs. "I guess lots of boys have done that. But I'd also go to the library and I'd look up books on how to improve yourself, how to improve your mind. Then, later in life, Dale Carnegie became a client of the Hammer Galleries and I used to enjoy talking to him. I liked his ideas. Then I knew Dr. [Norman Vincent] Peale very well. I was very fond of attending his sermons and of his positive thinking."

Maybe it's because of such inspiring influences that Dr. Hammer tends to have nice things to say about just about everybody. His autobiography limits its snideness to a mere few: chiefly his second wife (he's had three), his father's opponents, and Josef Stalin. (There is also his adopted niece. After the death of his brother Victor, Hammer sued the estate to get back $666,000 he had lent him for medical costs. This resulted in the cutoff of nursing home payments for his sister-in-law. His niece, who protested, was threatened with eviction from her home. He described her in a deposition as "ungrateful.")

When it comes to his heroes, Hammer writes most glowingly of President Franklin Roosevelt.

He wrote: "In FDR were to an unparalleled degree, all the most desirable qualities of the great statesman. Nobody could equal the speed of his mind, the warmth of his character and the charm of his personality, and to these attributes was added an unmatched capacity for decisive executive action."

It's easy to conclude that those are some of the traits for which Dr. Hammer would like best to be remembered. But we aren't so sure. And while one observer of the Hammer phenomenon suggested he is lobbying for sainthood, and another suggested that maybe the Nobel Prize folks could find it in their hearts to award him the Nobel Prize for Peace, just so he could retire, we subscribe to a different theory.

The driver waiting for his Koreans (who the previous day had ended their meetings and left without telling him) revealed that the doctor is known to interrupt a meeting just to relate a late-breaking joke. In our conversation about his international diplomacy, he detours momentarily to toss one in: "Before the first summit, Gorbachev told me he didn't want to meet Reagan. He said, 'Your president wants war. He calls us the evil empire.' I said, 'Mr. Gorbachev, you're mistaken, that was during an election.'" And yes, in his autobiography, he does take a few breaks from describing his various history-making roles to interject a quip or two.

So as he sits there (American flag to his rear), palms grasping the edge of his desk and looking out through glasses that seem too big, he suddenly resembles another Southern Californian in his nineties. And it hits: He's the George Burns of CEOs.

To test the theory, we ask him to tell his favorite jokes. Wouldn't you know it but there's suddenly a regenerative glow to his face. He assumes an actor's voice. As he talks, he lifts his palms from the desk to gesture in time with the jokes' cadence. And at the punchlines, he looks up. His eyes sparkle with mischievous glee. Here, then, is an exclusive. Dr. Armand Hammer's two favorite jokes. (Again: read with a Miami Beach accent): "People talk about my longevity. Well, the other night I was at the Ford Theater gala, where I'm one of the governors. During the intermission I had a chance to talk to President Reagan. I told him about Churchill, when he was ninety, the same age that I was, that a young officer said 'Mr. Churchill, I congratulate you on being ninety, I hope to see you when you're one hundred.' Churchill looked up and said, 'There's no reason why you shouldn't, you look pretty good to me.' I told that to Reagan and he said, 'I'm going to top that.' He said, [clears throat in dramatic preparation] 'A man who's ninety saw a friend of his who said, "I want to throw a party to commemorate your father." So the man said, "My father? Who told you he was dead? He's very much alive. He's a hundred and ten but he's still alive." His friend said, "Well, I'd still like to throw a party and commemorate your grandfather." He says, "Who told you my grandfather was dead? He's a hundred and thirty, and what's more, he's gonna marry a young girl." His friend said, "Well, that's wonderful, I'm glad," he says, "to think that he wants to marry at a hundred and thirty!" The man said, "Who said he *wants* to marry?" ' "

So Who Are CEOs' Heroes? THEIR FATHERS

Ask a CEO who his hero is and he's likely to wax sentimental about his father. That's one of the nice things CEOs have in common with small boys.

University of Wisconsin psychology professor Frank Farley has asked the hero question of thousands of people of vary-

STRAIGHT FROM ANTOINETTE'S KITCHEN– The K-Car King (or was it his ghostwriter/) wrote: "My mother makes the greatest pizzas in the country, if not the world." So when *Philadelphia* magazine dispatched writer Laurence R. Stains to Allentown, Pennsylvania, to sleuth around for Antoinette, the first thing he did was to ask her for that recipe. Writer Stains found the "Maker of the Maker of Chrysler" (the magazine's resulting article headline) living in the nice but not intimidating stone house in which she's lived for decades. She invited the writer in and revealed the following:

"I start from scratch. I make my own dough. My own tomatoes. Before, I used to can my own. Now, no more. But you take tomatoes and make a sauce that's your own way. Good sauce. I put a little garlic, a little oregano, a little olive oil. That's my recipe, really."

Who says a CEO's mother has to be as forthright as her son?

POSTSCRIPT In the Philadelphia Free Library, in search of every last published mention of Lee Iacocca, we crawl out of the business Reference Room after a long afternoon of work and come face-to-face with a poster on the door. At the top of the poster are the words GET A HEAD START AT THE LIBRARY. At the bottom is the word READ. And in the middle is none other than Iacocca himself, posing with an automotive manual (not reading it) looking straight out at us: (Just above that poster is one featuring a forlorn-looking dog among a pile of puppies and the message PREVENT A LITTER—SPAY OR NEUTER YOUR PET.)

A library regular takes notice of my special attention to the poster and says: "I hear he's on vacation now. He's over in Italy making wine."

ing ages and walks of life and the response often is the same: When it comes to male heroes, Dear Old Dad tops the list. And the percentage of people who cite their father as a personal hero remains relatively constant, particularly in the two age groups with whom Farley has conducted the vast majority of his research: five-to-eight-year olds and young adults.

Farley finds it significant that chief executives—who, as a group, are highly accomplished and worldly—often select the same candidate as kids who don't know all that many folks. "These people [chief executives] have done so much you'd think they'd look at other people of great accomplishment. So they must see in their fathers the qualities they admire," he said.

But, maybe it's *because* they have come to know so many individuals that they ultimately select their fathers. NYNEX chairman Delbert C. Staley has met thousands of potential

And we know Myles Martel is right.

Martel is a communications consultant, a member of the profession that trains business leaders and politicians to adopt a particular style. His most famous client was President Reagan, whom he coached before the debates with President Carter. When Martel watches a videotape of a CEO delivering a speech, he's capable of pinpointing the subtle yet sophisticated techniques the executive employs to produce a desired effect. He thinks Iacocca will be a hero to the general public for quite a long time.

When Martel read *Iacocca,* he saw "lots of common ground techniques." (Example: the constant reference to immigrant parents, the constant reference to early struggles and discrimination, the constant reference to getting fired ...) He saw a strong motivational message. He saw an executive who wants to demonstrate that he is not typical in terms of corporate America. He saw an executive who could demonstrate a genuine interest in employees, customers and the public. He saw an executive who emphasizes his energy and his courage and his philanthropy.

Iacocca's work on the Statue of Liberty project strengthened his image as a public citizen, according to Martel. It emphasized his humble roots. It rounded out his image as a hero, expanding it from the corporate to the public. "Iacocca fashioned the hero image over a number of years with a very strong, very publicly appealing style," said Martel. "It's definitely a very planned kind of thing."

As a result, even if Chrysler stock takes a nose dive, even if corporate profits dry up, there's one consolation: Lots of people are going to remember Lee Iacocca.

–DAVID DIAMOND

heroes over the decades, but he still worships his late father, who spent 30 years working as a laborer repairing sulfuric acid–damaged rail cars at Du Pont's East Chicago, Indiana, plant.

"I think like many youngsters, I suppose you had heroes that were athletes. At my age Babe Ruth and Lou Gehrig were heroes. As I went in the Army in World War II, I looked up to people like Eisenhower and MacArthur and Patton, people who turned out to be heroes at the moment during trying times. As you get older you tend to look back and realize that the true heroes are those that you look up to day in and day out, not just on special occasions, who taught you some of the basic qualities that are required of you as a CEO," says Staley.

General Motors' chairman Roger Smith cites former GM **THEIR PREDECESSORS** chairman Tom Murphy.

BLOWING IT
CEOS WHO CLIMBED TO THE TOP OF THE CORPORATE LADDER, THEN FELL OFF

1976: CBS president Arthur R. Taylor openly disagrees with chairman William Paley, tries to shape the company in his own image, and is forced to resign.

1977: As chairman and president of RCA Corporation, Anthony L. Conrad informs his company's board of directors that he had failed to file personal income tax returns to the IRS for the years 1971 through 1975. He is immediately forced to resign.

1978: Jerome Castle is forced to resign as chairman, president and chief executive officer of Penn-Dixie Industries, months before a grand jury indicts him and two associates in connection with the sale of Florida swampland to Penn Dixie for $5.8 million. He is later convicted in federal court of conspiracy, mail fraud and wire fraud for his part in a plot to defraud the cement and steel producer of more than $3 million. He was sentenced to 15 months at the "correctional center" at Eglin Air Force Base, Florida, and fined $12,000.

1980: Three years after CBS chairman William Paley confers on company president John D. Backe the title of chief executive (a title to which Paley has clung since 1947), Backe exerts his independence and indicates that he, and not Paley, is the real power at CBS. He is forced to resign.

1981: Ashland Oil Company chairman Orin E. Atkins leaves his company after repeatedly wrangling with the company's other directors. Later, U.S. Customs agents surreptitiously videotape him as he instructs an associate to sell two confidential Ashland memos to Iran for $600,000. (Iran's government was involved in a longstanding suit against Ashland.) In 1988, he is arrested and charged with stealing internal documents as part of what the company called an alleged conspiracy to sell the material to Iran. Late in that year, the U.S. government dismissed the arrest warrant, but the case is being investigated by the U.S. Attorney's office, Atkins's attorney says.

1986: Although CBS had fought off eight takeover attempts—including Ted Turner's much-publicized raid—and the board of directors made it clear to chairman Tom Wyman that it wanted the company to remain independent, Wyman waltzes into a September board meeting and asks the board for approval to explore a merger with Coca-Cola. It's his last meeting as a CBS employee.

1989: Robert Abboud gets yet one more chance to blow it. As chairman of First Chicago Bank in the mid-1970s, his clampdown on lending turned out to be a losing strategy; his abrasive style with the bank's officers earned him the nickname "Rude Abboud"; his feuding with management and such powerful customers as the Texas Hunt brothers and the Chicago Pritzkers not only got him fired in 1980, but made him the only First Chicago chairman in the bank's 124-year history to have his portrait removed from the 57th floor boardroom. He quickly resurfaced in Los Angeles at Occidental Petroleum, where chairman Armand Hammer named him president, chief operating officer and heir apparent. Abboud helped Oxy acquire IBP, the beef processor, and Cities Service Oil Company, but squabbles with the redoubtable Hammer led to Abboud's ouster in 1984. After three years of consulting, and keeping in touch with his banking sources, Abboud resurfaces again, this time as head of a group of investors that is buying up Houston's troubled First City Bancorp of Texas—and banking on an FDIC bailout. As of press time, Abboud once again is a banking CEO.

—DAVID DIAMOND

Ford CEO Donald E. Peterson admires former Ford CEO Henry Ford II. *Time*'s J. Richard Munro names company founder Henry Luce and former chairman Andrew Heiskell.

NYNEX chief Staley says that after his father, his heroes are former AT&T chairmen Charlie Brown and John De-Butts.

Such a reaction is not necessarily a public relations ploy, suggests psychologist Farley. "These are probably people who might have been mentors, who helped them out and for whom they have a lot of positive feelings." Indeed, perhaps that's partly what Peterson is trying to communicate when he says, "Henry Ford II was a world statesman who brought his own brand of personal leadership to Ford Motor Company and the worldwide automotive industry. He was a great force in business and I miss his candor, his humor, his wisdom and his dedicated pursuit of progress and fairness." (For an opposing view, read *Iacocca*.)

STATESMEN

"If I had to name one hero it would be Winston Churchill," said Drew Lewis, chairman of Union Pacific. "He made the greatest contribution to the free world of anybody in the 20th century and maybe in the history of mankind."

PEOPLE WHO HAVE OVERCOME ADVERSITY

Says Richard Morrow, CEO of Amoco: "The real heroes are the people who you see every day in the Loop, people who have lost their sight yet they manage to make their way into work every day. The real heroes are not people in the business community, they are people who have overcome adversity in this world. Or they are the people who risk their lives for others, the firemen and policemen."

BASEBALL MANAGERS

When asked about his heroes, General Motors chairman Roger Smith came up with Sparky Anderson of the Detroit Tigers. "He's someone who can take a group of talented individuals, with different and sometimes clashing personalities, and forge them into a smooth, winning team. And he does it with grace and good humor."

NOT OTHER BUSINESS LEADERS

If you've noticed something missing in this assemblage of heroes, you're right. Where (except for predecessors) are the businessmen?

Amazing as it sounds, ask a CEO who his business heroes are and he's likely to laugh in your face. Literally. That's what *Time* chairman Munro did. He chuckled and then he said: "maybe I take my heroes more seriously than you take your heroes."

"Heroic is a word that denotes a very rare breed of individual and I guess I look at heroism in terms of things like courage and patriotism and gallantry. I guess I have trouble equating heroism to business," he says. Munro swiftly points out the irony that he's in a business that does its share to create heroes out of businessfolk.

Question: "What about Armand Hammer?"

Answer: "Dr. Hammer gets an awful lot of respect for what he's accomplished but you're gonna have a tough time convincing me any American businessman's a hero," repeats Munro.

That's roughly the same as the response from Drew Lewis, who says he has no heroes in business, although there are people whom he respects and from whom he learns. Admittedly impatient, the Union Pacific chairman and former Transportation Secretary explains that he tries to learn patience by studying the behavior of American Express's James Robinson and Ford's Donald Peterson.

–DAVID DIAMOND

THE ADVENTURES
OF EMILY
POST-FEMINIST

Katharine Gra-
ham, chief executive officer of *The Washington Post* Company, refuses to discuss it.
Elizabeth Ortenberg, who headed Liz Claiborne, her own clothing manufacturing company, would not give interviews on the
subject. Ellen Hancock, president of IBM's
communications division, instructs her
spokesperson to turn down any reporter fool-
ish enough to ask about it.

What subject so offends these executives?
You might call it the F-question. It's sexual,
but not pornographic. It's personal, but also a
matter of public record. You see, these top
executives aren't just people, they're females.
And nothing ticks them off more than being
asked what it feels like to be a "female" chief
executive.

*The Problem
That Would
Rather Have
No Name*

At the beginning, in the mid- and late 1970s, business-women didn't mind the F-question. Those who found themselves staring down from on high in a corporation often enjoyed talking about being pioneers in their respective fields. But now the question of what it's like to be a woman seems hopelessly passé, and they're fed up. "C'mon guys!" they seem to be saying. "It's been a long time now—aren't you sick of asking me if I enjoy being a girl? Ask me about my job, not my gender."

Yet it is unlikely that business reporters will become totally gender-blind anytime in the next decade. Women who run very large public companies are rarer than happily married movie stars. Of the *Fortune*-500 largest industrial corporation CEOs, only two, Graham and Ortenberg, are female. Only one of *Fortune*'s Service 500, Marion O. Sandler of Golden West Financial Savings and Loan in Oakland, California, is a woman. Liz Claiborne Ortenberg started her business as an entrepreneurial fashion designer. Graham took over *The Washington Post* Company after her husband's death. And Sandler runs her company with her husband. So far, no female has actually come up through the ranks of a *Fortune*-500 company to become a CEO. Who can blame reporters for being fascinated by pioneers?

But it is only a matter of time before women reach the CEO level in large companies they didn't start, inherit or don't share with a spouse. Citing the influx of women into MBA programs in the mid-1970s, Harvard Business School professor Regina Herzlinger optimistically predicts that there will be 20 to 30 female big-company CEOs by 1997. "It's a matter of number, not gender," says Herzlinger. "The women are in the pipeline."

Who will be the first woman to break the tinted glass barriers to the CEO's limo? From which industry will she emerge? Will she go down in history with Amelia Earhart, Babe Didrikson Zaharias, Sally Ride, Florence Nightingale, Elizabeth Blackwell, Nellie Bly, and Geraldine Ferraro? Will she star in her company's television ads? Most importantly, will high school girls be rushing to buy her ghosted, best-selling autobiography?

No one can answer these questions with absolute certainty. But we can speculate. And it needn't be just idle speculation. All across the country, there are women waiting to be crowned the first genuine Ms. *Fortune*-500 CEO. Some won't make the final cut. They'll settle for senior vice-president or chief financial officer or other executive equivalents of Ms. Congeniality.

But one will be the first.

We can't predict who it will be. But experts on the subject have been able to piece together a composite sketch. From their observations—and in an effort to examine the anticipated personality traits of the first genuine Ms. *Fortune*-500 CEO, we've created a fictional personage.

Let's call her Emily Post-Feminist.

Headhunters, business professors, female CEOs of smaller companies, and top female executives on the CEO track themselves believe they know what Emily will be like, and, perhaps, more importantly, what she "won't" be like. They have been so specific in their comments that Emily has taken on a life of her own, and, like all upscale citizens on the cusp of the nineties, her chief characteristics can be boiled down into a trendy curriculum vitae.

Pretend the following is a scotch ad.

Job: CEO, FemFace International, a beauty and consumer products corporation with $3 billion in revenues.

Emily Post-Feminist, First Female CEO

Education: undergraduate degree in history, Radcliffe College; law degree from Georgetown University.

Age: 47

Personal: married, one adopted daughter.

Sports: tennis, skiing, running, horseback riding.

Hobbies: cooking, reading.

Cars: Jaguar and Jeep (Jaguar because of its sleek handleability; Jeep so the nanny can transport Katie to various stimulating activities).

Hired help: Housekeeper, nanny, gardener, personal shoppers.

Vacation home: In Aspen, Colorado.

Number of years with company: 15 (started at Procter & Gamble).

Favorite interview quote: "I think you just have to have drive—it doesn't matter if you're male or female or purple or green. I've always felt that being a woman is an advantage. I never really felt discriminated against. I really love what I do."

Emily's profile came about with the cooperation of the many women whose names surface repeatedly in those almost-annual "Corporate Women to Watch" articles that keep tabs on the nation's female CEO aspirants. (The articles themselves seem to trace roots to 1975, when *Business Week* splashed General Electric vice-president Marion Kellogg on its cover with the optimistic words, "The Corporate Woman: Up the Ladder, Finally.") Reading these articles, one gets the idea that social scientists and reporters go into business and professional schools each year, shoot a large number of women with tranquilizer guns, tag them with beeper devices, and then follow their progress through the corporate wilderness. Some of the women fall of cliffs and are lost forever, while others take side paths that lead nowhere. (Where is Kellogg now? A pioneer for her time, she retired as a GE vice-president in 1983.) Only the hardy survive to become Queen of the Pack.

Well, there is no official tagging and tracking. It's just that there are so few women out there in the upper echelons that they're loosely connected forever by their common aspiration of someday leading a *Fortune*-500 company. That's why they always pop up in the "contender" articles, and why they often know a lot about each other. Being CEO-bound binds women into an informal, exclusive club that at all times knows the successes and failures of its members.

Emily Through the Glass Ceiling   If you believe many experts, there comes a time in every executive woman's life when she must wake up and smell the Windex. The "glass ceiling" is now a common term used to describe the sometimes mysterious barriers that keep women from making it to the top in corporations. Will Emily, our first skirted CEO, have bumped her head and suffered the pains of the paned corporate ascent path?

Curiously, while executive recruiters and business researchers constantly mention the glass ceiling, women who are in power positions seldom do. The GC as a topic is a little like death or plastic surgery—powerful women acknowledge its existence for others, but they prefer not to speculate on its role in their own lives.

Talk with female executives who are moving toward the CEO position and you'll find that, when pressed, they explain the glass ceiling phenomenon in several ways.

1. The Bigfoot theory: The glass ceiling doesn't exist. "It's perception, not reality," says Linda Wachner, chief executive of Warnaco, an $800 million privately held clothing manufacturer.

2. The Right Stuff explanation: A lot of women just aren't good enough to make it and don't recognize the role their own inadequacy plays in career derailment. "Women are their own worst enemies," explains Bell South's director of corporate planning, Millye Bell. (Yes, that's her name.) "They excuse things that happen to them that could be a lack of background, style, or capability, and attribute it to prejudice. They're not as tough on themselves as they should be. It's tough at the top. A lot of *men* don't make it."

3. Fear of Commitment: Even though they are talented, some women never truly understand the level of commitment necessary for success. "Many women like a lot more personal time than is allowed at the senior level," says Ruth Smith, president of the First State Bank of Kansas. "They don't like working more than eight hours a day or weekends."

4. The Dreaded Chip-on-Her-Shoulder-Pad theory: Over and over, the women we interviewed said that they had learned "not to take things personally." "Things" included sexist jokes and leering remarks and an astonished attitude among men that women could get the job done. "A lot of it is attitude," believes Maria Monet, head of Ogden Financial Services, a division of Ogden International. "Men do have a tendency to test you."

A frequent conversational theme of female executives waiting in the wings for the CEO slot is the lack of discrimination they've experienced along the way. They describe themselves as optimists who don't dwell on bad things that happen to them. More than once, they matched the glass ceiling metaphor with a glass metaphor of their own. Several told us, "Some people see a half-empty glass, but I see a half-full one." Pollyanna seems alive and well in today's executive suites.

Don't expect to catch Emily Post-Feminist crying to *The Wall Street Journal, Fortune,* or *Business Week* about her encounters with barriers. It would be bad form for her to complain about discrimination while she's trying to hoist herself up the corporate ladder. And when she does make it to that first annual meeting as CEO, the glass ceiling will be so far below her that she will either deny its existence or forget any feelings of being discriminated against. As CEO, she will make a firm commitment to fostering the careers of other women, and maybe even take an interest in traditionally female issues, such as daycare and sexual harrassment, but she won't tolerate any sniveling in the female ranks from malcontents who believe they're not getting their fair share because of their sex.

Positive attitude and an unwillingness to waste time brooding over possible slights will be the dominant personality traits of the first Ms. *Fortune*-500 CEO. Headhunters describe the women they regard as CEO material as "emotionally mature" and "down-to-earth." Translation: no complaints.

Hold That Line . . . In the past, corporate women were fatally attracted to staff positions that excluded them from the race for the CEO suite. Emily Post-Feminist won't make that mistake.

"Women are smarter now," says Eugene Jennings, a business professor at Eastern Michigan State University who has studied female executives since 1964. "Ten or 15 years ago, they chose staff work and disappointed themselves. Now they know enough not to get stuck in staff positions and actively seek line experience."

The new, improved executive woman gets very excited talking about the line. "That's where the glory is," says Ogden's Maria Monet, referring to running a profit-and-loss operation. "I happen to love it," says Janice Stoney, president and CEO of Northwestern Bell in Omaha. "There's a vibrancy and an exhilaration in being in the thick of it." Millye Bell enjoys reminiscing about the years when she supervised the manufacturing of locomotives at General Electric. "Making locomotives was exciting. You could be welded three times just strolling the factory floor!"

It's not surprising that these women describe line positions in battle terms. "Corporations are like the military," explains Anne Morrison, director of the San Diego office of the Center for Creative Leadership. "The combat positions are prohibited to women, and yet that's where the awards are earned, and heroes are made." She believes that going out into the field in tough positions and turning things around can give a woman the visibility she needs to make it to the top. "Women are often seen as too narrow," says Morrison, "and that's what keeps them plateaued."

So, in an effort to keep her career from contracting a staff infection, our mythical CEO, Emily Post-Feminist, will have made a conscious decision to seek a variety of opportunities.

After graduating from law school, she starts in the trademark area of a big consumer products company's legal department but soon finds the work boring. After doing some of the paperwork on a trademark infringement case brought against one of the company's less profitable divisions, SquidInk Facial Fashions, she goes to the president of that division and offers to turn things around. Hired as an associate VP, she soon develops a marketing plan that triples sales for a troubled line of eye makeup based on natural squid ink. Her first act is to capitalize on consumer demand for European beauty products by changing the name of the line to Calamari Cosmetics. She then averts a raw-material shortage in Asia by transferring production to Haiti, where there was a squid glut. By the end of two years, the once-failing division is turning a $200 million profit.

Emily's success with Calamari captures the attention of the CEO at FemFace International, the nation's largest cosmetics company. He hires her away to become president of international operations, which are a mess. For eight years, Ms. Post-Feminist lives out of a suitcase, traveling to Europe, Asia, the Mideast, and South America.

At one point she supervises production at all South American plants, introducing computerized assembly lines and increasing productivity. She takes on the difficult project of breaking into the Islamic makeup market in the Mideast. And she increases sales of FemFace products by 300% in western Europe.

She is disappointed when her CEO yanks her back to the States to become senior vice-president in charge of human resources. While she worries that her staff function might jeopardize her ultimate goal of someday running FemFace, her fears turned out to be unjustified. The human resources position, which lasts three years, is just a stepping stone to the corporate officer level. She spends another three years as president and board member while her CEO grooms her for his post, which she assumes when he retired.

Clubs Without Walls Even though the barriers to formerly all-male clubs are fast tumbling down, few CEO-material women we interviewed indicated any strong cravings to sit around in dingy paneled rooms on rotting leather sofas.

"After wanting to belong to clubs or thinking about belonging to clubs but being unacceptable for membership, it's hard to say now, 'Oh, great, they finally changed the rules, I'm going to steam into that club,'" says USA Network founder and president, Kay Koplovitz. "You lose your enthusiasm for it, I suppose."

Koplovitz sums up the feelings of many women who might someday take the helm of a *Fortune*-500 company. Chances are that the old-time, old-boy clubs won't play a very significant role in Emily Post-Feminist's personal or professional life. Instead, she'll do her business entertaining in upscale restaurants and will rely on a loose network of associates she has met through sitting on nonprofit boards and participating in women's organizations such as the Women's Forum and the Committee of 200.

For women, the most practical club of all seems to be a club without walls.

Take the Committee of 200, for example. Based in Chicago, the national organization was originally only open to female entrepreneurs, but now accepts corporate women who run their own divisions. Everyone praises it for its agenda, and for the *joie de vivre* in evidence at its sponsored seminars and symposiums.

"I don't have any women coworkers," says member Millye Bell. "The Committee opens other avenues, it connected with some other organizations, and is a great business networking group. I think it's really just starting to get into long-range planning. Soon it will be the preeminent women's organization relative to business issues in the U.S. and world."

"I find as a group they have a marvelous sense of humor and a quest to have fun, and I like that," says Koplovitz, another member. "There's spunkiness and a 'let's-get-together-and-have-a-good-time' attitude that's more like men's organizations."

All the women we interviewed are glad that the dreary days when women self-consciously sought only "networking" groups—and humorless ones at that—are over. A woman like Linda Wachner, who engineered a takeover of Warnaco, a multimillion-dollar clothing manufacturer, looks to organizations for information, not job contacts. Like several others, she enthuses about the Women's Forum, a national business organization with local chapters, and the Young Presidents' Organization, a coed association of young CEOs. She calls the latter "a real plus," since many of the members are going through similar leadership challenges.

Since women executives historically haven't utilized private clubs and weekend sporting retreats as part of their business routine, Maria Monet thinks that Emily will have a hard time emulating the bonding process that's so crucial among male chief executives. "Once I was closing a deal for Ogden, and there were a lot of women there, and we started talking about networking and how the one thing women really don't do well is network. They really don't. For example, men will take clients and associates on fishing and golfing trips. Women don't do that with each other. We decided that if women could choose a pleasurable activity, we would go to a health spa together. Then we got a little embarrassed talking about it. But it's no different, really, than what men do. It's important, because you get to know the people you do business with better."

Emily Post-Feminist probably won't have enough female compatriots to make the health spa jaunt feasible (at least if she limits herself to socializing only with other CEOs). Like Cathleen Black, publisher of *USA Today,* who does her business entertaining at the Four Seasons restaurant in New York, or Kay Koplovitz, who belongs to the Rainbow Room eating club, Emily will have a few favorite restaurants that will function as quasi-clubs. Since she went to Radcliffe as an undergraduate, she'll belong to the Harvard Club. But the whole club experience will hold little mystique for her; it will seem a trifle old-fashioned, a remnant of the past, when people like her could never dream of seeing "Chief Executive Officer" beneath their names on a business card.

Even those whose only exposure to the business world is through the Blondie comic strip know that golf is *the* business game, one in which the leisurely pace fosters the perfect atmosphere for deal-making. It also happens to be a sport that women can play pretty well, too.

Being a Sport

Will Emily excel on the greens?

"If golf is the game the guys in the corporation play," says executive recruiter Millie McCoy, "then it's pretty important to learn it."

Certain businesses, such as banks and financial services companies, seem more golf-oriented than others. First Kansas State Bank president Ruth Smith has found golf useful "to build the kind of team support women need to feel comfortable. Deals are made across the desk, around the conference table, and sometimes on the golf course."

Rosemarie Greco, president of Philadelphia's Fidelity Bank, a subsidiary of Newark-based First Fidelity Corporation learned to play golf because the then-chairman mandated that all senior level executives be able to tee off with clients. But she balked at joining clubs with too-exclusive admissions requirements. "The last time I asked a group of people if I could play with them, I was about twelve years old," she says, laughing. "I finally found a club, Sunnybrook Golf Club in Plymouth Meeting, Pennsylvania, that has an admissions process, but it's not one where you sit in front of a group of people and they ask you all sorts of questions. Somebody who knows you may sponsor you, and then your name is sent around to the membership. The other thing is, they don't ask if you're married or single or divorced, or whatever. So single or divorced women can play as individuals, and they're not Mrs. So-and-So. When you go into many other clubs, women have no first names."

Greco has also come across antiquated rules in some clubs that bar women from playing at certain times. "At Sunnybrook, there are no tee-off times and no restrictions that women can't play after two o'clock. I can't tell you how many times a customer has asked me to play at two o'clock and I say, 'Let's play at my club instead.' "

If women see golf as an old-boy sport, many also see it as an old-style use of precious time. More seem to play tennis, another co-ed game that takes a lot less time. Nearly every female executive we interviewed knew her way around a court. "I'm not good, but I make up for it with cheap shots," kids Ogden's Maria Monet, who plays mostly with male friends and business associates. Kay Koplovitz prefers tennis because of its fast pace. Linda Wachner says she's embarrassingly bad at golf but can hold her own in tennis whites.

Ellen Gordon and her husband, Melvin, who jointly own and manage Tootsie Roll Company, play mixed doubles.

Many of the CEO-track women are runners. "Nowadays, we have so little time for fitness, we really tend to concentrate on the aerobic sports," says Northwestern Bell's Stoney, who jogs a few miles several times a week. Other macha sports for upper echelon businesswomen include skiing, hiking, and white-water rafting. Aspen, Colorado, is a favorite place to entertain business associates on the slopes; Wachner and Koplovitz have vacation homes there.

So, since the high energy levels required of anyone going for the top of the pyramid extend to the leisure hours, chances are that Emily P-F won't be a couch potato. Patricia Cook, a partner with the executive search firm of Ward Howell, thinks that Emily will only play a sport such as golf or tennis, primarily because it's beneficial for business. But most of the women we queried seemed to genuinely enjoy their chosen sport. (Even Greco, who did learn golf for business purposes, says she "rather likes it" now and looks forward to spending time in the fresh air.)

Emily will definitely play one "social" sport, probably tennis, and develop at least one other athletic passion to help her hone risk-taking skills and work off tension, perhaps even something as offbeat as horseback riding or windsurfing. But she won't pretend to know more about sports than she does. All the women we surveyed agreed that few experiences are more excruciating than entertaining a client with an excellent golf or tennis game when yours is below average. They will only use sports as a social lubricant when they feel confident about their abilities.

Says Linda Wachner, "I think that you should entertain people in a way that makes them comfortable, and if someone likes to play golf, then you can certainly take him to play golf. But more likely than not, I'm happy to have dinners and lunches with people. I don't think they look to me for a two handicap in a golf game or to be a double-diamond skier. I don't think it makes some men particularly comfortable to be invited out for a day of golf with somebody who's not a good golfer."

Cathie Black agrees. "I would probably say to a young person who is very ambitious, male or female, 'The more things that make you comfortable with people, they are all little notches that help.' But to say to somebody who's not that smart or not that terrific, 'Gee, if you learned golf, you're going to get ahead,' that's crazy. Would it have made any difference in my career if I played golf? Not in the least."

Give Me a Wife, Please

Like working women everywhere, women poised at the threshold of the CEO's office complain that they would like to have a stay-at-home wife to take care of the many niceties of life. After all, 93% of male CEOs are married to nonworking spouses, according to our *Wall Street Journal* survey. Country club memberships and countless other social necessities fit in better with a coupled life-style. Says Maria Monet, "Being married is an advantage socially, definitely." But male spouses, while often supportive, almost always have their own jobs. So they can't easily jump into the housewifely role. "Even when I was married," says Millye Bell, recently divorced after a seventeen-year marriage, "we *both* needed a wife."

"I think that's a wonderful arrangement, if you can have somebody at home who's dedicated totally to you and your personal responsibilities," says Fidelity Bank's Greco, who is single. While she hires people to take care of her house and depends on a sister to do food shopping, she still feels that she does more things that contribute to the management of her household than most men with stay-at-home wives do.

She remembers one conversation with her chairman, who tried to call her on a Saturday when she was running errands all day. "He left a message saying, 'You're never home, lady,'" says Greco. "When I talked to him, I said, 'Bernie, you never have to buy birdseed or weather-stripping!'"

One public relations man who has represented both male and female CEOs believes that the women "never lose sight of the niceties of life." Linda Wachner, a widow, takes time out from running an $800-million company to cook Thanksgiving dinner. Greco is also the chief turkey cook for her extended family. All the women we questioned believed themselves more acutely aware than men of the ways in which their safety nets of hired help contribute to the quality of life. "You can get off a plane and give a dinner party in two hours if you have the right help," says Millye Bell of Bell South, whom several executive recruiters have designated as a likely candidate for the first female to ascend to the top of a major communications company.

In an age when pantyhose and spouses are expected to be supportive, a logical solution for the CEO-bound woman is to marry a househusband. But it's an option that doesn't generate much enthusiasm among high-powered women.

"Never!" states Maria Monet, when asked if she ever entertained the notion. The 39-year-old executive, who is marrying a man who works outside the home, says, "The type of man I would want as a husband would have to be as successful, as strong as I am." All of the women echoed this sentiment, believing it was more sensible to hire the services than to marry a man to carry them out. Sensitive stay-at-homes, it seems, just don't turn on the CEO woman.

So just as Cathie Black is married to a Veterans Administration administrator, Emily will be married to a strong yet noncorporate guy, W. Hitching Post III, a 57-year-old United Nations executive whose old-money family has strong diplomatic ties. They will have many wife-equivalents to suit their many lives: a live-in housekeeper in their New York City apartment and at their Aspen, Colorado, vacation home; personal shoppers for major appliances and clothing; gardeners, and a chauffeur; and a staff to manage their most precious joint investment (but more on that next . . .).

Back in the late 1970s, Colorado congresswoman Patricia Schroeder made a splash by pronouncing, "I have a brain and a womb and I intend to use them both."

No Nervous (Biological) Ticks

While many women would agree that the use of these two organs need not be mutually exclusive, they also concede that combining motherhood with a high-echelon career can present difficulties. Will the first *Fortune*-500 CEO with a uterus be distracted by the ticking of the biological clock?

"No," believes executive recruiter Cook. "If the first female CEO is married, it will be a Margaret Thatcher–type marriage in which her career seems to come first. She will probably not have children, or, if she does, she will have had them a long time ago."

"I think it would be good if you gave her kids," says USA Network's Koplovitz, generously conferring motherhood on Emily Post-Feminist. "It's a part of the life experience, and why shouldn't a woman CEO have children?" asks Koplovitz, who is married but has decided to remain childless. Warnaco's Linda Wachner is another childless CEO who thinks that female chief executives of the future will be able to handle childrearing. "I wish I had had children," says Wachner, a 42-year-old widow, "but it wasn't in the cards for me." (If it *had* been in the cards, there may have been another issue to deal with. Wachner is bicoastal, commuting between her homes and offices in both Los Angeles and New York.)

Whether or not our mythical female CEO decides to have kids, she will not be publicly obsessive about her biological choices. Discretion is the better part of valor when it comes to executive childbearing. The corporate officer–level mothers we met fell into two groups: those who had their kids before they were 21 and then entered the workforce when the children were school-age; and those who postponed motherhood until the end of their third or beginning of their fourth decade. Janice Stoney, who had her son when she was 18 and now, at 48, runs Northwestern Bell, says she is glad that she never had to be pregnant on the job. "I talk to some of the younger women and they say that their pregnancies change the dynamics around the office, that being visibly pregnant puts them in a vulnerable position."

Waiting until one's career is firmly established works well if the woman doesn't mind gambling on her fertility. Adoption often fits in better with the work schedule of a busy executive. *USA Today*'s Cathie Black and her husband adopted an infant son when Black was 42. Despite the facts that she splits her week between New York and Washington, she is confident that her high-ranking job provides some flexibility for spending time with a baby. "In a way, it's easier when you're in the type of job I have. If I want to slip away to go to the pediatrician, I can." Black employs a full-time nanny to care for her son, Duffy.

"Nanny" and "money" are the two most important five-letter words for executive moms. If there's anything that will ease the way for the future of CEO maternity, it's hard, cold cash. "For many of these women, having children is not such a big deal, because they really are very rich," points out Harvard's Herzlinger. Those endless magazine articles about the difficulty of finding adequate child care are directed toward lower and mid-level managers, not women who make over a half million dollars a year.

The existence of children in a female CEO's life will not be a determining factor in her success, according to Felice

Schwartz, president of Catalyst, a nonprofit consulting firm specializing in women's business issues. "There are two kinds of women who work," notes Schwartz, "career-primary women and career-and-family women. A woman who wants to make it to the top as a *Fortune*-500 CEO would by necessity be a career-primary type. But this wouldn't preclude motherhood if she were willing to accept the fact that someone else would be raising her children for most of the time."

So Emily will have a child. But given her work schedule and age, adoption is the most sensible route. Then she needn't worry about any impact the physical disability of pregnancy could have on her day-to-day activities, or fertility problems that could crop up because she waited so long to conceive. Let's say that she and her husband, Hitch Post, waited until Emily was 43 to adopt a little girl, Katie Graham Post. Katie is cared for by a full-time American nanny *and* an au pair from France, who takes turns shuttling her to nursery school, Suzuki violin lessons, and water babies classes. Katie doesn't even know what a CEO is. She wants to be a ballerina when she grows up.

There are some refreshing images to look forward to with a female CEO. For one thing, the public will be spared countless magazine cover portraits of Emily Post-Feminist in shirtsleeves with red suspenders.

> *"Ain't it hard bein' a woman, but don't you just love the clothes?"*
>
> —From the **Randy Newman Song**

"She'll wear very expensive designer clothes," says headhunter Cook. "As women move up, they relax, and that manifests itself in their personal style," believes Professor Herzlinger. "When men become CEOs, they start wearing European-style suits and cuff links. The women become glamorous, which is a sure sign that the organization is permitting them to exhibit personal style."

"I've noticed that I no longer worry about wearing the uniform," admits Ogden Financial's Monet. She's referring to what Herzlinger calls the "costume" of the female middle-level manager: pinstriped suits and butterfly ties. On the afternoon we visit Monet in her spacious corner office in New York's Penn Plaza Center, she is wearing a vibrant purple shirtwaist dress cinched with a wide leather belt, a choker with four strands of natural pearls, and gold bracelets. Her long hair and expressive eyes and mouth make her look youthful. On out-of-the-office jaunts she wears a ski parka and carries an oversized canvas bag instead of a briefcase. "I even wear red nail polish now, which I would never do when I was starting out as a lawyer," she says.

"I've never worn the uniform," says Warnaco's Wachner. A small woman, she welcomes us into her country-decorated Park Avenue office wearing a tweed pantsuit with an Eisenhower jacket, lots of gold jewelry, and brown-and-white striped socks. Everything about her personal style is extravagant yet tasteful, from her whimsical hand-made black coffee mug with its animal-shaped handle to her very large emerald-and-diamond ring. At 31, Wachner was the youngest-ever president of a division of a *Fortune*-500 company, the Max Factor cosmetic concern. Now 42, she has been in the cosmetics and fashion industry all her working life, an industry that tolerates flamboyant style perhaps more than others.

Yet even industries not known for their stylishness, such as banking and newspaper publishing, harbor snappy dressers at the top. The day we met Fidelity president Rosemarie Greco, she was turned out very stylishly in a purple blouse, charcoal skirt, and amethyst jewelry.

"I think it's ridiculous to try to be a man in a pinstriped suit," says *USA Today*'s Black, who claims that she wears "about the same kind of things I always wore." For our interview, she is dressed casually in a suede skirt and black sweater. Black says that younger women often can't believe her cavalier attitude toward dress. Once when Black's niece, a mid-level manager at Sprint, was visiting her at home, the niece admired a red Chanel-type dress her aunt was wearing. "She said she loved my dress," recalls Black, "but that she could never wear it to work. I had just worn it to the office that day!"

When talking about style, USA Network's Kay Koplovitz likes to tell a story about Sid Sheinberg, president of MCA and a partner in USA Network. "Every time Sid sees me, he says things like, 'You look so pretty, you look fantastic—you don't look like the president of a company.' And I tell him, 'Sidney, this is what a president looks like!'"

Koplovitz, who started out as a television producer for a Milwaukee station, has ash-blond hair and piercing blue eyes that would serve her well as a television anchorwoman. Breakfasting on bran flakes and fresh raspberries at her regular table at the Intercontinental Hotel in Manhattan, she sports a periwinkle-blue dress that matches her eyes, a sapphire ring and earrings, and a handmade gold bracelet. The overcoat draped behind her is made of handsewn silk, and beside her sits a decidedly downscale canvas Land's End briefcase.

So, it appears that whatever pressures Emily Post-Feminist will have to face, a dress code won't be one of them. Spandex miniskirts and K-Mart blouses probably won't do in a CEO wardrobe, but beyond that, the sky's the limit, and she can expect to pay thousands a year for her stylish power ensembles.

Just as Emily will spend prolifically on her stylish duds, she will also probably employ one or more personal shoppers to keep her closet well stocked. Bank president Greco, who attends several formal business dinners per month, depends on a couple of department store saleswomen who keep a lookout for suitable evening dresses. Black buys almost all her clothes at one store, Harriet Kassman in Chevy Chase, where the owner knows her style. Wachner likes to shop by herself for big items, but uses a personal shopper to keep up inventories of lingerie, pantyhose, and other accessories.

There isn't a scruffy woman in the lot of CEO contenders, and not one who isn't trim and fit. No wonder 33-year-old Deborah Coleman, chief financial officer of Apple Computer, who has often been named as an eventual high-tech CEO contender, announced in the fall of 1988 that she was taking a leave of absence to get her weight under control. Designer clothes don't go above size 12.

One good thing about being a pioneer: Eventually, there are others. Emily Post-Feminist will be the first, but not the last, *Fortune*-500 CEO in pumps. Scores more of snappily dressed optimists with line experience and tennis-playing abilities will follow. Maybe so many that one day a book on CEO style will just naturally talk about co-ed habits and predilections.

Emily Over the Hill

But until that time, the women nearing the top will have to endure gender-based scrutiny as they create their own executive style. It is a style without pinstripes and wingtips, without moldy club locker rooms and Turkish towels, even without full-time spousal support.

"Successful women are the same as successful men," we

heard again and again from the women at the top. But are they? Women on the way to the CEO slot seem to have similar energy and drive, vacation homes, and the even-tempered traits and leadership abilities of male CEOs, plus a lot more. Ovaries, for example. And hairstylist appointments. And the added burden of always being interviewed about being women.

When will these additional factors be mitigated? "Things will change," says cable television entrepreneur Kay Koplovitz, sighing, "when the CEO's daughters are ready to take over."

By then, Emily will have taken early retirement to go sailing and skiing with Hitch. She'll sit on a few corporate boards. She'll go to see Katie dance for the City Ballet. And, being a good sport conditioned by years of corporate give-and-take, she will refuse interviews when Katie's autobiography, *CEO Kid: The Bottom Line Is Love,* bares all about her mother's personal life.

–CATHY CRIMMINS

IS IT
WORTH IT?

There arrives a moment in the life of any ambitious person when he suddenly feels a flash of revelation, looks at himself reflected in his marble shower and finds himself saying: "Holy Cow! I'm going to make it!" (Or, "I'm not going to make it." Or, if he has inherited his company, "I'm not going to send the family business down the tubes!")

The first time we asked, CEOs were a bit reluctant to share with us their own personal epiphanies. Who could blame them? They didn't achieve such success by blowing their cover of restraint to any old reporter who wandered by. (When was the last time you caught a chief exec smiling in his annual report photo?) So they would attempt to convince us that they never did feel a jolt of

> *"One of the things you have to do as a chief executive is to constantly remind yourself you're not king."*
>
> —**Thomas Watson, Jr.**
> **IBM former chairman**

joy—not even a little ripple—when it unexpectedly occurred to them that their years of sweat, toil, office politicking and missed Little League games would earn them their company's throne.

So we would ask again.

That was generally when the CEO would tell us it was the first time anyone had ever asked him that, instruct his secretary to hold all calls, prop his feet up on a coffee table and let his eyes dance.

Time's Dick Munro drifted back to the first of what he calls "sudden little signals that say 'Jesus!' " It was at a lunch with a colleague in the 1960s, at a little French restaurant. "My colleague said, 'There are rumors Dick, that you're hot,' " he recalled.

Another such moment occurred at a securities analysts' meeting at the Harvard Club in the early 1970s. At the time Munro was running *Time*'s small video group, which included the incipient Home Box Office. Few at the company were familiar with the intricacies of satellite transmission or pay-TV, and Munro found himself being asked all the questions. "After that meeting I said to myself, 'Holy Christ, here we're a magazine company, nobody asked a question about magazines. The whole meeting was on HBO and pay television and satellite transmission and I was the only guy who knew anything.' That was the second time I began to feel that [I had something up on other people]."

Southern California Edison's Howard Allen remembers excitedly phoning home the afternoon in 1962 that he *knew* he could become his company's CEO. It was the day he was made a vice-president. But his family didn't appear to attach a great deal of significance to the event.

"The phone was answered by my daughter, who was five years old. I said to her, 'Alisa, let me speak to your mother, I've just been made a vice-president of the Edison company!' She said, 'Daddy let me tell you about the Easter eggs we're coloring.' And my wife got on the phone and she said, 'That's fine, but the sink's plugged up and I hope you can get that fixed this evening. And the lawn needs to be mowed on Saturday.' "

Irving Shapiro recalls that in the meeting at which he was told he would head the nation's largest chemical company, he was so excited he had to painstakingly write down every word he was told, lest he forget something important (or think he had hallucinated the whole scene). He was informed that he couldn't tell anyone other than his wife of his impending rise to the chairmanship. He left work early, cautiously negotiating through the Wilmington traffic. And when he arrived home, his wife worriedly greeted him at the door, certain that, since he was home mid-day, some dreadful catastrophe had occurred.

We raise these memories not for nostalgia's sake, but to reinforce the hidden fact that for all their self-restraint and stability and white shirts, chief executive officers are—and we realize the point can be strongly argued otherwise—undeniably human.

And no report on the outside-of-work lives of our nation's top CEOs would be complete without addressing the obvious questions: 1) How can I use what I've just learned to make myself a CEO? and 2) Wait a minute, would I be any happier as a CEO?

We don't have the answer to Question Number One. Although we do have some advice from Tom Watson, Jr.: "I think the more careful people are with what they say and how they say it, the higher they get in the business. You have to be smart enough to know when to be outspoken and when to shut up." (For his part, Watson was smart enough to be born to the founder of IBM.)

As for Question Number Two, we've reduced the considerations to the quintessential pro and con of a chief executive's life.

Pro: A CEO never has to change a lightbulb.

Con: A CEO's time is so finely scheduled that he never has a moment to, say, drop in at lunchtime to catch the photography exhibit at International Center of Photography-Midtown that he read about in this morning's *New York Times*.

Our own assessment is that he probably was invited to the exhibit opening, anyway. And if you've seen one display of back-lit, stark flowers, you've seem them all.

When CEOs or retired CEOs discuss themselves—an activity, we've found, they seem to relish once they get going—it's fashionable for them to concentrate on the pleasure they derive from the challenges and to minimize the joys of power. (One rare exception, sort of. Irving Shapiro told us a war story from his early years at Du Pont. He had been passed over for a big promotion, and the fellow who was promoted over him managed to keep Shapiro from getting a raise for three years. When Shapiro's career eventually started to rise and he finally outstripped his rival, Shapiro allowed that it felt "nice.")

They also are extremely fond of underrating those wonderful perks that make the people below them so envious. Former Citicorp chairman Walter Wriston speaks for many CEOs when he explains: "In the sense that you ride a magic carpet—a corporate jet—it's nice. But it permits you to do what no sane person would do, get up at five A.M., fly to New Orleans for three calls, fly back to Washington for lunch, then back to New York to be in the office by three to get out at five and into a black tie for some function." (Probably a photography exhibit opening.)

Tom Watson, Jr., too, gives the impression that the perquisite business is highly overrated—and an exercise in overindulgence. "I'm driven batty by the black-windowed limousine that sneaks out from the small, dusty airport," he says, playfully adding: "Only gangsters had that car originally."

But Wharton School dean Russell Palmer, who in a previous incarnation served as chief executive officer of the Big Eight accounting firm of Touche, Ross, says: "I've seen a lot of CEOs rationalize their perks as a necessity of doing business. Not until they've stepped down and no longer have the perks do they realize how much they really liked them."

Moreover, some CEOs point out that while the challenges of running a major corporation rarely wear thin, some of the thrills of accomplishment quickly do. Southern California Edison chairman Howard Allen says: "I think after you've done something, the experience and satisfaction of doing it tends to diminish with time. Say you'd like to have a pair of Gucci loafers or a Mercedes, let's say, or to fly in the Concorde. But after you've done it, it's not as important the next time. I think this is just human nature. The first time I went in the West Wing of the White House, I was awestruck and humbled. The last time I was there it was kind of like going to 31 flavors."

So, how does it feel to be one of the beautiful people?

Are CEOs, with their career success and stock options and deed to the power table at the Fort Worth Club, any happier than everybody else?

"Happiness for me is a more personal thing in terms of being at peace with myself," responds AT&T's Robert Allen. "I don't have trouble going to sleep at night, but I didn't before I was a CEO." As for others, he says: "I don't know how happy other people are, but I doubt that CEOs are more or less happy than others just because they are CEOs. Being a CEO in itself has nothing to do with happiness."

"That's doubtful," responds Paul Hirsch, management professor at Northwestern University's Kellogg Graduate School of Management. "Being named a CEO is like winning all the marbles. There's definitely going to be euphoria. In careers, you're always real happy when you get a nod of approval. And becoming a CEO is the final nod and there's no way you cannot be happy, it's an affirmation of talent and self-esteem. If that doesn't get disconfirmed by a business or personal disaster at some point, you're certainly going to be happier than most people." And Wharton's Russell Palmer adds this evidence: "You don't talk to many CEOs who say 'I wish to hell I could get out of this job.' I don't hear a lot of them sitting around with great aspirations, talking about their next career."

Former IBM chief Thomas Watson, Jr., with his seasoned, postcareer perspective, concurs. "I think if you measure happiness over a long period of time, it's very much entwined with achievement. Probably it takes an awful lot to reduce that happiness of being the greatest. Reading it through those lenses, I'd say that CEOs are probably the happiest group of people I know of. Of course I connect happiness to achievement—not everybody would agree." We should note here that Watson, age 75, had to cut our interview short so he could spend the afternoon piloting his personal jet (he also pilots his own helicopter and sails).

With their excess free time, their unique perspective, their feeling that there's little to lose by being outspoken, and their eagerness to relive glory days, retired CEOs were particularly helpful in assessing the issue of CEO happiness. Former Citicorp chairman Walter Wriston, for instance, responded with a torrent of questions. "Is a division commander in a

PLACES TO SPOT A CEO

1. The Homestead, Hot Springs, Virginia, when the Business Council meets in May and October.

2. The Greenbrier, White Sulphur Springs, West Virginia, almost any time.

3. The Links, New York, when the Business Roundtable's 50-member policy committee convenes.

4. The Metropolitan Club, New York, when *Chief Executive* magazine hosts its annual Chief Executive of the Year award dinner in late June or early July.

5. Anywhere in Davos, Switzerland, when the World Economic Forum meets in late January.

6. Tikchik Narrows Lodge, Dillingham, Alaska, in late June and early July when the king salmon are available or in late August and early September when the silver salmon flourish.

7. Boca Raton Hotel and Club, Boca Raton, Florida, in the winter months.

8. Augusta National Golf Course, Augusta, Georgia, during Masters Tournament in April.

9. Hotel Stanford Court, San Francisco.

10. The Hub (Newstand), Nantucket, on summer mornings.

11. Hotel Okura, Tokyo.

12. Four Seasons restaurant, New York.

13. (Hotel) Connaught, London.

14. L'Orangerie restaurant, Beverly Hills.

15. Bohemian Grove Shrine of the Owl, Dining Circle, or Campfire Circle during July encampment (aka "greatest men's party on Earth").

16. Home of the New York Society of Security Analysts at 71 Broadway. In the second-floor meeting rooms, where, almost every business day, a CEO is making a lunch presentation before a Wall Street group.

—DAVID DIAMOND

battle happy? Not in the sense you think about it, but he may be able to deliver the job at hand, in that sense he may be happy. Would Henry Thoreau, sitting on the banks of Walden Pond, be happier than a guy running a company?

"I don't think that's determinable. I know CEOs who are happy guys, I know CEOs who are going through their third divorce. I know CEOs who are complete workaholics who have to take their fax machines with them in their cars. I know CEOs who are more reflective, who can take a few days off.

"I think if you say are they generally speaking well-adjusted people who take the knocks of the world with the flowers, they are. Otherwise they wouldn't last. But some of them mistake the flowers of the world for themselves."

At this point, there was a brief pause, after which Wriston added: "Depends whether they have a compatible spouse, or whether their stomach hurts that day."

Another pause. Then he concluded: "One of the happiest people I ever met was a person teaching arithmetic to high school dropouts."

"Anybody who's been a CEO is competitive with a strong desire for accomplishment and winning. I'd be astounded if you'd find one guy who would say he should have quit competing halfway up the ladder and concentrated on his fishing," concludes John Gallagher, former chief executive of Chemetron.

Gallagher is a fitting person with whom to end this report on CEOs. He was one of the first corporate heads to fall victim to that new, frightful fact of chief executive life, the hostile takeover. Gallagher traded his corporate career for one in academia (University of Chicago) after Allegheny International hostilely acquired his company in 1977.

Even from that vantage point, from the perspective of a CEO who got booted out of his corner office, he answers without hesitation that he has no regrets and even says: "I don't think any of these CEOs have any regrets. Faced with the question of whether they'd do it over again, I think you'd find a universal 'Hell, yes!' " Of course, he adds, corporate chiefs in general are not terribly introspective. If they had been, they probably would never have made it to the top.

–David Diamond

INDEX